A Fresh Look Based on Bronze Inscription Glyphs

Betsy Pearson

THE DÉ OF LAOZI: A FRESH LOOK BASED ON

BRONZE INSCRIPTION GLYPHS

Cover design: David Huebner, Back of Beyond Media, Sheridan, Wyoming

PUBLISHED BY SUNWARMED SAGE PRESS

650 SOUTH JEFFERSON STREET

SHERIDAN, WYOMING 82801

SUNWARMEDSAGEPRESS.COM

Ordering information:
Please visit sunwarmedsagepress.com/ordering
Or email sunwarmedsagepress@gmail.com

ISBN: 978-1-7357931-3-9

SUNWARMED SAGE

For John,
laughing like a dog in the grass

“Writing always means hiding something
in such a way that it then is discovered.”

Italo Calvino

CONTENTS

INTRODUCTION TO THE DÀO OF LAOZI, 2020

Laozi remains about as anonymous as a person can get and still have a name. Here's one of the most widely accepted stories about the master:

> Eminent court clerk and historian Laozi decided to leave the country, tired of the politics of the Zhou Dynasty. A border guard named Yinxi recognized the sage and asked that the master leave behind some wisdom before departing to the west, Laozi granted Yinxi's request, and the *Dào Dé Jīng* was born.

This common history was written by a court historian named Sima Qian around 85 BC during the Han dynasty. It places Laozi in the 6th century BC, and some versions even specify that Laozi was born in 601 BC and departed Zhou in 531 BC. These dates would mean Laozi lived during the Eastern Zhou Dynasty's Spring and Autumn period (770 – 476 BC).

Laozi's *Dào Dé Jīng* is a classic text (*Jīng*) about The Way (*Dào*) and its ethics system (*Dé*). In the common "received" version of the book, Chapters 1-37 describe the *Dào*, and Chapters 38-81 describe the *Dé*. I remember the day I learned that ancient versions of the text unearthed in the 1950s and 1990s presented the two sections in the opposite order. The *Dé* came first and ended with Laozi explaining that we really wouldn't need to know all that if we simply would follow the *Dào*. Then the following thirty-seven chapters explained the *Dào*.

That was the day I considered the fact that the *Dào Dé Jīng* translations I was reading were based on translations of modern Chinese characters and Mandarin pronunciations, whereas the original was certainly written in a glyph-type script of Old Chinese. I immediately wanted to see the ancient characters and learn about the pictures within those characters.

Here's my thinking. Like all languages, every variety and dialect of Chinese over the years has had synonyms. And each of those different versions of a concept has its own flavor—a subtlety—that's hard to translate. Given this array of options, any good writer's word choices matter. Poets' choices matter even more.

When each of those word choices is actually a unique pictorial glyph—and we know a picture is worth a thousand words—then it seems to me that the pictures inside Laozi's character choices are very important indeed. They give us not only a more full and nuanced immersion into what Laozi was writing but maybe an understanding of the master's own life experience. I find that possibility fascinating.

This book, then, is my interpretation of the Bronze Inscription glyphs associated with each Chinese character in the first 37 chapters of our received version of the *Dào Dé Jīng*.

~

There are many theories as to where, when, and even *if* Laozi really lived or wrote the *Dào Dé Jīng*. Most scholars don't agree with Sima Qian's biography and in fact believe the *Dào Dé Jīng* wasn't written by one single author at all. Devoted Taoists of course disagree.

Anthropologists have unearthed several versions of the *Dào Dé Jīng*. Many scholars and devotees have compared the various texts to one another as well as to the established received text. In doing so, they've generated theories about chapter sequencing, correlations between ancient and modern characters, whether the original was oral or written, and the fundamental nature of the *Dào Dé Jīng*'s topic—is this a book about politics, mythology, mystical experience, socioeconomic realities, philosophy, how to live, physics, other sciences, ultimate reality, or some combination of these topics?

There are also a large number of opinions as to how to go about answering such questions. Contextually? Personally? Traditionally—and, if so, through which Taoist lineage?

And then there's the real meat of the *Dào Dé Jīng*: what *does* it mean? In fact, what's the meaning of any particular chapter, line, or character?

By 1998 there were thought to be 250 translations or interpretations of this text. More have been published since then, and no two are identical. That's partly because the text is mysterious and partly because each translator brings their own lens and agenda to the project (some more consciously or determinedly than others). For a relatively short and very clear description of this academic history, I refer you to the *Stanford Encyclopedia of Philosophy* website.

~

You've already noted to yourself some of the many assumptions I've made and considerations I've chosen to ignore completely. When confronted with competing theories that can't be proven, I think you should believe whichever theory is most useful to you, whichever theory makes you deeply well and happy, or whichever theory feels like truth in your guts. I almost always find these three tests point me in the same direction.

In the case at hand, I find it helpful, fun, interesting, and solid yet exhilarating to believe that Laozi existed and authored the *Dào Dé Jīng*. The visual beauty, internal structure, and flow of characters convince me it originally was written and not oral. I choose to believe Sima Qian's origin story and dates. And I believe Laozi wrote the text in a script very close to Western Zhou Bronze Inscription.

I respect and flat-out love every Taoist scholar and devotee that has ever existed, and, at the same time, my own engagement with this text is a different kind of animal. It's very personal. I wanted to get as close to the original text as possible and see what happened to me when I did so. That's why even though I pay little attention to the kinds of context that scholars care about, I do care about the text's dates of origin because I want to know what kind of script the author used. I want to see what Laozi drew.

Chinese characters famously evolved from glyphs—pictorial representations of concrete things and abstract ideas. As in English or any other language, the meaning of individual words or characters evolved. A 21st century English speaker's definitions of certain words are very different from those of even a few hundred years ago when, for example, *quelling* something or someone meant *killing* it, not just calming it down. Grammar and syntax also evolve. That's why Old English texts like *Beowulf* are hard for the modern sensibility to decipher. Something similar holds true with Old Chinese scripts.

The study of the evolution of the Chinese language is vastly more complex and sophisticated than even the study of Laozi and the *Dào Dé Jīng*. What I don't know I don't know about the subject humbles me. For a short introduction, just check out Wikipedia entries for "Chinese language" and follow some of the links. It's mind-bogglingly fascinating and impressive.

If you delve into Old Chinese and consider its written aspect, you'll see that as the original glyphs evolved to convey an increasing number and complexity of words, compound characters were created. In compound characters, often one sub-component—a free-standing image within the overall image—gives the word its semantic meaning, and another sub-component gives the word its phonetic sound. The thing is: the phonetic part of a character is still conveyed by a drawing. Since we see that image, I find it at least subliminally contributes to and refines the meaning of the semantic part. This is another assumption incorporated into my interpretation of the *Dào*—my words for each glyph include descriptions of all its components. My reasoning is that there is almost always more than one sub-character that could carry the phonetic sound, so there may be a reason the author chose a character with that particular image to do that work in that particular place. The author knew we couldn't un-see or un-feel that image.

Another thing you learn immediately about Old Chinese is that there were regional differences, and, furthermore, several kinds of scripts were evolving simultaneously in each region for different uses and different socioeconomic classes. It's hard for scholars to piece it all together because of the sporadic sampling of texts we've found. Many of the original writing samples that survived the Spring and Autumn period (as well as the Warring States period that followed) are bronze inscriptions. Though most of the writing actually took place on perishable bamboo and wooden slips bound together by silk thread or leather thongs, these bronze texts were of course more durable. Originals of the more common "slip" texts often did not last long, and most of those that did survive were burned later during the Qin dynasty. Some texts, however, were copied and handed down through the ages. They were re-written in each new era's script and evolved into the received classic texts we read today.

The oldest known such copy of the *Dào Dé Jīng* was unearthed in the village of Guodian in 1993 near what was the capital of the ancient State of Chu where (probably coincidentally) Sima Qian claims Laozi was born. The text was written in the local Chu form of Small Seal Script on bamboo, and experts date it to sometime in the 300s BC.

It's hard to know what kind of writing system a Laozi of 531 BC would have used to write down an epic poem mid-departure at a border station. During this time, the Small Seal script was organically developing from the earlier Western Zhou dynasty (1066 – 770 BC) script which had been preserved on bronze inscriptions. As far as we can tell, the evolving seal script was not yet fully developed or codified, and during the 500's BC, it coexisted with a rougher, popular "vulgar" writing. Not only are the Western Zhou Bronze inscriptions the immediate etymological precursor of whatever script Laozi used, but also, they were most likely well known to Laozi in the role of court clerk and historian. That's why I look to those bronze inscription script characters for my interpretation. When no Western Zhou Bronze (WZB) inscription character is known for a compound character, I assemble the WZB versions of its various sub-components into one drawing. When no such images exist, I incorporate the older, original Oracle Bone Script characters. And if the only image available is the Small Seal script, we redrew that image with the blockier, more angular style of the WZB inscriptions.

~

I am not even a beginner in either Taoist or Chinese language studies, and yet I found I couldn't not do this project. I've been interested in the *Dào Dé Jīng* for 34 years—ever since I met my husband and came upon his original copy of Gia Fu Feng and Jane English's 1972 translation, beautifully amplified with Feng's calligraphy and English's photographs. But my daily practice of reading this text began later, 25 years ago, when a local writer introduced me to Stephen Mitchell's translation. Since that time, it's shaped my life and spiritual practice. In the last two years, baffled by the sometimes-dramatic differences between translations, I became interested in the characters that make up the text, then in their etymology, and finally in the author. The closer you get, the more you're awestruck by the elegance, humor, and craft of the *Dào Dé Jīng*... and puzzled by its mysteries. It's confusing no matter what.

When you're translating a text and run into a word, sentence, paragraph, or chapter that seems to contradict a previous point or to not compute at all, it's tempting to try to "make it make sense." I think this phenomenon is behind many of the big differences between translations. It's further complicated not just by the *Dào Dé Jīng*'s abstruse language but by the complexity of the Chinese language.

I know that the meaning of Chinese characters is contextual—the same is true in English. Consider a fork in the road, the fork you use to eat, a forked tongue, or, in this current moment's slang, "that forking jerk." When they understand these contextual differences, translators assign one character very different meanings in different parts of the book. Alas, I think when that happens, we the readers are deprived of seeing when and how Laozi chose to repeat certain characters.

The other side of this coin is that if several different characters are translated in the exact same way, we are led to believe that Laozi made the choice to use the same word in places where that's not the case.

There are many important differences between English and Chinese that make translation especially hard. In Chinese, you don't necessarily have to choose past or present tense for a verb or know the number of the subject. You don't have to choose a gender for pronouns. One word can be a noun, a verb, or an adjective—that's why I so often use gerunds. Add an "-ing" to most English words, and they too can be multi-functional.

Another big issue, maybe the biggest one you'll find as you read my translation, is syntax. Consider the phrase: "cat angry talking you luck good." If you were a Chinese speaker, you might decide it carries like a plough—carries the meaning of: "it's good luck if an angry cat's talking to you." The pauses and inflection upon delivery, as well as your ear for your own language, would serve as punctuation and context. Not only is the word-order different between languages, but the *Dào Dé Jīng* doesn't have the little in-between words English uses to convey connection and spaciousness. It can be frustrating. But when we try to make it more comfortable or certain, we really overlay our own ideas onto the translation. For example, if it makes no sense to you that a cat could be talking or that this would be good luck, you might translate that sentence as "when a cat's angry, you should talk about good luck." And maybe that was even the original meaning! It can be hard to tell. Naturally, native Chinese speakers have a huge advantage in translating Old Chinese. Except that Laozi's so obscure and puzzling even to native Chinese speakers—as evidenced by the radical differences between various translations—that I think something else is going on. It's just a very mysterious text for some reason, and I think the glyphs are complicit in those reasons.

My goal here is to assemble as objective a description of the glyphs as I can while also incorporating the traditional translations and the more modern and abstract meanings attributed to each character. In this way, I hope to let Laozi's evocative nature shine through.

I made some rules for myself. I decided to present the words in the same order as the received classic versions. I also decided to use the same translation for any particular character every time it appeared[1] and never to translate two different characters in the exact same way. So that the reader can get a sense of the layout, I start a new line in my translation for each character and a new paragraph for each line of the original *Dào*.[2] One advantage of this system is that you can turn to the

---

[1] Exceptions: In this version I made a few modifications such as sometimes eliminating the first word of "is breaking the little wings off." For the character *zhī*, 之 I've sometimes substituted "what it has," "what it had " "its," or even "'s" for its usual translation as "has this." These and similar modifications are discussed on my blog. The changes are so small that you can easily tell when the word is the same word used elsewhere.

[2] Exceptions: In the cases of "Heaven-Earth" and "Heaven-down-below," two characters share a line because those words have a long history of being combined into one term. I also put three-ten on one line since it's used to say "thirty." And when I translate *zhī* as "'s," then it's on the same line as the previous word.

Appendix and find the modern Chinese word and characters in the order in which they occur both in my translation and the received classics.

The only thing I've unabashedly improvised is capitalization and punctuation—the oldest versions have none of the former and very, very little of the latter. I have followed the chapter sequence of the Mawangdui Silk Texts which carries like a plough—carries the meaning of that Chapter 24 comes between Chapter 21 and Chapter 22. In the Appendix and on my website, you see my most uncompromising translations which follow these rules strictly. If you compare those to the main body of this book, you'll see where I did add a few little connecting words here and there. On the website, you can follow my process in assembling glyph sub-components, translating them, and turning those drawings into images suitable for this book: thedaooflaozi.com.

~

I figured once I assembled this bare-bones, pictorial version, then I could stop, step back, look at the book in a form as close to how Laozi wrote it as I can imagine, and then... then what? Then have an experience more like what Laozi had or what Laozi intended. I trusted something would happen in and to me, and it did. That's described elsewhere including on my website. But to begin with, I just want you to have access to the same kind of raw engagement that I got to have which is why I've made this book. It's not a simple read. But it's one you can use as a resource if you've been reading the *Dào Dé Jīng* in different translations and trying to form a clearer picture of what it says. And it's a rather dreamy one if you just let it wash over you.

As of this publication date, the book's companion website—thedaooflaozi.com—is still in its early phase. In its final form it will give you a place to engage with the text more easily. There you will be able to see my interpretations alongside others, choose the translation you prefer for each character, and then, best of all, build your own translation.

Meanwhile, I hope you use this book to do that very thing. Scribble in it, make it your own. Have your own personal encounter with Laozi and the images and ideas in the *Dào*, and interesting things will happen. That's what I want for you and for Laozi, to whom I offer this book with great thanks.

NOTES FOR *THE DÉ*

These Chapters 38-81 of *The Dào Dé Jīng* include some of the most-often quoted stanzas of the classic text. My hope for you (and me) is that reading them in the context of their original glyphs may help reveal some over-arching structure to the way Laozi laid out the *Dé*. Then again, maybe it really is simply a collection of aphorisms.

Line-numbering extends through the entire text so that you more easily can use the Index to find each line's Modern Chinese characters and their Pinyin transcriptions. Each Pinyin word is cross-refenced in the Glossary which also contains each character's reconstructed glyph image and a list of where it occurs in this book as well as in its companion volume, *The Dào of Laozi*. The close reader will notice some changes in my interpretations of characters from that 2020 work to this one. An upcoming updated version of *The Dào* will reflect those same changes.

I hope you enjoy adding this fresh look to your previous ponderings. Please do use the email address listed in the front of the book to let me know what you find.

BP 1/17/2022

THANK YOU

I offer my heartfelt thanks to the same people who have been vital to the success of this project and my life and happiness:

Caitlin, Annie, and Trace Addlesperger were my first readers and cheerleaders. I'm so grateful for—and lucky to have—not only their interest in the Tao Te Ching but also their interest in my interest in it. This is equally true of Erik Hoversten. We are so grateful in so many ways that he came into our family. I especially thank him for his technical expertise, curiosity, and incredible generosity in helping me move my composition books and index cards into an elegant part of the digital realm.

Renée Ballard and Kimberly Gee have also been with me through this whole journey, and their love, enthusiasm, and unconditional support is one of the greatest surprise gifts of my life. That they are both wildly creative and wildly successful creatives is perhaps no surprise, and I must say, it is a huge plus.

Wendy Mead Hammond inspires me daily and was kind enough to ask for and receive a rambling 100-page account of my exploration of the Tao Te Ching. Check out her work if you're ready for effective, compassionate therapy or coaching.

John Addlesperger not only introduced me to Lao Tzu 36 years ago but provides me literal life support as well as love during this project just as solidly as he has done for our entire relationship.

The writer Sam Western first introduced me to Stephen Mitchell as his favorite Rilke translator in 1996 in a bookstore then co-owned and operated by the poet and photographer Dainis Hazners. (I remember it was April because that's National Poetry Month, so Dainis had free poems for every visitor. He and Sam conspired to find a Mitchell-Rilke poem for me in the stack of snippets from earlier in the month.) That book led me to Mitchell's other books including his interpretation of the Tao Te Ching which I've had within reach ever since. It's true that the little exchanges you have with others—events and dates you probably don't even remember—may influence them more profoundly than you know!

Indeed, I extend to Stephen Mitchell a great deal of thanks.

Hilmar Alquiros, PhD—a poet, psychologist, philosopher, and self-described "happy master-survivor in the beautiful Phillipines"—built a useful Tao Te Ching resource website (tao-te-king.org) that I've used for hours and hours and hours most weeks in the last two years. It was there that I first encountered an etymological reference that made me wonder... and thereby changed everything for me. (The character was *shēn*, 身, which is commonly translated as "self". The bronze inscription glyph shows a pregnant woman in profile.) Ralf Schlüter, PhD—a physicist and Dr. Alquiros' friend, proofreader, and collaborator—helps maintain the site. I have not run my approach (nor my startling conclusions!) past these two gentlemen-scholars, so they should not be held responsible for any of it, but I am grateful for their work.

James Schindler-Ord's late Tao Te Ching website (taoteching.org.uk) was such an elegant, beautiful, and useful passion project. It was my go-to, and I was sorry to see it cease. There I discovered my favorite translation, that of Dr. Yi Wu, professor emeritus at the California Institute of Integral Studies. It feels to me so clear, humble, strong, and based in a sincere effort to represent Lao Tzu.

Special thanks to Annie Addlesperger for her research into the sub-components of compound charcters and her careful hand-drafting and assembling of those components when needed. She not only dove fearlessly into one etymological rabbit hole after another but did so enthusiastically—in other words she became a true collaborator. That's a tremendous gift.

My friends who themselves love the Tao Te Ching and have expressed enthusiasm for this project, thank you. Diane Redman may have been the first person to know about and support my intentions to complete this translation—I can't exactly remember when we first talked about it because we've shared everything as it happened for so many fortunate years.

My new friends and colleagues in The Art School provide me with the creative community that turns out to be essential even for lone wolves. Of course, the not-so-secret ingredient in the massive magic of The Art School is its founder, my friend and coach, the artist, writer, and podcaster Leah Campbell Badertscher. She is a wonder, and I'm so lucky to know her

THE DÈ OF LAOZI:

A FRESH LOOK BASED ON BRONZE INSCRIPTION GLYPHS

38.

Higher, ruling level *38.1.1*

Dé—the ethical, straight way of walking awhile and stopping awhile, eye directed forward over the heart-core...[3] *38.1.2*

the husk of the initial protective bud casing—the sepal—but not really the true inner flower of *38.1.3*

Dé—the ethical, straight way of walking awhile and stopping awhile, eye directed forward over the heart-core; *38.1.4*

the sun—walking across the sundial a while, stopping a while—sees indeed *38.2.5*

this carries like a plough—carries the meaning of *38.2.6*

flesh-and-blood, meat-handling Being[4] *38.2.7*

Dé—the ethical, straight way of walking awhile and stopping awhile, eye directed forward over the heart-core. *38.2.8*

Down below, lower level *38.3.9*

Dé—the ethical, straight way of walking awhile and stopping awhile, eye directed forward over the heart-core... *38.3.10*

the husk of the initial protective bud casing—the sepal—but not really the true inner flower of *38.3.11*

dropping something—losing[5] *38.3.12*

Dé—the ethical, straight way of walking awhile and stopping awhile, eye directed forward over the heart-core; *38.3.13*

the sun—walking across the sundial a while, stopping a while—sees indeed *38.4.14*

this carries like a plough—carries the meaning of *38.4.15*

Not-Being—nobody trance-dancing with long tails flowing from her wrists—[6] *38.4.16*

Dé—the ethical, straight way of walking awhile and stopping awhile, eye directed forward over the heart-core. *38.4.17*

---

[3] This character first appeared in *The Dào of Laozi* in Chapters 10, 21, 23, and 28.

[4] This character first appeared in Chapter 1.

[5] From Chapters 13, 23, 26, 29, and 33. In Chapter 23 it occurs close to a reference to "*Dé*." In Chapter 33, it precedes the character "*Dé*."

[6] This character first appeared in Chapter 1.

Higher, ruling level *38.5.18*
Dé—the ethical, straight way of walking awhile and stopping awhile, eye directed forward over the heart-core... *38.5.19*
Not-Being—nobody trance-dancing with long tails flowing from her wrists— *38.5.20*
efforting—like lifting up an elephant...[7] *38.5.21*
    and yet now, bearded, [8] *38.5.22*
    Not-Being—nobody trance-dancing with long tails flowing from her wrists... *38.5.23*
        the husk of the initial protective bud casing—the sepal—but not really the true inner flower of *38.5.24*
        efforting—like lifting up an elephant. *38.5.25*

Down below, lower level *38.6.26*
Dé—the ethical, straight way of walking awhile and stopping awhile, eye directed forward over the heart-core... *38.6.27*
efforting—like lifting up an elephant— *38.6.28*
has this... *38.6.29*
    and yet now, bearded, *38.6.30*
    flesh-and-blood, meat-handling Being... *38.6.31*
        this carries like a plough—carries the meaning of *38.6.32*
        efforting—like lifting up an elephant. *38.6.33*

Higher, ruling level *38.7.34*
being a personable person relating to others...[9] *38.7.35*
efforting—like lifting up an elephant— *38.7.36*
has this... *38.7.37*
    and yet now, bearded, *38.7.38*
    Not-Being—nobody trance-dancing with long tails flowing from her wrists... *38.7.39*
        this carries like a plough—carries the meaning of *38.7.40*
        efforting—like lifting up an elephant. *38.7.41*

---

[7] This is one of several different characters Laozi uses to describe doing/acting. It first appeared in Chapter 2.
[8] This character first appeared in Chapter 1.
[9] From Chapters 5, 8, 18, and 19.

Higher, ruling level *38.8.42*
righteous generosity—sacrificing a ram to the poor each year with that rake-like weapon we use to defend ourselves and our opinions...[10] *38.8.43*
efforting—like lifting up an elephant— *38.8.44*
has this... *38.8.45*
"and yet now, bearded, *38.8.46*
flesh-and-blood, meat-handling Being... *38.8.47*
this carries like a plough—carries the meaning of *38.8.48*
efforting—like lifting up an elephant." *38.8.49*

Higher, ruling level *38.9.50*
making ritual offerings at the altar with strings of jade and a drum with feathers on top...[11] *38.9.51*
efforting—like lifting up an elephant— *38.9.52*
has this... *38.9.53*
and yet now, bearded, *38.9.54*
must not—eh, like the lost-in-the-bushes , eh?— *38.9.55*
has this... *38.9.56*
as it ought to be—like the heart of a person as ugly as a short-tailed bird in a habitable cave in a cliff. *38.9.57*

After following this sacrificial blade-and-cauldron-like ritual example or regulation... *38.10.58*
their hand helping to undress, rolling up the sleeves, disturbs—throws into disorder— *38.10.59*
their arm—like the meat of a ruler or dead husband who administered and punished, marked a kneeling slave or criminal with a chisel, *38.10.60*
and yet now, bearded, *38.10.61*
your hand unexpectedly throwing away what it has... *38.10.62*
has this. *38.10.63*

[10] From Chapters 18 and 19.
[11] From Chapter 31.

Anciently, for ten generations, this lightly hits and leaves a mark of reason: *38.11.64*

"dropping something—losing" *38.11.65*

The Way of the loose-haired headperson—walking a while, stopping a while, and speaking of it all,[12] *38.11.66*

and yet now, bearded, *38.11.67*

afterwards—what remains when stepping slowly with only one's left leg leading the way, leaving the tiniest of silk thread footprints, that is, one's descendants... *38.11.68*

Dé—the ethical, straight way of walking awhile and stopping awhile, eye directed forward over the heart-core; *38.11.69*

"dropping something—losing *38.12.70*

Dé—the ethical, straight way of walking awhile and stopping awhile, eye directed forward over the heart-core," *38.12.71*

and yet now, bearded, *38.12.72*

afterwards—what remains when stepping slowly with only one's left leg leading the way, leaving the tiniest of silk thread footprints, that is, one's descendants... *38.12.73*

"being a personable person relating to others;" *38.12.7*

"dropping something—losing" *38.13.75*

"being a personable person relating to others" *38.13.76*

and yet now, bearded, *38.13.77*

afterwards—what remains when stepping slowly with only one's left leg leading the way, leaving the tiniest of silk thread footprints, that is, one's descendants... *38.13.78*

"righteous generosity—sacrificing a ram to the poor each year with that rake-like weapon we use to defend ourselves and our opinions;" *38.13.79*

[12] This character first appeared in Chapter 1.

"dropping something—losing" *38.14.80*
"righteous generosity—sacrificing a ram to the poor each year with that
rake-like weapon we use to defend ourselves and our opinions—"
38.14.81
and yet now, bearded, *38.14.82*
afterwards—what remains when stepping slowly with only one's
left leg leading the way, leaving the tiniest of silk thread
footprints, that is, one's descendants... *38.14.83*
"making ritual offerings at the altar with strings of jade
and a drum with feathers on top." *38.14.84*

That is to say, this particular grown man with a hairpin and public
courtesy name[13] *38.15.85*
"making ritual offerings at the altar with strings of jade and a drum with
feathers on top..." *38.15.86*
—now this is cooking with fire!— *38.15.87*
faithful as a centered heart-core like the drum with a flagpole placed in the
middle of a field to gather the people,[14] *38.15.88*
truth-speaking—speaking words like slaves or criminals, branded by a
chisel, emerging from a mouth of good luck that's as empty and quiet
as a mouth with a soldier's axe above it, speaking of grass,[15] *38.15.89*
has this *38.15.90*
thinning—weak like foliage covering a great man reduced to a
round-hung spindle of one inch; *38.15.91*

and yet now, bearded... *38.16.92*
confused anxiety—one's tongue is like twisted threads
with one remnant string hanging out—[16] *38.16.93*
has this *38.16.94*
head—the loose-haired headperson.[17] *38.16.95*

[13] This character first appeared in Chapter 3.
[14] From Chapter 18.
[15] From Chapters 8, 17, 21, and 23.
[16] From Chapters 3 and 18.
[17] From Chapter 14.

Forward—the front place in battle where a step could mean one's feet get cut off as punishment...[18] *38.17.96*
intimately knowing with the mind—recognizing those words on that weapon on a pole and saying what it carries like a plough, what it carries the meaning of...[19] *38.17.97*
—now this is cooking with fire!— *38.17.98*
The Way of the loose-haired headperson—walking a while, stopping a while, and speaking of it all— *38.17.99*
has this *38.17.100*
decorative brilliant magnificence of a flower blooming; *38.17.101*

and yet now, bearded, *38.18.102*
having a heart-core as foolish as that trampling monkey with the head of a ghost[20] *38.18.103*
has this *38.18.104*
beginning—like conception in and by a woman.[21] *38.18.105*

The sun—walking across the sundial a while, stopping a while—sees indeed *38.19.106*
this carries like a plough—carries the meaning of *38.19.107*
great giant[22] *38.19.108*
respected man or husband—as in, you stay ten feet from them, *38.19.109*
that is to say, this particular grown man with a hairpin and public courtesy name:[23] *38.19.110*

dwelling here—staying, as someone at home at the tea table, chaste and unmarried, someone being followed from behind by a tiger-fur head...[24] *38.20.111*
what it holds a basket of... *38.20.112*
thick like a generous cliff with a habitable cave that opposes the flow of the river, housing a baby with a large head, spread arms and swaddled legs under the sun... *38.20.113*

---

[18] From Chapter 2.
[19] From Chapter 15.
[20] From Chapter 20.
[21] From Chapters 1, 14, and 32.
[22] This character first appeared in Chapter 13.
[23] This character first appeared in Chapter 2.
[24] From Chapters 2, 8, 24, 26, 30, and 31.

"the husk of the initial protective bud casing—the sepal—but not really
the true inner flower of *38.21.114*
abiding—dwelling where birthed, sitting over ten mouths..."[25] *38.21.115*
what it holds a basket of... *38.21.116*
"thinning—weak like foliage covering a great man reduced to a
round-hung spindle of one inch;" *38.21.117*

dwelling here—staying, as someone at home at the tea table,
chaste and unmarried, someone being followed from behind
by a tiger-fur head... [26] *38.22.118*
what it holds a basket of... *38.22.119*
really filling—like a building with strings of solid
cowry-like riches...[27] *38.22.120*

"the husk of the initial protective bud casing—the sepal—but not really
the true inner flower of *38.23.121*
abiding—dwelling where birthed, sitting over ten mouths..." *38.23.122*
what it holds a basket of... *38.23.123*
"decorative brilliant magnificence of a flower blooming." *38.23.124*

Anciently, for ten generations, this lightly hits and leaves a mark of reason: *38.24.125*
"*withdrawing—like a person with a mouth or cave between their legs leaving*[28] *38.24.126*
*that—that fur stripped by hand from its pelt on the road where you stepped slowly, only
the left leg leading the way... 38.24.127*
grabbing the ear of—like marrying[29]*— 38.24.128*
this here—the foot stops a person here on their footprint."[30] *38.24.129*

39.

Ancient times, when the floods covered the sun, *39.1.1*
has this *39.1.2*
hand-picking, like-cowry-shell-riches-along-the-road, *39.1.3*
One[31] *39.1.4*
—now this is cooking with fire! *39.1.5*

---

[25] From Chapter 2. The second character also appears in Chapters 8, 25, and 31.
[26] From Chapters 2, 8, 24, 26, 30, and 31.
[27] From Chapter 3.
[28] From Chapters 2, 12, 20, 21, and 29.
[29] From Chapters 12, 29, and 30.
[30] This expression was used in Chapter 12.
[31] From Chapters 10, 11, 14, 22, and 25.

Heaven (that sky level above the human head) *39.2.6*
"hand-picking, like-cowry-shell-riches-along-the-road, *39.2.7*
One," *39.2.8*
this carries like a plough—carries the meaning of *39.2.9*
clear like still blue-green water—the color resembling the growth
of that sedative cinnabar plant.[32] *39.2.10*

Earth (this soil vagina) *39.3.11*
"hand-picking, like-cowry-shell-riches-along-the-road, *39.3.12*
One," *39.3.13*
this carries like a plough—carries the meaning of *39.3.14*
settled as when a married woman visits her parents' home—her heart
under their roof with food and wine—and she exhales. *39.3.15*

A lightning god[33] *39.4.16*
"hand-picking, like-cowry-shell-riches-along-the-road, *39.4.17*
One," *39.4.18*
this carries like a plough—carries the meaning of *39.4.19*
nimbly effective as a rain shaman *39.4.20*

Within that valley mouth between two mountains[34] *39.5.21*
"hand-picking, like-cowry-shell-riches-along-the-road, *39.5.22*
One," *39.5.23*
this carries like a plough—carries the meaning of *39.5.24*
full to overflowing its vessel.[35] *39.5.25*

The myriad, scorpion-medicine-dancing Ten Thousand *39.6.26*
Things cut off—all matter external to oneself like seeds, cows etc.[36] *39.6.27*
"hand-picking, like-cowry-shell-riches-along-the-road, *39.6.28*
One," *39.6.29*
this carries like a plough—carries the meaning of *39.6.30*
birthing—a bud sprouting from the ground.[37] *39.6.31*

---

[32] From Chapter 15.
[33] From Chapters 6 and 29.
[34] From Chapters 6, 15, 28, and 32.
[35] From Chapters 4, 9, 15, and 22.
[36] "The Ten Thousand Things" characters are often linked and first appeared like this in Chapter 1.
[37] From Chapters 2, 7, 10, 15, 25, 30, and 34.

A marquis—'arrow in the cave'—king—connecting
heaven, man, and earth[38] *39.7.32 & 33*
"hand-picking, like-cowry-shell-riches-along-the-road, *39.7.34*
One," *39.7.35*
this carries like a plough—carries the meaning of *39.7.36*
efforting—like lifting up an elephant— *39.7.37*
Heaven (that sky level above the human head)—Down
Below (lower level)[39] *39.7.38 & 39*
pure, chaste, and virtuous as an ancient divination cauldron. *39.7.40*

What it holds a basket of... *39.8.41*
causing—lightly hitting and leaving a mark— *39.8.42*
has this. *39.8.43*

"Heaven (that sky level above the human head)" *39.9.44*
Not-Being—nobody trance-dancing with long tails flowing from
her wrists, *39.9.45*
this carries like a plough—carries the meaning of *39.9.46*
"clear like still blue-green water—the color resembling the growth
of that sedative cinnabar plant" *39.9.47*
soon will be—as if offering a meat tribute by hand
on a table— *39.9.48*
afraid—your heart like commonplace dishes being scraped
with a blade—of... *39.9.49*
rending like using a blade to tear clothing—like a robe, especially
on the torso, or the placental afterbirth hanging from a
recently pregnant woman—from human remains. *39.9.50*

[38] This character first appeared in Chapters 32 and 37.
[39] "Heaven-Below" characters are often linked and first appeared like this in Chapter 1.

"Earth (this soil vagina)" *39.10.51*
Not-Being—nobody trance-dancing with long tails flowing from
her wrists, *39.10.52*
this carries like a plough—carries the meaning of *39.10.53*
"settled as when married woman visits her parents'
home—her heart under their roof with food and
wine—and she exhales" *39.10.54*
soon will be—as if offering a meat tribute by hand on
a table— *39.10.55*
afraid—your heart like commonplace dishes being scraped with
a blade—of ... *39.10.56*
shot like by a bow launching 'thwang!' and levelling grass with
one's feet as effectively as if by hand with a halberd. *39.10.57*

"A lightning god" *39.11.58*
Not-Being—nobody trance-dancing with long tails flowing from
her wrists, *39.11.59*
this carries like a plough—carries the meaning of *39.11.560*
"nimbly effective as a rain shaman" *39.11.61*
soon will be—as if offering a meat tribute by hand on
a table— *39.11.62*
afraid—your heart like commonplace dishes being scraped
with a blade—of ... *39.11.63*
yawning—like a man deficient and lacking breath—
and resting, relaxing. *39.11.64*

"Within that valley mouth between two mountains" *39.12.65*
Not-Being—nobody trance-dancing with long tails flowing from
her wrists, *39.12.66*
this carries like a plough—carries the meaning of *39.12.67*
"full to overflowing its vessel" *39.12.68*
soon will be—as if offering a meat tribute by hand on
a table— *39.12.69*
afraid—your heart like commonplace dishes being scraped
with a blade—of ... *39.12.70*
drained, exhausted—a person standing on solid ground making
a yawning sound. *39.12.71*

"The myriad, scorpion-medicine-dancing Ten Thousand *39.13.72*
Things cut off—all matter external to oneself like seeds, cows etc." *39.13.73*
Not-Being—nobody trance-dancing with long tails flowing from her wrists, *39.13.74*
this carries like a plough—carries the meaning of *39.13.75*
"birthing—a bud sprouting from the ground—" *39.13.76*
soon will be—as if offering a meat tribute by hand on a table— *39.13.77*
afraid—your heart like commonplace dishes being scraped with a blade—of ... *39.13.78*
obliterating like water extinguishing a fire sheltered by a cliff with a habitable cave as surely as any weapon on a pole. *39.13.79*

A marquis—'arrow in the cave'—king—connecting heaven, man, and earth *39.14.80 & 81*
Not-Being—nobody trance-dancing with long tails flowing from her wrists— *39.14.82*
this carries like a plough—carries the meaning of *39.14.83*
treasuring—as if as valuable as cowry-shell-riches,[40] *39.14.84*
high above (a two-story building in the city outskirts) *39.14.85*
soon will be—as if offering a meat tribute by hand on a table— *39.14.86*
afraid—your heart like commonplace dishes being scraped with a blade—of ... *39.14.87*
toppling or overthrown—like stumbling or fainting as a disobedient, upside-down person yawning in a habitable cave on a cliff. *39.14.88*

Anciently, for ten generations, this lightly hits and leaves a mark of reason: *39.15.89*
"treasuring—as if as valuable as cowry-shell-riches," *39.15.90*
this carries like a plough—carries the meaning of *39.15.91*
appearing to accumulate cheap inferior "riches"—like several tiny weapons on a pole next to a cowry— *39.15.92*
efforting—like lifting up an elephant— *39.15.93*
the source foundation of a rooted tree; *39.15.94*

[40] From Chapters 3, 9, 13, 17, 20, 27, and 31.

"high above (a two-story building in the city outskirts)," *39.16.95*
this carries like a plough—carries the meaning of *39.16.96*
down below, lower level *39.16.97*
efforting—like lifting up an elephant— *39.16.98*
the foundation of native earth or clay under what it holds a
basket of. *39.16.99*

The sun—walking across the sundial a while, stopping a while—sees indeed *39.17.100*
this carries like a plough—carries the meaning of *39.17.101*
a marquis—'arrow in the cave'—king—connecting heaven, man,
and earth *39.17.102 & 103*
of course—one's self personally, right on one's nose, *39.17.104*
what it's called when speaking from the gut—words, like slaves or criminals
branded by a chisel emerging from a mouth:[41] *39.17.105*
orphaned like a big-headed, legs-swaddled baby left as a melon on
the vine, *39.17.106*
scant as one widowed, alone—separating them from the kneeling head of
the household with a blade...[42] *39.17.107*
the husk of the initial protective bud casing—the sepal—
but not really the true inner flower of *39.17.108*
hub of a wheel on the carriage used for harvesting.[43] *39.17.109*

This here—the foot stops a person here on their footprint— *39.18.110*
breaking the little wings off,[44] *39.18.111*
this carries like a plough—carries the meaning of *39.18.112*
"appearing to accumulate cheap inferior "riches"—like several tiny
weapons on a pole next to a cowry *39.18.113*
efforting—like lifting up an elephant— *39.18.114*
the source foundation of a rooted tree..." *39.18.115*
of disastrous nature—like that disease-causing environment around
Tusk Town; *39.18.116*

"breaking the little wings off..." *39.19.117*
—pah, can you?! *39.19.118*

---

[41] This is one of several characters that Laozi used to describe how we name something. It first appeared in Chapter 1.
[42] From Chapter 19.
[43] From Chapter 11.
[44] From Chapters 1, 7, and 31.

Anciently, for ten generations, this lightly hits and leaves a mark of reason: *39.20.119*
causing—lightly hitting and leaving a mark of *39.20.120*
counting up—like a mother, lightly hitting, scolding her daughter— *39.20.121*
such a good public reputation—that is, what's being spoken with words like a slave or criminal branded by a chisel about one's support, about one's offers to carry things on one's shoulders like a broker whose fame is everything...[45] *39.20.122*
Not-Being—nobody trance-dancing with long tails flowing from her wrists— *39.20.123*
"such a good public reputation—that is, what's being spoken with words like a slave or criminal branded by a chisel about one's support, about one's offers to carry things on one's shoulders like a broker whose fame is everything..." *39.20.124*

the husk of the initial protective bud casing—the sepal—but not really the true inner flower of *39.21.125*
wanting—missing what's been eroded from this ravine...[46] *39.21.126*
a string of carved jade-like stone totems, *39.21.127*
a string of carved jade-like stone totems *39.21.128*
'as if—like a woman just doing as told— *39.21.129*
jade totems;[47] *39.21.130*

each and every pedestrian jade, *39.22.131*
each and every pedestrian jade *39.22.132*
'as if—like a woman just doing as told— *39.22.133*
a hard stone beneath a cliff with a habitable cave *39.22.134*

40.

Making someone return, with one's right hand, to the habitable cave in the cliff[48] *40.1.1*
—now this is cooking with fire!— *40.1.2*
The Way of the loose-haired headperson—walking a while, stopping a while, and speaking of it all *40.1.3*
has this *40.1.4*
laboring—like moving heavy bags with great strength.[49] *40.1.5*

---

[45] From Chapter 17.
[46] First introduced in Chapter 1.
[47] From Chapter 9.
[48] From Chapter 25.
[49] Another kind of doing/acting. From Chapters 5, 8, and 15.

To be as fragile as a matching pair of decorative bows or little wings[50] *40.2.6*
—now this is cooking with fire!— *40.2.7*
The Way of the loose-haired headperson—walking a while, stopping a while, and speaking of it all *40.2.8*
has this *40.2.9*
doing truly useful work like a water bucket—by means of carrying-capacity.[51] *40.2.10*

Heaven (that sky level above the human head)-Down Below (lower level): *40.3.11 &12*
the myriad, scorpion-medicine-dancing Ten Thousand *40.3.13*
Things cut off—all matter external to oneself like seeds, cows etc. *40.3.14*
birthing—a bud sprouting from the ground [52]*40.3.15*
here—oh, black, icy raven...[53] *40.3.16*
flesh-and-blood, meat-handling Being; *40.3.17*

flesh-and-blood, meat-handling Being *40.4.18*
birthing—a bud sprouting from the ground *40.4.19*
here—oh, black, icy raven... *40.4.20*
Not-Being—nobody trance-dancing with long tails flowing from her wrists. *40.4.21*

41.

Higher, ruling level *41.1.1*
bachelor soldier-scholar-official appointed by the emperor—a yeoman...[54] *41.1.2*
hearing at the double-winged gateway[55] *41.1.3*
The Way of the loose-haired headperson—walking a while, stopping a while, and speaking of it all... *41.1.4*
exerting with force—working hard with the strength of an arm, a bladed tool, or a plough on the soil...[56] *41.1.5*
and yet now, bearded, *41.1.6*
on a public road, practicing—moving with—[57] *41.1.7*
has this. *41.1.8*

---

[50] From Chapters 3 and 36.
[51] Another kind of doing/acting. From Chapters 4, 6, 11, 27, 28, 31, and 35.
[52] See the previous chapter for more on "The Ten Thousand Things birthing."
[53] Introduced in Chapter 8.
[54] This character first appeared in Chapter 15.
[55] From Chapters 14 and 35.
[56] Another kind of doing/acting. From Chapter 6.
[57] From Chapters 2, 12, 24, 25, 26, 27, 29, and 33.

In the center—like that drum with a flagpole placed in the middle of a field to gather the people, detect the wind—[58] *41.2.9*
"bachelor soldier-scholar-official appointed by the emperor—a yeoman... *41.2.10*
hearing at the double-winged gateway *41.2.11*
The Way of the loose-haired headperson—walking a while, stopping a while, and speaking of it all..." *41.2.12*
"A Certain Someone compliantly combing their loose hair seems to be saying: 'this is as if...'[59] *41.2.13*
surviving—on the plane of a baby with health issues, maybe a large head, but still sprouting..."[60] *41.2.14*
A Certain Someone compliantly combing their loose hair seems to be saying: 'this is as if...' *41.2.15*
past—perished.[61] *41.2.16*

Down below, lower level *41.3.17*
"bachelor soldier-scholar-official appointed by the emperor—a yeoman... *41.3.18*
hearing at the double-winged gateway *41.3.19*
The Way of the loose-haired headperson—walking a while, stopping a while, and speaking of it all..." *41.3.20*
great giant... *41.3.21*
laughing like a dog in the grass *41.3.22*
has this. *41.3.23*

The husk of the initial protective bud casing—the sepal—but not really the true inner flower of *41.4.24*
"laughing like a dog in the grass..." *41.4.25*
the husk of the initial protective bud casing—the sepal—but not really the true inner flower of *41.4.26*
enough—the full leg-cut of the animal,[62] *41.4.27*
this carries like a plough—carries the meaning of... *41.4.28*
efforting—like lifting up an elephant... *41.4.29*
The Way of the loose-haired headperson—walking a while, stopping a while, and speaking of it all. *41.4.30*

[58] From Chapters 5, 21 and 25.
[59] This character was first introduced in Chapter 6.
[60] This character is from Chapters 4, 6, & 7. This entire two-character expression was used in Chapter 6.
[61] From Chapter 33.
[62] From Chapter 17, 19, 23, 28, 33, and 35.

Anciently, for ten generations, this lightly hits and leaves a mark of reason: *41.5.31*
Expertly—hand-built by a striding person with a bamboo brush— *41.5.32*
speaking—words, like slaves or criminals branded by a chisel emerging from a mouth... *41.5.33*
flesh-and-blood, meat-handling Being *41.5.34*
has this. *41.5.35*

As bright as dawn rising on a crescent moon—enlightened,[63] *41.6.36*
The Way of the loose-haired headperson—walking a while, stopping a while, and speaking of it all... *41.6.37*
A Certain Someone compliantly combing their loose hair seems to be saying: 'this is as if...' *41.6.38*
dark—as if the sun's behind a tree with two layers of branches, tree tops not yet fully grown.[64] *41.6.39*

Walking forward awhile and stopping awhile like a 'short-tailed bird,' *41.7.40*
The Way of the loose-haired headperson—walking a while, stopping a while, and speaking of it all... *41.7.41*
A Certain Someone compliantly combing their loose hair seems to be saying: 'this is as if...' *41.7.42*
withdrawing—walking awhile and stopping a while, retreating from the sun.[65] *41.7.43*

As foreign as that tribe in the east—the great barbarians with bows—leveled and razed by destruction,[66] *41.8.44*
The Way of the loose-haired headperson—walking a while, stopping a while, and speaking of it all... *41.8.45*
A Certain Someone compliantly combing their loose hair seems to be saying: 'this is as if...' *41.8.46*
blemished as an ill head that's as bright white as husked raw rice kernels, knotted like a skein of silk. *41.8.47*

---

[63] From Chapters 10, 16, 22, 24, 27, 33, and 36.
[64] From Chapter 14.
[65] From Chapter 9.
[66] From Chapter 14.

"Higher, ruling level *41.9.48*
Dé—the ethical, straight way of walking awhile and stopping awhile, eye directed forward over the heart-core..."[67] *41.9.49*
A Certain Someone compliantly combing their loose hair seems to be saying: 'this is as if...' *41.9.50*
in the common practices of the people from that difficult position in the valley between two mountains.[68] *41.9.51*

Great giant, *41.10.52*
white-clear as acorn flesh...[69] *41.10.53*
A Certain Someone compliantly combing their loose hair seems to be saying: 'this is as if...' *41.10.54*
disgracing—like vibrating oneself to life in one tiny inch as when life begins to stir.[70] *41.10.55*

Wide like a person with a large belly in a habitable cave in a cliff *41.11.56*
Dé—the ethical, straight way of walking awhile and stopping awhile, eye directed forward over the heart-core... *41.11.57*
A Certain Someone compliantly combing their loose hair seems to be saying: 'this is as if...' *41.11.58*
"the husk of the initial protective bud casing—the sepal—but not really the true inner flower of *41.11.59*
enough—the full leg-cut of the animal." *41.11.60*

"Expertly—hand-built by a striding person with a bamboo brush—" *41.12.61*
Dé—the ethical, straight way of walking awhile and stopping awhile, eye directed forward over the heart-core *41.12.62*
A Certain Someone compliantly combing their loose hair seems to be saying: 'this is as if...' *41.12.63*
covertly sneaking, like a man standing with his back to someone gathering themselves together from three sides after a blade cut off their foot as punishment, like from adultery. *41.12.64*

---

[67] From Chapter 38.
[68] From Chapter 20.
[69] From Chapter 28.
[70] From Chapters 13 and 28.

Matter mattering—with the keen and weighty quality of two axes over a cowry... *41.13.65*
genuine—using your fork to get food right from the cauldron...[71] *41.13.66*
A Certain Someone compliantly combing their loose hair seems to be saying: 'this is as if...' *41.13.67*
as changeable as a river flowing against someone gathering themselves together from three sides after a blade cut off their foot as punishment, like from adultery. *41.13.68*

Great giant, *41.14.69*
like the parallel side of a tipped blade... *41.14.70*
Not-Being—nobody trance-dancing with long tails flowing from her wrists... *41.14.71*
a corner like that remote place by the big soil mound with that trampling monkey with the head of a ghost. *41.14.72*

Great giant, *41.15.73*
set of valuable vessels with lots of capacity—worthy of a guard dog...[72] *41.15.74*
late evening when the sun on a man in a hat is being removed... *41.15.75*
completing—that final nail in the weapon on a pole.[73] *41.15.76*

Great giant, *41.16.77*
one tone—one note from a mouth...[74] *41.16.78*
sparse—as spare as the interconnecting threads in that square cloth men wrap around their 'little bird' top knots and heads...[75] *41.16.79*
many sounds—hitting chimes with one's right hand and hearing them.[76] *41.16.80*

Great giant, *41.17.81*
likeness—like an elephant skeleton letting us see a living elephant...[77] *41.17.82*
Not-Being—nobody trance-dancing with long tails flowing from her wrists... *41.17.83*
shaping with measuring lines of hair's breadth.[78] *41.17.84*

---

[71] From Chapter 21.
[72] From Chapters 11, 28, 29, 31, and 36.
[73] From Chapters 2, 7, 15, 17, 25, and 34.
[74] From Chapters 2 and 12.
[75] From Chapters 14 and 23.
[76] From Chapter 2 where it also was juxtaposed to "one tone."
[77] From Chapters 4, 14, 21, and 35!
[78] From Chapters 2 and 24.

The Way of the loose-haired headperson—walking a while, stopping a while,
and speaking of it all... *41.18.85*
hidden—a soil mound as careful and compassionate as a claw-like hand
grabbing from above the real work from the force of a bladed tool over a
pig-head heart: *41.18.86*
"Not-Being—nobody trance-dancing with long tails flowing from
her wrists— *41.18.87*
personal, childhood naming—what it whispers to identify itself
by moonlight."[79] *41.18.88*

That is to say, this particular grown man with a hairpin and public
courtesy name, *41.19.89*
essentially and only—like the mouth of 'the short-tailed bird'— *41.19.90*
The Way of the loose-haired headperson—walking a while, stopping
a while, and speaking of it all: *41.19.91*
virtue—such as offering up a ram's head while back and forth
speaking words that are emerging from a mouth like slaves or
criminals branded by a chisel—[80] *41.19.92*
lending like a retrievable arrow attached to a
string with cowry riches... *41.19.93*
abiding for a long time—like the erect penis of a
male ancestor—[81] *41.19.94*
"completing—that final nail in the weapon on a pole." *41.19.95*

42.

The Way of the loose-haired headperson—walking a while, stopping a while, and
speaking of it all— *42.1.1*
birthing—a bud sprouting from the ground... *42.1.2*
One; *42.1.3*

One— *42.2.4*
birthing—a bud sprouting from the ground... *42.2.5*
Two; *42.2.6*

---

[79] Another kind of naming. It appeared first in Chapter 1 including paired with "Not-Being" as it is here. There it was "Heaven-Down Below's conception."
[80] First introduced in Chapter 2.
[81] From Chapter 7.

Two— *42.3.7*
birthing—a bud sprouting from the ground... *42.3.8*
three; *42.3.9*

three— *42.4.10*
birthing—a bud sprouting from the ground... *42.4.11*
the myriad, scorpion-medicine-dancing Ten Thousand *42.4.12*
Things cut off—all matter external to oneself like seeds, cows etc.; *42.4.13*

the myriad, scorpion-medicine-dancing Ten Thousand *42.5.14*
Things cut off—all matter external to oneself like seeds, cows etc. *42.5.15*
carrying as cowry-riches with a much smaller person or knife—that kind of load-bearing that can lead to suffering, to neglect, to betrayal, to repudiation— *42.5.16*
that feminine yīn principle of what's hidden and overcast as when what's being said—in the mouth now, in modern times—is said when it's dusky, like clouds covering a big soil mound,[82] *42.5.17*
and yet now, bearded... *42.5.18*
bundling it all up together—in one's arms... *42.5.19*
that male principle *yáng* of sun shining on a big soil mound; *42.5.20*

pouring water from the center—like from the hollow drum at the base of the flagpole,[83] *42.6.21*
the breath of life—that vital *qì* energy, that air flow that's like rice given as a gift...[84] *42.6.22*
this carries like a plough—carries the meaning of *42.6.23*
efforting—like lifting up an elephant— *42.6.24*
harmonizing as a mouth organ.[85] *42.6.25*

That person *42.7.26*
has this *42.7.27*
'place'—somewhere intentionally created, like a door chopped with an axe...[86] *42.7.28*
a house's inferior-hearted evil—seen from overhead:[87] *42.7.29*

---

[82] From Chapter 41.
[83] From Chapter 4.
[84] From Chapter 10.
[85] From Chapters 2, 4, and 18.
[86] First introduced in Chapter 7.
[87] From Chapters 24 and 31.

essentially and only—like the mouth of 'the short-tailed bird'— *42.8.30*
"orphaned like a big-headed, legs-swaddled baby left as a melon on the vine, *42.8.31*
scant as one widowed, alone—separating them from the kneeling head of the household with a blade... *42.8.32*
the husk of the initial protective bud casing—the sepal—but not really the true inner flower of *42.8.33*
hub of a wheel on the carriage used for harvesting;"[88] *42.8.34*

and yet now, bearded... *42.9.35*
king—connecting heaven, man, and earth—[89] *42.9.36*
as publicly fair and impartial as a high ranking old big-balled man—a duke...[90] *42.9.37*
this carries like a plough—carries the meaning of *42.9.38*
efforting—like lifting up an elephant— *42.9.39*
being weighed, like a claw-like hand grabbing from above, holding rice or grain on a scale and called out as that.[91] *42.9.40*

Anciently, for ten generations, this lightly hits and leaves a mark of reason: *42.10.41*
Things cut off—all matter external to oneself like seeds, cows etc... *42.10.42*
this particular territory—this enclave, defended by a weapon on a pole, plus its surroundings...[92] *42.10.43*
diminishing like hands and fingers injured by the top edge of the cauldron that is the monarchy government *42.10.44*
has this... *42.10.45*
and yet now, bearded... *42.10.46*
overflowing like water from a vessel; *42.10.47*

this particular territory—this enclave, defended by a weapon on a pole, plus its surroundings... *42.11.48*
"overflowing like water from a vessel," *42.11.49*
has this... *42.11.50*
and yet now, bearded, *42.11.51*
"diminishing like hands and fingers injured by the top edge of the cauldron that is the monarchy government." *42.11.52*

[88] From Chapter 39 where it described the marquis-king.
[89] From Chapters 16, 25, 32, 37, and 39.
[90] From Chapter 16.
[91] Another kind of naming.
[92] From Chapters 4, 24, 29, and 31.

"That person *42.12.53*
has this *42.12.54*
'place'—somewhere intentionally created, like a door chopped with an axe..." *42.12.55*
this teaching—instructing a child in counting or divination, lightly hitting with a teaching cane...[93] *42.12.56*

I/we—holding a rake-like weapon to defend ourselves and our opinion—[94] *42.13.57*
—both armpits sweat this too!— *42.13.58*
"this teaching—instructing a child in counting or divination, lightly hitting with a teaching cane..."*42.13.59*
has this: *42.13.60*

> *Strengthening like an insect—revolving oneself as a venomous snake-like bow—*[95] *42.14.61*
> *wood bridging water—with a brutal double-edged sword injury in there too—like the state of* Liáng *42.14.62*
> *—now this is cooking with fire!—* *42.14.63*
> *the husk of the initial protective bud casing—the sepal—but not really the true inner flower of* *42.14.64*
> *hand-picking, like-cowry-shell-riches-along-the-road,* *42.14.65*
> *what it holds a basket of...* *42.14.66*
> *dying—going from a standing person to a pile of bones.*[96] *42.14.67*

I/we—our five mouths— *42.15.68*
soon will be—as if offering a meat tribute by hand on a table, *42.15.69*
this carries like a plough—carries the meaning of, *42.15.70*
efforting—like lifting up an elephant— *42.15.71*
"this teaching—instructing a child in counting or divination, lightly hitting with a teaching cane..." *42.15.72*
as a beginning—the father who works by hand with a stone axe.[97] *42.15.73*

---

[93] From Chapter 2.
[94] This character first appeared in Chapters 17 and 20.
[95] From Chapters 3, 15, 25, 29, 30, 33, and 36.
[96] This last character is from Chapters 6 and 33. (Yi Wu says the proverb in italics was a popular maxim adopted by Laozi and translates it as "the man of violence will not die well.")
[97] From Chapter 21.

43.

Heaven (that sky level above the human head)-Down Below (lower level), *43.1.1 & 2*
what it has... *43.1.3*
reaching the extreme—like an arrow straight into the clay soil— *43.1.4*
softening—to be like a tree that can be cut with a spear...[98] *43.1.5*

> "galloping—'oh yeah, vagina!'— *43.2.6*
> galloping all over—like a horse given free rein by a chivalrous knight with frank words on a sob"[99] *43.2.7*
> Heaven (that sky level above the human head)-Down Below (lower level), *43.2.8 & 43.2.9*
> what it has... *43.2.10*
> reaching the extreme—like an arrow straight into the clay soil—*43.2.11*
> hard and solid as a right hand through an eye cast down in surrender over solid clay soil; *43.2.12*

Not-Being—nobody trance-dancing with long tails flowing from her wrists... *43.3.13*
flesh-and-blood, meat-handling Being... *43.3.14*

> entering like an arrow *43.3.15*
> Not-Being—nobody trance-dancing with long tails flowing from her wrists— *43.3.16*
> interstice—space where moonlight's peeking leisurely through the double-winged gateway.[100] *43.3.17*

I/we—our five mouths, *43.4.18*
the sun—walking across the sundial a while, stopping a while—sees indeed, *43.4.19*
this carries like a plough—carries the meaning of: *43.4.20*

> firing arrows from the mouth, sure... *43.4.21*
> Not-Being—nobody trance-dancing with long tails flowing from her wrists— *43.4.22*
> efforting—like lifting up an elephant,[101] *43.4.23*
> what it has... *43.4.24*
>
> > flesh-and-blood, meat-handling Being *43.4.25*
> > overflowing like water from a vessel.[102] *43.4.26*

---

[98] From Chapters 10 and 36.
[99] From Chapter 12.
[100] From Chapter 5.
[101] From Chapter 38.
[102] From Chapter 42.

"The husk of the initial protective bud casing—the sepal—but not really the true inner flower of 43.5.27
speaking—words, like slaves or criminals branded by a chisel emerging from a mouth, 43.5.28
what it has... 43.5.29
this teaching—instructing a child in counting or divination, lightly hitting with a teaching cane..."[103] *43.5.30*

"Not-Being—nobody trance-dancing with long tails flowing from her wrists— *43.6.31*
efforting—like lifting up an elephant, *43.6.32*
what it has... " *43.6.33*
"overflowing like water from a vessel..." *43.6.34*

> "Heaven (that sky level above the human head)-Down Below (lower level)... " *43.7.35 & 36*
> sparse—as spare as the interconnecting threads in that square cloth men wrap around their 'little bird' top knots and heads—[104] *43.7.37*
> are reaching—like grabbing a person—[105] *43.7.38*
> what it has. *43.7.39*

44.

Personal, childhood naming—what it whispers to identify itself by moonlight... *44.1.1*
supporting—offering to carry on one's shoulders—[106] *44.1.2*
one's pregnant self...[107] *44.1.3*

> whoever—which person, like a baby with a slanting mouth of enjoyment is this[108] *44.1.4*
> intimate—like a beloved that one sees closely even in suffering like from that chisel used to mark slaves and criminals?[109] *44.1.5*

---

[103] This last character is from Chapters 2 and 42. The entire line is from Chapter 2.
[104] From Chapters 14, 23, and 41.
[105] From Chapters 13 and 21.
[106] First introduced in Chapter 8.
[107] This character first appeared in Chapter 7.
[108] From Chapters 15 and 23.
[109] From Chapters 17 and 18.

"One's pregnant self..." *44.2.6*
supporting—offering to carry on one's shoulders— *44.2.7*
transformation of cowry-shell-riches—like from a right-side-up person to an upside-down person...[110] *44.2.8*
whoever—which person, like a baby with a slanting mouth of enjoyment is this *44.2.9*
much more—like a double serving of meat?[111] *44.2.10*

Hand-picking, like-cowry-shell-riches-along-the-road... *44.3.11*
supporting—offering to carry on one's shoulders— *44.3.12*
past—perished...[112] *44.3.13*
whoever—which person, like a baby with a slanting mouth of enjoyment is this *44.3.14*
ill as one carried on a stretcher on the third heavenly stem? *44.3.15*

The sun—walking across the sundial a while, stopping a while—sees indeed *44.4.16*
anciently, for ten generations, this lightly hits and leaves a mark of reason: *44.4.17*
in the extreme—something pleasing in the mouth, matched so it's doubly pleasing—[113] *44.4.18*
loving—your heart-core stuck in your throat,[114] *44.4.19*
analytically—hands over heart-core...[115] *44.4.20*
great giant... *44.4.21*
lavishly expending like two sticks tied together to start a fire over cowry-riches; *44.4.22*

"much more—like a double serving of meat—" *44.5.23*
hiding—like storing weapons on a pole that can kill by piercing the eye under a bamboo bed below grass as is right and generous, *44.5.24*
analytically—hands over heart-core... *44.5.25*
thick like a generous cliff with a habitable cave that opposes flow of the river, housing a baby with a large head, spre arms and swaddled legs under the sun[116] *44.5.26*
"past—perished." *44.5.27*

---

[110] From Chapters 3 and 12.
[111] From Chapters 5 and 22.
[112] From Chapters 33 and 41.
[113] From Chapters 21 and 29.
[114] From Chapters 13 and 27.
[115] From Chapters 30 and 36.
[116] From Chapter 38.

Firing arrows from the mouth, sure *44.6.28*
enough—the full leg-cut of the animal...[117] *44.6.29*
the husk of the initial protective bud casing—the sepal—but not really the true inner flower of *44.6.30*
disgracing—like vibrating oneself to life in one tiny inch as when life begins to stir;[118] *44.6.31*

firing arrows from the mouth, sure *44.7.32*
stopping on their footprint...[119] *44.7.33*
the husk of the initial protective bud casing—the sepal—but not really the true inner flower of *44.7.34*
endangered—evil like human remains, spoken of privately, revolving around yourself;[120] *44.7.35*

[illegible]out which one can purse one's lips like a piece of cane and puff: 'Yup, that's it, definitely,' *44.8.36*
carries like a plough—carries the meaning of... *44.8.37*
long as hair that has to be tied with a brooch...[121] *44.8.38*
enduring through time—like someone receiving moxibustion treatments with mugwort used for cramps, turning a breech baby, or other health issues.[122] *44.8.39*

45.

[illegible]ant *45.1.1*
[illegible]ing—that final nail in the weapon on a pole,[123] *45.1.2*
A Certain Someone compliantly combing their loose hair seems to be saying: 'this is as if...' *45.1.3*
[illegible]acking—like a lidded earthen pot with a gap broken by a resolute hand with a fork... *45.1.4*

---

[117] From Ch[illegible] 17, 19, 23, 28, 33, 35, and 41.
[118] From Ch[illegible] 13, 28, and 41.
[119] From Cha[illegible] 20, 32, and 35.
[120] From Cha[illegible] 16, 25, and 32.
[121] From Chap[illegible] 2, 7, and 9.
[122] From Chapt[illegible] 7, 15, 16, 23, and 33.
[123] From Chapte[illegible], 7, 15, 17, 25, 34 and 41.

what it holds a basket of.. *45.2.5*
doing truly useful work like a water bucket—by means of carrying-capacity: *45.2.6*
the husk of the initial protective bud casing—the sepal—but not really the true inner flower of *45.2.7*
fraud like both hands supporting tattered cloth that's been hit lightly. *45.2.8*

Great giant *45.3.9*
full to overflowing its vessel, *45.3.10*
A Certain Someone compliantly combing their loose hair seems to be saying: 'this is as if...' *45.3.11*
pouring water from the center, like from the hollow drum at the base of the flagpole...[124] *45.3.12*

what it holds a basket of... *45.4.13*
doing truly useful work like a water bucket—by means of carrying-capacity: *45.4.14*
the husk of the initial protective bud casing—the sepal—but not really the true inner flower of *45.4.15*
being used up and destitute—your pregnant self, buried with a bow.[125] *45.4.16*

Great giant *45.5.17*
looking straight on, straight ahead,[126] *45.5.18*
A Certain Someone compliantly combing their loose hair seems to be saying: 'this is as if...' *45.5.19*
bending—like one who represents the dead in a rite flexing to step out of a cave.[127] *45.5.20*

Great giant *45.6.21*
craftiness—using a bladed tool on exhaled air,[128] *45.6.22*
A Certain Someone compliantly combing their loose hair seems to be saying: 'this is as if...' *45.6.23*
clumsy—stepping out of their cave all hands and fingers. *45.6.24*

[124] From Chapter 4.
[125] From Chapter 5.
[126] From Chapter 22.
[127] From Chapter 5.
[128] From Chapter 19.

Great giant *45.7.25*
debating—speaking words that are emerging from a mouth like slaves or criminals branded by a chisel while surrounded by more chisels on each side, *45.7.26*
A Certain Someone compliantly combing their loose hair seems to be saying: 'this is as if...' *45.7.27*
mumbling or stammering—words that are emerging from a mouth like slaves or criminals branded by a chisel entering a city through its outskirts. *45.7.28*

Impetuous, the irritable—three birds chirping in a tree along the way of walking a while and stopping a while...[129] *45.8.29*
forcing a victory over—using a blade to mend a boat or roll rice into a ball under moonlight—[130]*45.8.30*
cold as a humble person sleeping under a desolate roof in the grass to protect themselves from winter chill. *45.8.31*

Calm peace—when the clear blue-green growth of that sedative cinnabar plant quiets a dispute between two hands on a ploughshare...[131] *45.9.32*
"forcing a victory over—using a blade to mend a boat or roll rice into a ball under moonlight—"*45.9.33*
hot like a fire under a tree tipped and planted by a person in the clay soil. *45.9.34*

Clear like still blue-green water—the color resembling the growth of that sedative cinnabar plant—[132] *45.10.35*
"calm peace—when the clear blue-green growth of that sedative cinnabar plant quiets a dispute between two hands on a ploughshare..." *45.10.36*
efforting—like lifting up an elephant— *45.10.37*
Heaven (that sky level above the human head)-Down Below (lower level) *45.10.38 & 39*
straight—upright as a nail in a footprint.[133] *45.10.40*

---

[129] From Chapter 26.
[130] From Chapters 31, 33, and 36.
[131] From Chapters 15, 16, 26, and 37.
[132] From Chapters 15 and 39.
[133] From Chapter 8.

46.

Heaven (that sky level above the human head)-Down Below (lower level)... *46.1.1 & 2*
flesh-and-blood, meat-handling Being *46.1.3*
The Way of the loose-haired headperson—walking a while, stopping a while, and
speaking of it all... *46.1.4*
withdrawing like a kneeling person from within that valley mouth between
two mountains... *46.1.5*
going—like a running young man who will die young on foot, *46.1.6*
a horse, *46.1.7*
this carries like a plough—carries the meaning of, *46.1.8*
manure—like rice kernels through a differently-
masked person. *46.1.9*

Heaven (that sky level above the human head)-Down Below
(lower level)... *46.2.10 & 11*
Not-Being—nobody trance-dancing with long tails flowing from her wrists— *46.2.12*
The Way of the loose-haired headperson—walking a while, stopping a while, and
speaking of it all... *46.2.13*
armed like with a shield and a weapon on a pole, *46.2.14*
a horse *46.2.15*
birthing—a bud sprouting from the ground— *46.2.16*
here—oh, black, icy raven... *46.2.17*
outside of town where someone sits with crossed legs at a big
soil mound. *46.2.18*

A sin or crime like a net breaking the little wings off something... *46.3.19*
must not—eh, like the lost-in-the-bushes , eh?— *46.3.20*
great giant *46.3.21*
here—oh, black, icy raven... *46.3.22*
about which one can purse one's lips like a piece of cane and puff:
'Yup, that's it, definitely' *46.3.23*
wanting—missing what's been eroded from this ravine. *46.3.24*

Disaster—slanting mouth of a skull on a sacrifice altar... *46.4.25*
"must not—eh, like the lost-in-the-bushes , eh?— *46.4.26*
great giant *46.4.27*
here—oh, black, icy raven..." *46.4.28*
the husk of the initial protective bud casing—the sepal—but not
really the true inner flower of *46.4.29*
"firing arrows from the mouth, sure *46.4.30*
enough—the full leg-cut of the animal."[134] *46.4.31*

---

[134] See Chapter 44.

Calamity—a person, something with two legs being followed from behind...[135] *46.5.32*
"must not—eh, like the lost-in-the-bushes , eh?— *46.5.33*
great giant *46.5.34*
here—oh, black, icy raven..." *46.5.35*
wanting—missing what's been eroded from this ravine— *46.5.36*
hand-picking, like-cowry-shell-riches-along-the-road. *46.5.37*

Anciently, for ten generations, this lightly hits and leaves a mark of reason: *46.6.38*
"firing arrows from the mouth, sure *46.6.39*
enough—the full leg-cut of the animal" *46.6.40*
has this *46.6.41*
enough—the full leg-cut of the animal... *46.6.42*

the ever-present square fabric—like that which our grown men wrap around the 'little bird' top knots on their heads after receiving their public courtesy-names—or what we know as the timeless, whole head-cloth 'ji' version of[136] *46.7.43*
enough—the full leg-cut of the animal— *46.7.344*
—swearing on an arrow revolving around oneself, that's it! *46.7.45*

47.

The husk of the initial protective bud casing—the sepal—but not really the true inner flower of *47.1.1*
stepping out of their cave,[137] *47.1.2*
the single-gate-doorway to a household... *47.1.3*
firing arrows from the mouth, sure, *47.1.4*
Heaven (that sky level above the human head)-Down Below (lower level). *47.1.5 & 6*

---

[135] From Chapter 9.
[136] This character first appeared in Chapter 1.
[137] From Chapters 1, 5, 18, and 35.

The husk of the initial protective bud casing—the sepal—but not really the true inner flower of *47.2.7*

flashing a look—that is to say, this particular grown man with a hairpin and public courtesy name seeing with one big eye for a head—through the double-winged gateway, *47.2.8*

a window—like a boudoir window's sliver of wood that's half of a double-winged gateway and lets the moon shine in on the family's primordial father... ten hung, round spindles...[138] *47.2.9*

seeing—one big eye for a head, *47.2.10*

Heaven (that sky level above the human head) *47.2.11*

The Way of the loose-haired headperson—walking a while, stopping a while, and speaking of it all. *47.2.12*

What it holds a basket of... *47.3.13*

"stepping out of their cave," *47.3.14*

far—a bow relaxing like cloth on a loom... *47.3.15*

remote—not intimately close but a profound way in which you walk a while, stop a while, shaped like a big round spindle with a long robe, like the afterbirth hanging from a recently pregnant woman,[139] *47.3.16*

what it holds a basket of... *47.4.17*

"firing arrows from the mouth, sure," *47.4.18*

"far—a bow relaxing like cloth on a loom..." *47.4.19*

reducing to few—four little dots.[140] *47.4.20*

The sun—walking across the sundial a while, stopping a while—sees indeed *47.5.21*

this carries like a plough—carries the meaning of *47.5.22*

a grounded sage—listening and speaking, standing connected to earth as well as the heavens,[141] *47.5.23*

that person: *47.5.24*

the husk of the initial protective bud casing—the sepal—but not really the true inner flower of *47.5.25*

on a public road, practicing—moving with,[142] *47.5.26*

and yet now, bearded... *47.5.27*

"firing arrows from the mouth, sure;" *47.5.28*

---

[138] From Chapter 11.

[139] From Chapter 25.

[140] From Chapters 19 and 22.

[141] This character first appeared in Chapter 2.

[142] Introduced in Chapter 2; most recently appeared in Chapter 41.

the husk of the initial protective bud casing—the sepal—but not really the true inner flower of *47.6.29*
"seeing—one big eye for a head—" *47.6.30*
and yet now, bearded... *47.6.31*
personal, childhood naming—what it whispers to identify itself by moonlight; *47.6.32*

the husk of the initial protective bud casing—the sepal—but not really the true inner flower of *47.7.33*
efforting—like lifting up an elephant— *47.7.34*
and yet now, bearded... *47.7.35*
completing—that final nail in the weapon on a pole.[143] *47.7.36*

48.

Efforting—like lifting up an elephant— *48.1.1*
learning—like hands-on teaching a child gets in school...[144] *48.1.2*
the sun—the day...[145] *48.1.3*
overflowing like water from a vessel;[146] *48.1.4*

efforting—like lifting up an elephant— *48.2.5*
The Way of the loose-haired headperson—walking a while, stopping a while, and speaking of it all... *48.2.6*
the sun—the day... *48.2.7*
diminishing like hands and fingers injured by the top edge of the cauldron that is the monarchy government...[147] *48.2.8*

"diminishing like hands and fingers injured by the top edge of the cauldron that is the monarchy government," *48.3.9*
what it has... *48.3.10*
again—on the right hand *48.3.11*
"diminishing like hands and fingers injured by the top edge of the cauldron that is the monarchy government." *48.3.12*

---

[143] Introduced in Chapter 2; most recently appeared in Chapters 41 and 45.
[144] From Chapters 19 and 20.
[145] From Chapters 23 and 26.
[146] From Chapters 42 and 43.
[147] From Chapter 42.

This carries like a plough—carries the meaning of *48.4.13*
reaching the extreme—like an arrow straight into the clay soil—[148] *48.4.14*
here—oh, black, icy raven... *48.4.15*
    Not-Being—nobody trance-dancing with long tails flowing from her wrists— *48.4.16*
    efforting—like lifting up an elephant... *48.4.17*

"Not-Being—nobody trance-dancing with long tails flowing from her wrists— *48.5.18*
efforting—like lifting up an elephant," *48.5.19*
and yet now, bearded... *48.5.20*
    Not-Being—nobody trance-dancing with long tails flowing from her wrists— *48.5.21*
    the husk of the initial protective bud casing—the sepal—but not really the true inner flower of *48.5.22*
    efforting—like lifting up an elephant— *48.5.23*

Fetching—carrying in your hand the ear of an enemy *48.6.24*
Heaven (that sky level above the human head)-Down Below (lower level), *48.6.25 & 26*
the ever-present square fabric—like that which our grown men wrap around the 'little bird' top knots on their heads after receiving their public courtesy-names—or what we know as the timeless, whole head-cloth 'ji' version, *48.6.27*
this carries like a plough—carries the meaning of *48.6.28*
    Not-Being—nobody trance-dancing with long tails flowing from her wrists... *48.6.29*
    one's personal, manual role—what one does with a weapon, a flag, or a pen;[149] *48.6.30*

reaching—like grabbing a person,[150] *48.7.31*
what it holds a basket of... *48.7.32*
    flesh-and-blood, meat-handling Being *48.7.33*
    one's personal, manual role—what one does with a weapon, a flag, or a pen... *48.7.34*

---

148 From Chapter 43.
149 First introduced in Chapter 2.
150 From Chapters 13, 21, and 43.

"the husk of the initial protective bud casing—the sepal—but not really the true inner flower of *48.8.35*
enough—the full leg-cut of the animal,"[151] *48.8.36*
this carries like a plough—carries the meaning of, *48.8.37*
"fetching—carrying in your hand the ear of an enemy *48.8.38*
Heaven (that sky level above the human head)-Down Below (lower level)." *48.8.39 & 40*

49.

A grounded sage—listening and speaking, standing connected to earth as well as the heavens, *49.1.1*
that person... *49.1.2*
Not-Being—nobody trance-dancing with long tails flowing from her wrists... *49.1.3*
the ever-present square fabric—like that which our grown men wrap around the 'little bird' top knots on their heads after receiving their public courtesy-names—or what we know as the timeless, whole head-cloth 'ji' version of *49.1.4*
heart-core:[152] *49.1.5*

this carries like a plough—carries the meaning of *49.2.6*
"a hundred *49.2.7*
family names—that women, kneeling with breasts, sprout from the ground—the common people"[153] *49.2.8*
heart-core... *49.2.9*
efforting—like lifting up an elephant— *49.2.10*
heart-core. *49.2.11*

Virtue—such as offering up a ram's head while back and forth speaking words that are emerging from a mouth like slaves or criminals branded by a chisel... *49.3.12*
—now this is cooking with fire!— *49.3.13*
I/we—our five mouths... *49.3.14*
"virtue—such as offering up a ram's head while back and forth speaking words that are emerging from a mouth like slaves or criminals branded by a chisel"*49.3.15*
has this; *49.3.16*

[151] See Chapter 46.
[152] From Chapters 3, 8, 12, and 20.
[153] From Chapters 5 and 17.

the husk of the initial protective bud casing—the sepal—but not really the true inner flower of *49.4.17*

"virtue—such as offering up a ram's head while back and forth speaking words that are emerging from a mouth like slaves or criminals branded by a chisel..." *49.4.18*

—now this is cooking with fire!— *49.4.19*

I/we—our five mouths... *49.4.20*

—both armpits sweat this too!— *49.4.21*

"virtue—such as offering up a ram's head while back and forth speaking words that are emerging from a mouth like slaves or criminals branded by a chisel *49.4.22*

has this..." *49.4.23*

Dé—the ethical, straight way of walking awhile and stopping awhile, eye directed forward over the heart-core— *49.5.24*

"virtue—such as offering up a ram's head while back and forth speaking words that are emerging from a mouth like slaves or criminals branded by a chisel." *49.5.25*

Truth-speaking—speaking words like slaves or criminals, branded by a chisel, emerging from a mouth of good luck that's as empty and quiet as a mouth with a soldier's axe above it, speaking of grass...[154] *49.6.26*

—now this is cooking with fire!— *49.6.27*

I/we—our five mouths... *49.6.28*

"truth-speaking—speaking words like slaves or criminals, branded by a chisel, emerging from a mouth of good luck that's as empty and quiet as a mouth with a soldier's axe above it, speaking of grass" *49.6.29*

has this; *49.6.30*

---

[154] From Chapters 8, 17, 21, 23, and 38.

the husk of the initial protective bud casing—the sepal—but not really the true inner flower of *49.7.31*

"truth-speaking—speaking words like slaves or criminals, branded by a chisel, emerging from a mouth of good luck that's as empty and quiet as a mouth with a soldier's axe above it, speaking of grass..." *49.7.32*

—now this is cooking with fire!— *49.7.33*

I/we—our five mouths... *49.7.34*

—both armpits sweat this too!— *49.7.35*

"truth-speaking—speaking words like slaves or criminals, branded by a chisel, emerging from a mouth of good luck that's as empty and quiet as a mouth with a soldier's axe above it, speaking of grass" *49.7.36*

has this..." *49.7.37*

Dé—the ethical, straight way of walking awhile and stopping awhile, eye directed forward over the heart-core—*49.8.38*

"truth-speaking—speaking words like slaves or criminals, branded by a chisel, emerging from a mouth of good luck that's as empty and quiet as a mouth with a soldier's axe above it, speaking of grass." *49.8.39*

A grounded sage—listening and speaking, standing connected to earth as well as the heavens, *49.9.40*

that person... *49.9.41*

"existing sprouting—of seedlings, talents, here on earth—[155] *49.9.42*

Heaven (that sky level above the human head)-Down Below (lower level):" *49.9.43 & 44*

sucking in—when finally a gathering of little wings isn't a sufficient target for a blade...[156] *49.10.45*

sucking in—when finally a gathering of little wings isn't a sufficient target for a blade— *49.10.46*

here—this place where that yellow bird lives around the Yangtze and Huai Rivers...[157] *49.10.47*

efforting—like lifting up an elephant— *49.10.48*

Heaven (that sky level above the human head)-Down Below (lower level)... *49.10.49 & 50*

---

[155] From Chapters 24 and 32. This particular two-character phrase combining it with "Heaven-Below" was used in Chapter 32.

[156] From Chapter 36.

[157] From Chapters 2, 25, and 34.

muddied like a river spouting from an army of surrounding carts... *49.11.51*
what it holds a basket of... *49.11.52*
"heart-core;" *49.11.53*

"a hundred *49.12.54*
family names—that women, kneeling with breasts, sprout from the ground—the common people..." *49.12.55*
public opinion—that clear, plain back and forth between people...[158] *49.12.56*
pouring, filling with attention like a river master—the owner and host of the lamp's flame— *49.12.57*
what it holds a basket of... *49.12.58*
ear,[159] *49.12.59*
what the eye sees;[160] *49.12.60*

a grounded sage—listening and speaking, standing connected to earth as well as the heavens, *49.13.61*
that person... *49.13.62*
public opinion—that clear, plain back and forth between people... *49.13.63*
a baby animal, giggling,[161] *49.13.64*
has this. *49.13.65*

50.

Stepping out of their cave...[162] *50.1.1*
birthing—a bud sprouting from the ground; *50.1.2*
entering like an arrow...[163] *50.1.3*
dying—going from a standing person to a pile of bones.[164] *50.1.4*

"Birthing—a bud sprouting from the ground" *50.2.5*
has this *50.2.6*
followers—foot soldiers, walking awhile and stopping a while on the clay soil: *50.2.7*
ten *50.2.8*
flesh-and-blood, meat-handling Being, *50.2.9*
three; *50.2.10*

---

[158] From Chapters 2, 17, and 20. It was used with the previous two characters in Chapter 17.
[159] From Chapter 12. This character is the second part of Lǎo Zǐ's personal name, Lǐ Ěr.
[160] From Chapter 12.
[161] From Chapter 20.
[162] From Chapters 1, 5, 18, 35, and 47.
[163] From Chapter 43.
[164] From Chapters 6, 33, and 42.

"dying—going from a standing person to a pile of bones... *50.3.11*
has this *50.3.12*
followers—a foot soldier, walking awhile and stopping a while on the clay soil: *50.3.13*
ten *50.3.14*
flesh-and-blood, meat-handling Being, *50.3.15*
three; *50.3.16*

that person *50.4.17*
has this... *50.4.18*
"birthing—a bud sprouting from the ground..." *50.4.19*
laboring—like moving heavy bags with great strength,[165] *50.4.20*
has this... *50.4.21*
"dying—going from a standing person to a pile of bones..." *50.4.122*
Earth (this soil vagina):[166] *50.4.23*

—both armpits sweat this too!— *50.5.24*
ten *50.5.25*
flesh-and-blood, meat-handling Being *50.5.26*
three. *50.5.27*

That is to say, this particular grown man with a hairpin and public courtesy name, *50.6.28*
that very one about whom you can purse your lips around a cane and puff, 'yup, that's the person,' *50.6.29*
anciently, for ten generations, this lightly hits and leaves a mark of reason... *50.6.30*

this carries like a plough—carries the meaning of *50.7.31*
what it holds a basket of... *50.7.32*
"birthing—a bud sprouting from the ground..." *50.7.33*
"birthing—a bud sprouting from the ground" *50.7.34*
has this... *50.7.35*
thick like a generous cliff with a habitable cave that opposes the flow of the river, housing a baby with a large head, spread arms and swaddled legs under the sun.[167] *50.7.36*

---

[165] From Chapters 5, 8, 15, and 40.
[166] First introduced in Chapter 1.
[167] From Chapters 38 and 44.

Indeed covering—like grass and clay soil thatch over a chalice— *50.8.37*
hearing at the double-winged gateway,[168] *50.8.38*
virtue—such as offering up a ram's head while back and forth speaking words that are emerging from a mouth like slaves or criminals branded by a chisel: *50.8.39*
'taking well in hand, hearing three times over: *50.8.40*
"birthing—a bud sprouting from the ground..."' *50.8.41*
—now this is cooking with fire!— *50.8.42*

on the land—many divided pieces of soil and big soil mound... *50.9.43*
on a public road, practicing—moving with... *50.9.44*
the husk of the initial protective bud casing—the sepal—but not really the true inner flower of *50.9.45*
encountering—like walking a while, stopping a while around that trampling monkey with the head of a ghost— *50.9.46*
fearsome buffalo, *50.9.47*
fierce tiger; *50.9.48*

"entering like an arrow..." *50.10.49*
army of surrounding carts...[169] *50.10.50*
the husk of the initial protective bud casing—the sepal—but not really the true inner flower of *50.10.51*
wearing like clothing—especially like a robe on the torso, like the placental afterbirth hanging from a recently pregnant woman, made of fur stripped by hand from its pelt— *50.10.52*
shield—a turtle shell, *50.10.53*
carrying a short ax with two hands like a soldier or pawn.'[170] *50.10.54*

"Fearsome buffalo..." *50.11.55*
Not-Being—nobody trance-dancing with long tails flowing from her wrists— *50.11.56*
'place'—somewhere intentionally created, like a door chopped with an axe... *50.11.57*
throwing expertly by hand—like handling a *shū* weapon— *50.11.58*
what it holds a basket of... *50.11.59*
an angled horn. *50.11.60*

[168] From Chapters 14, 35, and 41.
[169] From Chapters 30 and 31.
[170] From Chapters 30 and 31.

"Fierce tiger..." *50.12.61*
"Not-Being—nobody trance-dancing with long tails flowing from
her wrists— *50.12.62*
'place'—somewhere intentionally created, like a door chopped with an axe..." *50.12.63*
arranging—like hand-placing strips of meat to dry in the sun — *50.12.64*
what it holds a basket of... *50.12.65*
a claw like a hand grabbing from above. *50.12.66*

"Carrying a short ax with two hands like a soldier or pawn..." *50.13.67*
"Not-Being—nobody trance-dancing with long tails flowing from
her wrists— *50.13.68*
'place'—somewhere intentionally created, like a door chopped with an axe..." *50.13.69*
outward public container of private parts—like a building housing an
important, older, man with big testicles, a duke[171] *50.13.70*
what it holds a basket of... *50.13.71*
a blade. *50.13.72*

"That is to say, this particular grown man with a hairpin and public
courtesy name *50.14.73*
that very one about whom you can purse your lips around a cane and puff, 'yup,
that's the person'— *50.14.74*
anciently, for ten generations, this lightly hits and leaves a mark of reason... *50.14.75*

this carries like a plough—carries the meaning of *50.15.76*
what it holds a basket of..." *50.15.77*
Not-Being—nobody trance-dancing with long tails flowing from her wrists... *50.15.78*
"dying—going from a standing person to a pile of bones... *50.15.79*
Earth (this soil vagina)." *50.15.80*

51.

The Way of the loose-haired headperson—walking a while, stopping a while, and
speaking of it all... *51.1.1*
birthing—a bud sprouting from the ground— *51.1.2*
has this. *51.1.3*

---

[171] From Chapters 15, 16, 21, and 28.

Dé—the ethical, straight way of walking awhile and stopping awhile, eye directed forward over the heart-core... *51.2.4*
tying animals and raising them in a pen *51.2.5*
has this. *51.2.6*

Things cut off—all matter external to oneself like seeds, cows etc... *51.3.7*
shaping with measuring lines of hair's breadth[172] *51.3.8*
has this. *51.3.9*

Planting power—like holding a forceful arm, a bladed tool, or a plough on the soil to seed like testicles... *51.4.10*
completing—that final nail in the weapon on a pole—[173] *51.4.11*
has this. *51.4.12*

The sun—walking across the sundial a while, stopping a while—sees indeed *51.5.13*
this carries like a plough—carries the meaning of *51.5.14*
the myriad, scorpion-medicine-dancing Ten Thousand *51.5.15*
Things cut off—all matter external to oneself like seeds, cows etc... *51.5.16*
must not—like the lost-in-the-bushes sinking sun, eh?... *51.5.17*

the husk of the initial protective bud casing—the sepal—but not really the true inner flower of *51.6.18*
honoring—like offering by hand the *yi* ritual alcohol vessel with the chief charged with its preparation *51.6.19*
The Way of the loose-haired headperson—walking a while, stopping a while, and speaking of it all, *51.6.20*
and yet now, bearded... *51.6.21*
treasuring—as if as valuable as cowry-shell-riches—[174] *51.6.22*
Dé—the ethical, straight way of walking awhile and stopping awhile, eye directed forward over the heart-core. *51.6.23*

The Way of the loose-haired headperson—walking a while, stopping a while, and speaking of it all *51.7.24*
has this... *51.7.25*
"honoring—like offering by hand the yi ritual alcohol vessel with the chief charged with its preparation..." *51.7.26*

---

172 From Chapters 2, 24, and 41.
173 From Chapters 2, 7, 15, 17, 25, 34, 41, 45, and 47.
174 From Chapters 3, 9, 13, 17, 20, 27, 31, and 39.

Dé—the ethical, straight way of walking awhile and stopping awhile,
eye directed forward over the heart-core *51.8.27*
has this... *51.8.28*
"treasuring—as if as valuable as cowry-shell-riches..." *51.8.29*

that is to say, this particular grown man with a hairpin and public courtesy name... *51.9.30*
must not—like the lost-in-the-bushes sinking sun, eh?— *51.9.31*
has this... *51.9.32*
what has to be—like a command from a magistrate speaking, joining from three sides over a kneeling person,[175] *51.9.33*
and yet now, bearded... *51.9.34*
the ever-present square fabric—like that which our grown men wrap around the 'little bird' top knots on their heads after receiving their public courtesy-names—or what we know as the timeless, whole head-cloth 'ji' version of *51.9.35*
of course—one's self personally, right on one's nose, *51.9.36*
accomplished thus, in this manner: as naturally as dog meat over a fire.[176] *51.9.37*

Anciently, for ten generations, this lightly hits and leaves a mark of reason: *51.10.38*
"The Way of the loose-haired headperson—walking a while, stopping a while, and speaking of it all... *51.10.39*
birthing—a bud sprouting from the ground— *51.10.40*
has this; *51.10.41*

"Dé—the ethical, straight way of walking awhile and stopping awhile, eye directed forward over the heart-core... *51.11.42*
tying animals and raising them in a pen *51.11.43*
has this:" *51.11.44*

"long-haired elder" *51.12.45*
has this... *51.12.46*
birthing like an upside down baby below the moon *51.12.47*
has this; *51.12.48*

---

[175] From Chapter 16.
[176] From Chapters 17, 23, 25, and 26.

sheltering like a person in a pavilion or in a checkpoint *51.13.49*
has this... *51.13.50*
poisoning—like using that toxic plant that's as virtueless as an axe-bearing soldier not-being a mother *51.13.51*
has this; *51.13.52*

feeding a meal—mouth over a rice bowl, as beautiful as a ram's head—[177] *51.14.53*
has this... *51.14.54*
covering by walking forth and then back again, stepping slowly with only one's left leg leading the way, *51.14.55*
has this. *51.14.56*

"Birthing—a bud sprouting from the ground, 51.15.57
and yet now, bearded... 51.15.58
the husk of the initial protective bud casing—the sepal—but not really the true inner flower of 51.15.59
flesh-and-blood, meat-handling Being; 51.15.60

efforting—like lifting up an elephant, 51.16.61
and yet now, bearded, 51.16.62
the husk of the initial protective bud casing—the sepal—but not really the true inner flower of 51.16.63
expecting that will be holding one's heart-core like a mother;"[178] *51.16.64*

"long-haired elder," 51.17.65
and yet now, bearded, 51.17.66
the husk of the initial protective bud casing—the sepal—but not really the true inner flower of 51.17.67
dominating—like the house of that chisel used to mark slaves and criminals. 51.17.68

The sun—walking across the sundial a while, stopping a while—sees indeed 51.18.69
what it's called when speaking from the gut—words, like slaves or criminals branded by a chisel emerging from a mouth: 51.18.70
hard-to-see dark structure—like a figure-eight skein of string-dyed-black—[179] *51.18.71*
Dé—the ethical, straight way of walking awhile and stopping awhile, eye directed forward over the heart-core"[180] *51.18.71*

---

[177] From Chapter 34.
[178] From Chapters 2 and 10. The last character also appears in Chapter 34.
[179] From Chapters 1, 6, 10, and 15.
[180] These four italicized lines match the last four lines of Chapter 10.

52.

Heaven (that sky level above the human head)-Down Below (lower level)... *52.1.1 & 2*
flesh-and-blood, meat-handling Being *52.1.3*
beginning—like conception in and by a woman,[181] *52.1.4*

> this carries like a plough—carries the meaning of *52.2.5*
> efforting—like lifting up an elephant— *52.2.6*
> Heaven (that sky level above the human head)-Down Below (lower level) *52.2.7 & 8*
> suckling—like being nursed by a woman.[182] *52.2.9*

'Done'—as de facto as a kneeling person turning away after eating a bowl of rice—done[183] *52.3.10*
hand-picking, like-cowry-shell-riches-along-the-road, *52.3.11*
what it holds a basket of... *52.3.12*
"suckling—like being nursed by a woman—" *52.3.13*

> this carries like a plough—carries the meaning of *52.3.14*
> firing arrows from the mouth, sure *52.3.15*
> what it holds a basket of... *52.3.16*
> baby—arms wide open and legs swaddled.[184] *52.3.17*

---

[181] From Chapters 1, 14, 32, 3 and 8.
[182] From Chapters 1, 20, and 25.
[183] From Chapters 32 and 35.
[184] This character is the second part of Lǎo Zī's honorific name and was used in Chapters 4 and 31.

'Done'—as de facto as a kneeling person turning away after eating a bowl of rice—done *52.4.18*
"firing arrows from the mouth, sure *52.4.19*
what it holds a basket of... *52.4.20*
baby—arms wide open and legs swaddled," *52.4.21*
walking forth and then back again[185] *52.4.22*
hand-defending this—one's building,[186] *52.4.23*
what it holds a basket of... *52.4.24*
"suckling—like being nursed by a woman;" *52.4.25*
"without—because one would have to dive into the water, wrap one's hands around it to get it—[187]*52.4.26*
one's pregnant self... 52.4.27
the husk of the initial protective bud casing—the sepal—but not really the true inner flower of 52.4.28
endangered—evil like human remains, spoken of privately, revolving around yourself."[188] *52.4.29*

Cramming—both hands stuffing items into the house... *52.5.30*
what it holds a basket of... *52.5.31*
open mouth like that of a smiling, breathy older brother, *52.5.32*

blocking entry—like obstructing the double-winged gateway with the sprouting of seeds...[189] *52.6.33*
what it holds a basket of... *52.6.34*
double-winged gateway:[190] *52.6.35*

ending—the knot at the end of a thick silk skein in winter—[191] *52.7.36*
one's pregnant self... *52.7.37*
the husk of the initial protective bud casing—the sepal—but not really the true inner flower of *52.7.38*
exerting with force—working hard with the strength of an arm, a bladed tool, or a plough on the soil.[192] *52.7.39*

---

[185] From Chapters 14, 16, 19, and 28.
[186] From Chapters 5, 9, 16, 28, 32, and 37.
[187] From Chapter 16.
[188] This phrase was used in Chapter 16
[189] From Chapter 27.
[190] From Chapters 6 and 10.
[191] From Chapters 23, 26, and 34.
[192] Another kind of doing/acting. From Chapters 6 and 41.

Unlatching the double-winged gateway with a pair of hands... [193] *52.8.40*
"what it holds a basket of... *52.8.41*
open mouth like that of a smiling, breathy older brother," *52.8.42*

helping like ferrying across that river Qi that's as even as a field of grain... *52.9.43*
what it holds a basket of... *52.9.44*
one's personal, manual role—what one does with a weapon, a flag, or a pen: *52.9.45*

> "ending—the knot at the end of a thick silk skein in winter *52.10.46*
> one's pregnant self... *52.10.47*
> the husk of the initial protective bud casing—the sepal—but not really the
> true inner flower of" *52.10.48*
> rescuing—lightly hitting upon request someone in a fur coat.[194] *52.10.49*

Seeing—one big eye for a head—[195] *52.11.50*
very little, like three grains of sand,[196] *52.11.51*

> what it's called when issued on a breath from the mouth...[197] *52.11.52*
> 'as bright as dawn rising on a crescent moon—enlightened;'[198] *52.11.53*

"hand-defending this—one's building—" *52.12.54*
softening—to be like a tree that can be cut with a spear,[199] *52.12.55*

> what it's called when issued on a breath from the mouth... *52.12.56*
> 'strengthening like an insect—revolving oneself as a
> venomous snake-like bow.'[200] *52.12.57*

---

[193] From Chapters 10 and 27.
[194] From Chapter 27.
[195] From Chapters 3, 14, 19, 22, 24, 29, 35, and 47.
[196] From Chapters 32 and 34.
[197] This breathy version of naming first appeared in Chapter 14 and is often juxtaposed with "what it's called when speaking from the gut" or "when spoken of altogether in integrity."
[198] From Chapters 10, 16, 22, 24, 27, 33, 36, and 41.
[199] From Chapters 10, 36, and 43.
[200] "Softening" and "strengthening" were also paired in Chapter 36.

Doing truly useful work like a water bucket—by means of carrying-capacity... *52.13.58*
what it holds a basket of... *52.13.59*
brilliant—that shining fire over the head of a kneeling person,[201] *52.13.60*
"walking forth and then back again" *52.13.61*
returning after sweeping troops out of the hills to this...[202] *52.13.62*
what it holds a basket of... *52.13.63*
"as bright as dawn rising on a crescent moon—enlightened." *52.13.64*

Not-Being—nobody trance-dancing with long tails flowing from her wrists... *52.14.65*
leaving behind cowry-like riches—like after dying—on this way of walking a while, stopping for a while,[203] *52.14.66*
one's pregnant self... *52.14.67*
bringing harm—like bone remnants ending in the center that's pleading as a person with their head in the middle of a pole over their shoulders with two things on either end. *52.14.68*

The sun—walking across the sundial a while, stopping a while—sees indeed: *52.15.69*
efforting—like lifting up an elephant... *52.15.70*
practicing like flapping both wings in the sun *52.15.71*
the ever-present square fabric—like that which our grown men wrap around the 'little bird' top knots on their heads after receiving their public courtesy-names—or what we know as the timeless, whole head-cloth 'ji' version. *52.15.72*

53.

Breeding—like a gentleman holding a fountain pen making something happen,[204] *53.1.1*
I/we—holding a rake-like weapon to defend ourselves and our opinion... *53.1.2*
a person lying in between, *53.1.3*
accomplished thus, in this manner, as naturally as dog meat over a fire: *53.1.4*
flesh-and-blood, meat-handling Being *53.1.5*
firing arrows from the mouth, sure... *53.1.6*

---

[201] From Chapter 4.
[202] This character is from Chapters 14, 16, 20, 22, 28, and 34. In 14 and 16, it was used with the same preceding character.
[203] From Chapters 9 and 20.
[204] From Chapter 3.

on a public road, practicing—moving with— *53.2.7*
here—oh, black, icy raven... *53.2.8*
great giant, *53.2.0*
The Way of the loose-haired headperson—walking a while, stopping a while, and speaking of it all... *53.2.10*

essentially and only—like the mouth of 'the short-tailed bird'— *53.3.11*
putting it in place like flags flying over a corpse—yes, that too, vagina, *53.3.12*
the sun—walking across the sundial a while, stopping a while—sees indeed *53.3.13*
fearing—like when there's a ghost holding a stick or maybe part of a tiger with its claw.[205] *53.3.14*

"Great giant *53.4.15*
The Way of the loose-haired headperson—walking a while, stopping a while, and speaking of it all..." *53.4.16*
in the extreme—something pleasing in the mouth, matched so it's doubly pleasing...[206] *53.4.17*
as foreign as that tribe in the east—the great barbarians with bows—leveled and razed by destruction,[207] *53.4.18*

and yet now, bearded... *53.5.19*
civilians—like the Mín people enslaved by blinding with a dagger—[208] *53.5.20*
as good as—like a woman with a child—[209] *53.5.21*
a short-cut pathway straight across—stepping slowly with only the left leg across an underground stream. *53.5.22*

The morning—when the sun's just rising out of the grass with a crescent moon in the sky...[210] *53.6.23*
in the extreme—something pleasing in the mouth, matched so it's doubly pleasing... *53.6.24*
a new posting—like moving me to a different thatched cottage on a soil mountain;[211] *53.6.25*

---

[205] From Chapters 15, 17, and 20.
[206] From Chapters 21, 29, and 44.
[207] From Chapters 14 and 41.
[208] This character first appeared in Chapter 3.
[209] From Chapter 30.
[210] From Chapter 23.
[211] From Chapter 10.

a field... *53.7.26*
in the extreme—something pleasing in the mouth, matched so it's
doubly pleasing... *53.7.27*
thick grass of an unused field; *53.7.28*

granaries—food stored in one's house... *53.8.29*
in the extreme —something pleasing in the mouth, matched so it's
doubly pleasing... *53.8.30*
empty—like a tiger head upon a hill...[212] *53.8.31*

wearing clothes—like mourning dress as earthly and mortal as commonplace
plates—subdued like a kneeling person by hand... *53.9.32*
written description—a tattooed chest or, nowadays, literature
or texts—[213] *53.9.33*
a skein of silk dyed many colors as in with fruit hand-picked
from a tree, *53.9.34*

belt, like the ever-present square fabric we know as the timeless, whole head-cloth
'ji' but around a person's waist... *53.10.35*
benefiting, like by reaping grain with a sharp-edged blade[214] *53.10.36*
a sword all together unanimous like two mouthy people walking together,
gathering themselves from three sides; *53.10.37*

sated like by some sweet dog meat in the mouth... *53.11.38*
drinking a beverage—leaning over a vase for making alcohol with
one's mouth, *53.11.39*
having a meal—mouth over a bowl of rice on a stand,[215] *53.11.40*

riches—sprouting cowry currency like seeds... *53.12.41*
transformation of cowry-shell-riches—like from a right-side-up person to
an upside down person—[216] *53.12.42*
flesh-and-blood, meat-handling Being *53.12.43*
having leftovers—excess food remains in one's house.[217] *53.12.44*

---

[212] From Chapters 3, 5, 16, and 22.
[213] From Chapter 19.
[214] From Chapters 8, 11, 19, and 36.
[215] From Chapters 20 and 24.
[216] From Chapters 3, 12, and 44.
[217] From Chapters 20 and 24.

The sun—walking across the sundial a while, stopping a while—sees indeed *53.13.45*
what it's called when speaking from the gut—words, like slaves or criminals branded by a chisel emerging from a mouth... *53.13.46*
thievery—spitting into a bowl as an oath among thieves—[218] *53.13.47*
as extravagant as a great giant blowing air... *53.13.48*

breaking the little wings off *53.14.49*
The Way of the loose-haired headperson—walking a while, stopping a while, and speaking of it all... *53.14.50*
—yes, that too, vagina!— *53.14.51*
I say, 'Oh, indeed! That hurts like a weapon on a pole wounding sprouting seeds, talents.'[219] *53.14.52*

54.

Virtue—such as offering up a ram's head while back and forth speaking words that are emerging from a mouth like slaves or criminals branded by a chisel—[220] *54.1.1*
expertly hand-built by a striding person with a bamboo brush...[221] *54.1.2*
—now this is cooking with fire!— *54.1.3*
the husk of the initial protective bud casing—the sepal—but not really the true inner flower of *54.1.4*
pulling up so expertly by hand that it's like a running dog arriving. *54.1.5*

Virtue—such as offering up a ram's head while back and forth speaking words that are emerging from a mouth like slaves or criminals branded by a chisel— *54.2.6*
bundling it all up together—in one's arms...[222] *54.2.7*
—now this is cooking with fire!— *54.2.8*
the husk of the initial protective bud casing—the sepal—but not really the true inner flower of *54.2.9*
they're leaving—freely stripping like a smiling breathy older brother by moonlight.[223] *54.2.10*

---

[218] From Chapters 3 and 19. Pronounced *dào*.
[219] From Chapters 20, 21, and 22.
[220] From Chapters 2, 8, 15, 20, 27, 30, 41, 49, and 50.
[221] From Chapter 41.
[222] From Chapters 10, 19, 22, and 42.
[223] From Chapter 36.

Baby—arms wide open and legs swaddled,[224] *54.3.11*
baby boy—maybe a grandson like a thin silk thread, *54.3.12*
this carries like a plough—carries the meaning of *54.3.13*
a ceremony making a meat offering by hand at an altar *54.3.14*
sacrificing—something like a fetus or a snake upon an altar... *54.3.15*
    the husk of the initial protective bud casing—the sepal—but not really the true inner flower of *54.3.16*
    halting like a chariot by four hands connecting repeatedly. *54.3.17*

Studying, mastering—as when washing on a person's back and hair, hitting it lightly with water during a purification ceremony... *54.4.18*
what it has *54.4.19*
here—oh, black, icy raven... *54.4.20*
one's pregnant self, *54.4.21*
    what it holds a basket of... *54.4.122*
    Dé—the ethical, straight way of walking awhile and stopping awhile, eye directed forward over the heart-core... *54.4.23*
    you, then, *54.4.24*
        genuine—using your fork to get food right from the cauldron.[225] *54.4.25*

Studying, mastering—as when washing on a person's back and hair, hitting it lightly with water during a purification ceremony... *54.5.26*
what it has *54.5.27*
here—oh, black, icy raven... *54.5.28*
home—a pig under your roof,[226] *54.5.29*
    what it holds a basket of... *54.5.30*
    Dé—the ethical, straight way of walking awhile and stopping awhile, eye directed forward over the heart-core... *54.5.31*
    you, then, *54.5.32*
        having leftovers—excess food remains in one's house.[227] *54.5.33*

---

[224] This character is the second part of Lǎo Zǐ's honorific name.
[225] From Chapters 21 and 41.
[226] From Chapter 18.
[227] From Chapters 20, 24, and 53.

Studying, mastering—as when washing on a person's back and hair, hitting it lightly with water during a purification ceremony... *54.6.34*
what it has *54.6.35*
here—oh, black, icy raven... *54.6.36*
a village -- a rural community where people face one another over a food vessel, feasting, *54.6.37*
what it holds a basket of... *54.6.38*
Dé—the ethical, straight way of walking awhile and stopping awhile, eye directed forward over the heart-core... *54.6.39*
you, then, *54.6.40*
long as hair that has to be tied with a brooch.[228] *54.6.41*

Studying, mastering—as when washing on a person's back and hair, hitting it lightly with water during a purification ceremony... *54.7.42*
what it has *54.7.43*
here—oh, black, icy raven... *54.7.44*
this nation—this particular territory, this enclave defended by a weapon on a pole plus its surroundings,[229] *54.7.45*
what it holds a basket of... *54.7.46*
Dé—the ethical, straight way of walking awhile and stopping awhile, eye directed forward over the heart-core *54.7.47*
you, then, *54.7.48*
as luxuriant and lush as a pot full of flowers. *54.7.49*

Studying, mastering—as when washing on a person's back and hair, hitting it lightly with water during a purification ceremony... *54.8.50*
what it has *54.8.51*
here—oh, black, icy raven... *54.8.52*
Heaven (that sky level above the human head)-Down Below (lower level), *54.8.53 & 54*
what it holds a basket of... *54.8.55*
Dé—the ethical, straight way of walking awhile and stopping awhile, eye directed forward over the heart-core... *54.8.56*
you, then, *54.8.57*
universally widespread—side by side over the sun, rendering it lusterless. *54.8.58*

[228] From Chapters 2, 7, 9, and 44.
[229] From Chapters 10, 18, and 36.

Anciently, for ten generations, this lightly hits and leaves a mark of reason: *54.9.59*
this carries like a plough—carries the meaning of *54.9.60*
"one's pregnant self..." *54.9.61*
keeping watch from the temple tower for *54.9.62*
one's pregnant self; *54.9.63*

this carries like a plough—carries the meaning of *54.10.64*
"home—a pig under your roof..." *54.10.65*
keeping watch from the temple tower for *54.10.66*
home—a pig under your roof; *54.10.67*

this carries like a plough—carries the meaning of *54.11.68*
"a village—a rural community where people face one another over a food vessel, feasting..." *54.11.9*
keeping watch from the temple tower for *54.11.70*
a village—a rural community where people face one another over a food vessel, feasting; *54.11.71*

this carries like a plough—carries the meaning of *54.12.72*
"this nation—this particular territory, this enclave defended by a weapon on a pole plus its surroundings..." *54.12.73*
keeping watch from the temple tower for *54.12.74*
this nation—this particular territory, this enclave defended by a weapon on a pole plus its surroundings; *54.12.75*

this carries like a plough—carries the meaning of *54.13.76*
"Heaven (that sky level above the human head)-Down Below (lower level)" *54.13.77& 78*
keeping watch from the temple tower for *54.13.79*
Heaven (that sky level above the human head)-Down Below (lower level). *54.13.80 & 81*

I/we—our five mouths, *54.14.82*
that very one about whom you can purse your lips around a cane and puff,
'yup, that's the person,' *54.14.83*
this carries like a plough—carries the meaning of... *54.14.84*
firing arrows from the mouth, sure[230] *54.14.85*
"Heaven (that sky level above the human head)-Down Below
(lower level)" *54.14.86 & 87*
accomplished thus, in this manner: as naturally as dog meat over a fire?[231] *54.14.88*
I say, 'Oh, indeed! That hurts like a weapon on a pole wounding sprouting
seeds, talents.' *54.14.89*

This carries like a plough—carries the meaning of... *54.15.90*
this here—the foot stops a person here on their footprint.[232] *54.15.91*

55.

To keep what's being said, in the mouth now, in modern times, in the mouth—
staying stuffed in like jade, pearls, and gems in a corpse's mouth... *55.1.1*
Dé—the ethical, straight way of walking awhile and stopping awhile, eye directed
forward over the heart-core... *55.1.2*
has this... *55.1.3*
thick like a generous cliff with a habitable cave that opposes the flow of the
river, housing a baby with a large head, spread arms and swaddled legs
under the sun... [233] *55.1.4*

it compares, like two people right next to each other, to *55.2.5*
here—oh, black, icy raven... *55.2.6*
bare naked and red as a great giant by a fire *55.2.7*
baby—arms wide open and legs swaddled.[234] *55.2.8*

---

[230] See previous chapter's first line.
[231] From Chapters 17, 23, 25, 26, 51, and 53.
[232] From Chapters 1, 12, 14, 19, 23, 38, and 39.
[233] From Chapters 38, 44, and 50.
[234] This character is the second part of Lǎo Zī's honorific name.

A bee—an insect following something from behind on two legs like the knot at the end of a thread through lush grown of plants, *55.3.9*
a scorpion, *55.3.10*
a venomous snake that will cut off one's foot, *55.3.11*
a serpent, a crooked snake—including certain crooked gentlemen or emperors... *55.3.12*
the husk of the initial protective bud casing—the sepal—but not really the true inner flower of *55.3.13*
stinging—both armpits sweat this too!—when hit lightly by a snake. *55.3.14*

Vigorous and ferocious as a dog of an eldest brother—that baby son in the chalice *55.4.15*
animal—as a dog on a beast ... *55.4.16*
the husk of the initial protective bud casing—the sepal—but not really the true inner flower of *55.4.17*
taking possession of like an expert hand with tigers or boars fighting one another, *55.4.18*
grabbing like an expert hand with a nervously-looking-around-with-two-eyes, bird in hand, *55.4.19*
a bird with a dangling tail, paying attention already... *55.4.20*
the husk of the initial protective bud casing—the sepal—but not really the true inner flower of *55.4.21*
monopolizing expertly by hand—like a big round spindle over an inch-sized spot that's as small as where you measure the radial artery pulse in your wrist. *55.4.22*

That bony will that comes from a skeleton framework...[235] *55.5.23*
as fragile as a matching pair of decorative bows or little wings;[236] *55.5.24*
sinew—tendons, muscles, or even veins that stand out like two bamboo stalk on the meat of one's arm that sticks out from the body like a plough... *55.5.25*
softening—to be like a tree that can be cut with a spear,[237] *55.5.26*
and yet now, bearded... *55.5.27*
gripping—holding expertly in hand like a shelter made from a cloth draped over an arrow stuck in the ground— *55.5.28*
solidly, anciently—for ten generations of mouths, keeping as firm to what happened in the first place as this land surrounding and holding this nation since ancient times. *55.5.29*

---

[235] From Chapter 3.
[236] From Chapters 3, 36, and 40.
[237] From Chapters 10, 36, 43, and 52.

Not yet—a tree whose top branches aren't yet fully grown—[238] *55.6.30*
firing arrows from the mouth, sure *55.6.31*
of a mother's lap—a cow with an arrow... a vagina,[239] *55.6.32*
a bull soil... male genitals *55.6.33*
has this *55.6.34*
joining together from three sides over a mouth—having sex,[240] *55.6.35*
and yet now, bearded, *55.6.36*
whole like a piece of pure jade, entire as it arrived,[241] *55.6.38*
getting up and going to work.[242] *55.6.38*

Essence or spirit—like polished rice or semen or like spring's blue-green lush, ripening of that sedative cinnabar plant—[243] *55.7.39*
has this *55.7.40*
reaching the extreme—like an arrow straight into the clay soil,[244] *55.7.41*
—yes, that too, vagina!— *55.7.42*

ending—the knot at the end of a thick silk skein in winter—[245] *55.8.43*
the sun—the day, *55.8.44*
roaring like a puffing tiger, *55.8.45*
and yet now, bearded, *55.8.46*
the husk of the initial protective bud casing—the sepal—but not really the true inner flower of *55.8.47*
hoarse—mouth like a man under a scorching sun. *55.8.48*

Harmonizing as a mouth organ—[246] *55.9.49*
has this *55.9.50*
reaching the extreme—like an arrow straight into the clay soil, *55.9.51*
—yes, that too, vagina!— *55.9.52*

[238] From Chapter 20.
[239] From Chapter 6.
[240] From Chapter 32
[241] From Chapter 22.
[242] From Chapter 2, 16, and 37.
[243] From Chapter 21.
[244] From Chapter 43 and 48.
[245] From Chapters 23, 26, 34, and 52.
[246] From Chapters 2, 4, 18, and 42.

Firing arrows from the mouth, sure *55.10.53*
"harmonizing as a mouth organ..." *55.10.54*
"what it's called when issued on a breath from the mouth: *55.10.55*
'the ever-present square fabric—like that which our grown men wrap around the 'little bird' top knots on their heads after receiving their public courtesy-names—or what we know as the timeless, whole head-cloth "ji" version;'"[247] *55.10.56*

"firing arrows from the mouth, sure *55.11.57*
the ever-present square fabric—like that which our grown men wrap around the 'little bird' top knots on their heads after receiving their public courtesy-names—or what we know as the timeless, whole head-cloth 'ji' version..." *55.11.58*
"what it's called when issued on a breath from the mouth: *55.11.59*
'as bright as dawn rising on a crescent moon—enlightened;'"[248] *55.11.60*

overflowing like water from a vessel[249] *55.12.61*
birthing—a bud sprouting from the ground... *55.12.62*
what it's called when issued on a breath from the mouth: *55.12.63*
'a good omen—a ram's head at an altar;'[250] *55.12.64*

heart-core *55.13.65*
breeding—like a gentleman holding a fountain pen making something happen— *55.13.66*
the breath of life—that vital *qì* energy, that air flow that's like rice given as a gift...[251] *55.13.67*
what it's called when issued on a breath from the mouth: *55.13.68*
'strengthening like an insect—revolving oneself as a venomous snake-like bow;' *55.13.69*

Things cut off—all matter external to oneself like seeds, cows etc. 55.14.70
just passing their prime—a robust bachelor soldier-scholar-official appointed by the emperor in his bed...55.14.71
after following this sacrificial blade-and-cauldron-like ritual example or regulation...55.14.72
an old man with long hair and a cane...[252]*55.14.73*

---

[247] This two-character expression is from Chapter 16.

[248] From Chapters 10, 16, 22, 24, 27, 33, 36, 41, and 52. It's used with the previous character in Chapter 52. This whole line is from Chapter 16.

[249] From Chapters 42, 43, and 48. This is the last place it occurs.

[250] From Chapter 31.

[251] From Chapter 10 and 42.

[252] From Chapter 30. This character is the first part of Lǎo Zǐ's name. This entire italicized section is from Chapter 30 where it follows a discussion about the implications of going to war and carrying an axe with the admonishment, "do *not* be strengthening like an insect."

what it's called when speaking from the gut—words, like slaves or criminals branded by a chisel emerging from a mouth... 55.15.74
has this... 55.15.75
the husk of the initial protective bud casing—the sepal—but not really the true inner flower of 55.15.76
The Way of the loose-haired headperson—walking a while, stopping a while, and speaking of it all. 55.15.77

"The husk of the initial protective bud casing—the sepal—but not really the true inner flower of 55.16.78
The Way of the loose-haired headperson—walking a while, stopping a while, and speaking of it all..." 55.16.78
early, premature—like sunrise above an acorn on the jujube, that thorny plant that's used for insomnia and contraception and causes midterm miscarriages,[253] *55.16.78*
already... finishing it in the womb.[254] *55.16.78*

56.

Firing arrows from the mouth, sure... *56.1.1*
—now this is cooking with fire!— *56.1.2*
"the husk of the initial protective bud casing—the sepal—but not really the true inner flower of *56.1.3*
speaking—words, like slaves or criminals braded by a chisel emerging from a mouth..."[255] *56.1.4*
speaking—words, like slaves or criminals branded by a chisel emerging from a mouth... *56.1.5*
—now this is cooking with fire!— *56.1.6*
the husk of the initial protective bud casing—the sepal—but not really the true inner flower of *56.1.7*
firing arrows from the mouth, sure. *56.1.8*

"Cramming—both hands stuffing items into the house, *56.2.9*
what it holds a basket of... *56.2.10*
open mouth like that of a smiling, breathy older brother; *56.2.11*

---

[253] From Chapter 30.
[254] From Chapters 2, 9, 29, 30, and 31. This is the last place it occurs.
[255] From Chapters 2 and 43.

blocking entry—like obstructing the double-winged gateway with the sprouting of
seeds,[256] *56.3.12*
what it holds a basket of… *56.3.13*
double-winged gateway;"[257] *56.3.14*

"pushing down to a sitting position on the ground, 56.4.15
what it holds a basket of... 56.4.16
a person speaking like an axe on metal—sharpening; 56.4.17

removing it—like a blade cutting the horn from an ox,[258] *56.5.18*
what it holds a basket of... 56.5.19
unravelling—separating thin silk with a blade into disorderliness; 56.5.20

harmonizing as a mouth organ,[259] *56.6.21*
what it holds a basket of... 56.6.22
brilliant—that shining fire over the head of a kneeling person;[260] *56.6.23*

when spoken of altogether in integrity—like all earthly, mortal,
commonplace plates,[261] *56.7.24*
what it holds a basket of... 56.7.25
leaving dusty footprints in the dirt—like a deer streaked with soil..."[262] *56.7.26*

the sun—walking across the sundial a while, stopping a while—sees indeed *56.8.27*
what it's called when speaking from the gut—words, like slaves or criminals
branded by a chisel emerging from a mouth… *56.8.28*
hard-to-see dark structure—like a figure-eight skein of string-
dyed-black…[263] *56.8.29*
"when spoken of altogether in integrity—like all earthly, mortal,
commonplace plates." *56.8.30*

---

[256] From Chapters 27 and 52.
[257] These two lines are from Chapter 52. This last character is also in Chapters 6 and 10.
[258] From Chapters 4 and 27.
[259] From Chapters 2, 4, 18, 42, and 55.
[260] From Chapters 4 and 52.
[261] From Chapters 1, 4, and 23.
[262] These four lines are from Chapter 4 where it was discussing "this particular territory surviving" and a baby whose bears a likeness to "God of Heaven."
[263] From Chapters 1, 6, 10, 15, and 51.

Anciently, for ten generations, this lightly hits and leaves a mark of reason: *56.9.31*
the husk of the initial protective bud casing—the sepal—but not really the true inner flower of *56.9.32*
about which one can purse one's lips ike a piece of cane and puff: 'Yup, that's it, definitely' *56.9.33*
hand-picking—like-cowry-shell-riches-along-the-road— *56.9.34*
and yet now, bearded... *56.9.35*

intimates—like a beloved that one sees closely even in suffering like from that chisel used to mark slaves and criminals;[264] *56.9.36*

"the husk of the initial protective bud casing—the sepal—but not really the true inner flower of *56.10.37*
about which one can purse one's lips like a piece of cane and puff: 'Yup, that's it, definitely' *56.10.38*
hand-picking—like-cowry-shell-riches-along-the-road— *56.10.39*
and yet now, bearded, ..." *56.10.40*

distant and sparse—picture a foot with a thigh above it and an upside-down baby with amniotic fluid streaming down below its head; *56.10.41*

"the husk of the initial protective bud casing—the sepal—but not really the true inner flower of *56.11.42*
about which one can purse one's lips like a piece of cane and puff: 'Yup, that's it, definitely' *56.11.43*
hand-picking—like-cowry-shell-riches-along-the-road— *56.11.44*
and yet now, bearded, ..." *56.11.45*

benefiting, like by reaping grain with a sharp-edged blade; *56.11.46*

"the husk of the initial protective bud casing—the sepal—but not really the true inner flower of *56.12.47*
about which one can purse one's lips ike a piece of cane and puff: 'Yup, that's it, definitely' *56.12.48*
hand-picking—like-cowry-shell-riches-along-the-road—" *56.12.49*
and yet now, bearded... *56.12.50*

being harmed, like speaking and tallying many lies within the house;[265] *56.12.51*

---

264 From Chapters 17, 18, and 44.
265 From Chapter 35.

"the husk of the initial protective bud casing—the sepal—but not really the true inner flower of *56.13.52*
about which one can purse one's lips like a piece of cane and puff: 'Yup, that's it, definitely' *56.13.53*
hand-picking—like-cowry-shell-riches-along-the-road— *56.13.54*
and yet now, bearded, ..." *56.13.55*
treasuring—as if as valuable as cowry-shell-riches;[266] *56.13.56*

"the husk of the initial protective bud casing—the sepal—but not really the true inner flower of *56.14.57*
about which one can purse one's lips like a piece of cane and puff: 'Yup, that's it, definitely' *56.14.58*
hand-picking—like-cowry-shell-riches-along-the-road— *56.14.59*
and yet now, bearded, ..." *56.14.60*
appearing to accumulate cheap inferior "riches" that are like several tiny weapons on a pole next to a cowry.[267] *56.14.61*

Anciently, for ten generations, this lightly hits and leaves a mark of reason: *56.15.62*
efforting—like lifting up an elephant... *56.15.63*
Heaven (that sky level above the human head)-Down Below (lower level)... *56.15.64 & 65*
"treasuring—as if as valuable as cowry-shell-riches." *56.15.66*

57.

This carries like a plough—carries the meaning of *57.1.1*
straight—upright as a nail in a footprint...[268] *57.1.2*
governing—regulating by harnessing the river named Happy or speaking of turning oneself—[269] *57.1.3*
this nation—this particular territory, this enclave defended by a weapon on a pole plus its surroundings; *57.1.4*

---

[266] From Chapters 3, 9, 13, 17, 20, 27, 31, 39, and 51.
[267] From Chapter 39 where it also was associated with treasuring.
[268] From Chapters 8 (where it's also used to discuss governing) and 45.
[269] From Chapters 3, 8 and 10.

this carries like a plough—carries the meaning of, *57.2.5*
remarkably cunning—like the great giant about which one can purse one's lips like a piece of cane and puff: 'Yup, that's it, definitely'... *57.2.6*
"doing truly useful work like a water bucket—by means of carrying-capacity— *57.2.7*
carrying a short ax with two hands like a soldier or pawn;"[270] *57.2.8*

this carries like a plough—carries the meaning of *57.3.9*
Not-Being—nobody trance-dancing with long tails flowing from her wrists... *57.3.10*
one's personal, manual role—what one does with a weapon, a flag, or a pen... *57.3.11*
"grabbing the ear of—like marrying—[271] *57.3.12*
Heaven (that sky level above the human head)-Down Below (lower level)." *57.3.13 & 14*

"I/we—our five mouths, 57.4.15
that very one about whom you can purse your lips around a cane and puff, 'yup, that's the person,' 57.4.16
this carries like a plough—carries the meaning of 57.4.17
firing arrows from the mouth, sure 57.4.18
what it holds a basket of... 57.4.19
accomplished thus, in this manner: as naturally as dog meat over a fire? 57.4.20
I say, 'Oh, indeed! That hurts like a weapon on a pole wounding sprouting seeds, talents.' 57.4.21

This carries like a plough—carries the meaning of 57.5.22
this here—the foot stops a person here on their footprint."[272] *57.5.23*

[270] From Chapter 31. The second character also appears in Chapters 30 and 50.
[271] From Chapters 12, 29, and 30. It occurs with the following character ("Heaven-Below") in Chapter 29.
[272] From Chapters 1, 12, 14, 19, 23, 39, and 54. These last two lines are from Chapter 54. This last character is from Chapters 20, 21, 22, 53, and 54. This is its last appearance.

Heaven (that sky level above the human head)-Down Below (lower level) *57.6.24 & 25*
much more—like a double serving of meat—[273] *57.6.26*
abstaining from—binding one's heart like with a silk rope— *57.6.27*
taboo words—words like slaves or criminals branded by a chisel emerging from a mouth to be avoided like footsteps around an enclosure as with the name of a deceased emperor or elder... *57.6.28*
and yet now, bearded, *57.6.29*
civilians—like the Mín people enslaved by blinding with a dagger... *57.6.30*
far—a bow relaxing like cloth on a loom—[274] *57.6.31*
poor—separated by a knife from cowry-riches; *57.6.32*

civilians—like the Mín people enslaved by blinding with a dagger— *57.7.33*
"much more—like a double serving of meat—" *57.7.34*
benefiting—like by reaping grain with a sharp-edged blade—[275] *57.7.35*
set of valuable vessels with lots of capacity—worthy of a guard dog...[276] *57.7.36*
this nation—this particular territory, this enclave defended by a weapon on a pole plus its surroundings— *57.7.37*
home—a pig under your roof...[277] *57.7.38*
increasing as a river of double hard-to-see dark structured—like figure-eight skeins of string-dyed-black— *57.7.39*
darkening—getting dusky as the sun bows like a person with back-swept hands;[278] *57.7.40*

that person *57.8.41*
"much more—like a double serving of meat—" *57.8.42*
underhanded tricky—like that person with their right hand supporting ten *57.8.43*
craftiness—using a bladed tool on exhaled air—[279] *57.8.44*
"remarkably cunning—like the great giant about which one can purse one's lips like a piece of cane and puff: 'Yup, that's it, definitely...'" *57.8.45*
Things cut off—all matter external to oneself like seeds, cows etc. *57.8.46*
flowing like a river of hard-to-see dark structure—a figure-eight skein of string-dyed-black— *57.8.47*
coming up like a young man who will die young running from a snake or fetus; *57.7.48*

---

[273] From Chapters 5, 22, and 44.
[274] From Chapter 47.
[275] From Chapters 8, 11, 19, 36, 53, and 56. In Chapter 19 it's used with the "civilins" character.
[276] From Chapters 11, 28, 29, 31, 36, and 41. Used with the previous character in Chapter 36.
[277] From Chapters 18 and 54.
[278] From Chapters 18 and 20. In Chapter 18 it was used directly after the character "home."
[279] From Chapters 19 and 45.

following standards, regulations, rules—like water coming out of a mouth between a person's legs—of[280] *57.9.49*
controlling—joining together from three sides over a kneeling person and ordering them to do something, perhaps sending them somewhere—[281] *57.9.50*
"increasing as a river of double hard-to-see dark structured—like figure-eight skeins of string-dyed-black—" *57.9.51*
shining forth—as obviously clear and 'enlightened' as the hair on a person standing on the ground in the early morning sun over the jujube, that thorny plant that's used for insomnia and contraception and causes midterm miscarriages...[282] *57.9.552*
thievery—spitting into a bowl as an oath among thieves,[283] *57.9.53*
using a weapon on a pole in a blade-and-cauldron ritual standard to damage or rob...[284] *57.9.54*
"much more—like a double serving of meat" *57.9.55*
flesh-and-blood, meat-handling Being. *57.9.56*

Anciently, for ten generations, this lightly hits and leaves a mark of reason: *57.10.57*
a grounded sage—listening and speaking, standing connected to earth as well as the heavens *57.10.58*
that person, *57.10.59*
saying like a cloud... *57.10.60*

I/we—holding a rake-like weapon to defend ourselves and our opinion— *57.11.61*
"Not-Being—nobody trance-dancing with long tails flowing from her wrists— *57.11.62*
efforting—like lifting up an elephant,"[285] *57.11.63*
and yet now, bearded... *57.11.64*
civilians—like the Mín people enslaved by blinding with a dagger— *57.11.65*
of course—one's self personally, right on one's nose... *57.11.66*
transforming—a right-side-up person into an upside down person;[286] *57.11.67*

---

[280] From Chapter 25.
[281] From Chapters 12, 19, and 32.
[282] From Chapters 22 and 24.
[283] From Chapters 3, 19, and 53.
[284] From Chapter 19 where it was used with the previous character.
[285] From Chapters 38 and 43.
[286] From Chapter 37 (the final chapter of the *Dào*)

I/we—holding a rake-like weapon to defend ourselves and
our opinion— *57.12.68*
as good as—like a woman with a child—[287] *57.12.69*
calm peace—when the clear blue-green growth of that sedative cinnabar
plant quiets a dispute between two hands on a ploughshare,[288] *57.12.70*
and yet now, bearded... *57.12.71*
civilians—like the Mín people enslaved by blinding
with a dagger— *57.12.72*
of course—one's self personally, right on one's nose... *57.12.73*
"straight—upright as a nail in a footprint;"[289] *57.12.74*

I/we—holding a rake-like weapon to defend ourselves and
our opinion— *57.13.75*
"Not-Being—nobody trance-dancing with long tails flowing from
her wrists— *57.13.76*
one's personal, manual role—what one does with a weapon, a flag, or
a pen," *57.13.77*
and yet now, bearded... *57.13.78*
civilians—like the Mín people enslaved by blinding with
a dagger— *57.13.79*
of course—one's self personally, right on one's nose... *57.13.80*
wealth—a house full of valuable vessels with lots
of capacity;[290] *57.13.81*

I/we—holding a rake-like weapon to defend ourselves and
our opinion— *57.14.82*
"Not-Being—nobody trance-dancing with long tails flowing from
her wrists— *57.14.83*
wanting—missing what's been eroded from this ravine,"[291] *57.14.84*
and yet now, bearded... *57.14.85*
civilians—like the Mín people enslaved by blinding with
a dagger— *57.14.86*
of course—one's self personally, right on one's nose... *57.14.87*
natural state—like a piece of wood one can hold in one's hands,
straight from a thicket, uncarved and unpolished.[292] *57.14.88*

---

[287] From Chapters 30 and 53.
[288] From Chapters 15, 16, 26, 37, and 45.
[289] From Chapters 8 and 45.
[290] From Chapters 9 and 33.
[291] This phrase is used in several places including Chapter 1.
[292] From Chapters 15, 19, 28, 32, and 37 (the last chapter of the *Dào*).

58.

What it holds a basket of... *58.1.1*
politics and regulations of governing—lightly hitting to straight as if nailing setting out by foot on a long journey or campaign... *58.1.2*
gloomy—bored as a heart-core within the double-winged gateway—[293] *58.1.3*
gloomy—bored as a heart-core within the double-winged gateway: *58.1.4*

> what it holds a basket of... *58.2.5*
> civilians—like the Mín people enslaved by blinding with a dagger... *58.2.6*
> honest—thick-tasting and flowing enjoyment like a river, like a baby with a slanting mouth at an ancestral shrine— *58.2.7*
> honest—thick-tasting and flowing enjoyment like a river, like a baby with a slanting mouth at an ancestral shrine. *58.2.8*

"What it holds a basket of... *58.3.9*
politics and regulations of governing—lightly hitting to straight as if nailing setting out by foot on a long journey or campaign—" *58.3.10*
carefully discerning—studying at home like making a meat offering by hand at an altar—[294] *58.3.11*
carefully discerning—studying at home like making a meat offering by hand at an altar: *58.3.12*

> what it holds a basket of... *58.4.13*
> civilians—like the Mín people enslaved by blinding with a dagger... *58.4.14*
> lacking like a lidded earthen pot with a gap broken by a resolute hand with a fork—[295] *58.4.15*
> lacking like a lidded earthen pot with a gap broken by a resolute hand with a fork. *58.4.16*

Disaster—slanting mouth of a skull on a sacrifice altar...[296] *58.5.17*
—Oh! A breath, like wind through tree branches!— *58.5.18*
blessings and good fortune—like a full vessel on display on an altar *58.5.19*
has this... *58.5.20*
'place'—somewhere intentionally created, like a door chopped with an axe— *58.5.21*
to lean—to rely on a person who's remarkable like the great giant about which one can purse one's lips like a piece of cane and puff: 'Yup, that's it, definitely.' *58.5.22*

---

[293] From Chapter 20.
[294] From Chapter 20.
[295] From Chapter 45.
[296] From Chapter 46.

"Blessings and good fortune—like a full vessel on display on an altar..." *58.6.23*
—Oh! A breath, like wind through tree branches!— *58.6.24*
"disaster—slanting mouth of a skull on a sacrifice altar —" *58.6.25*
has this... *58.6.26*
'place'—somewhere intentionally created, like a door chopped with an axe— *58.6.27*
lying in wait like a dog waiting to ambush a person. *58.6.28*

Whoever—which person, like a baby with a slanting mouth of enjoyment is this *58.7.29*
firing arrows from the mouth, sure... *58.7.30*
what it holds a basket of... *58.7.31*
in the utmost—to the highest position of a double-beamed wooden ridgepole?[297] *58.7.32*

What it holds a basket of... *58.8.33*
Not-Being—nobody trance-dancing with long tails flowing from her wrists— *58.8.34*
straight—upright as a nail in a footprint:[298] *58.8.35*

"straight—upright as a nail in a footprint—" *58.9.36*
walking forth and then back again... *58.9.37*
efforting—like lifting up an elephant— *58.9.38*
remarkably cunning like the great giant about which one can purse one's lips like a piece of cane and puff: 'Yup, that's it, definitely;'[299] *58.9.39*

virtue—such as offering up a ram's head while back and forth speaking words that are emerging from a mouth like slaves or criminals branded by a chisel— *58.10.40*
walking forth and then back again... *58.10.41*
efforting—like lifting up an elephant— *58.10.42*
spooky, evil like gorgeous demons—a woman with breasts, kneeling... a running young man who will die young. *58.10.43*

---

[297] From Chapters 16 and 28.
[298] From Chapters 8, 45, and 57.
[299] From Chapter 57.

That person *58.11.44*
has this... *58.11.45*
getting lost—like raw rice scattered on the way of walking a while, stopping a while... bewitched, infatuated...[300] *58.11.46*

what it holds a basket of... *58.12.47*
the sun—the day, *58.12.8*
solidly, anciently—for ten generations of mouths, keeping as firm to what happened in the first place as this land surrounding and holding this nation since ancient times— *58.12.49*
enduring through time—like someone receiving moxibustion treatments with mugwort used for cramps, turning a breech baby, or other health issues.[301] *58.12.50*

The sun—walking across the sundial a while, stopping a while—sees indeed *58.13.51*
this carries like a plough—carries the meaning of *58.13.52*
a grounded sage—listening and speaking, standing connected to earth as well as the heavens, *58.13.53*
that person... *58.13.54*

like the parallel side of a tipped blade,[302] *58.14.55*
and yet now, bearded... *58.14.56*
"the husk of the initial protective bud casing—the sepal—but not really the true inner flower of *58.14.57*
splitting apart—like cutting open a house already harmed, dense with spoken and tallied lies;"[303] *58.14.58*

clean and incorruptible as that hand holding two stalks of grain—doing two things at once—in a habitable cliff cave, *58.15.59*
and yet now, bearded... *58.15.60*
the husk of the initial protective bucasing—the sepal—but not really the true inner flower of *58.15.61*
stabbing with a knife like pacing off distance, one foot in front of the other, marking the passage of time like a year on a calendar; *58.15.62*

---

[300] From Chapter 27.
[301] From Chapters 7, 15, 16, 23, 33, and 44.
[302] From Chapter 41.
[303] From Chapter 28.

looking straight on, straight ahead,[304] *58.16.63*
and yet now, bearded... *58.16.64*
the husk of the initial protective bud casing—the sepal—but not really the true inner flower of *58.16.65*
undisciplined—like the long hair that has to be tied with a brooch of one who once was skillful with a bamboo brush; *58.16.66*

brilliant—that shining fire over the head of a kneeling person,[305] *58.17.67*
and yet now, bearded... *58.17.68*
the husk of the initial protective bud casing—the sepal—but not really the true inner flower of *58.17.69*
brilliant—that shining fire over the head of a kneeling person as the plumes of a long-tailed pheasant. *58.17.70*

59.

Governing—regulating by harnessing the river named Happy or speaking of turning oneself—[306] *59.1.1*
that person... *59.1.2*
one's personal, manual role—what one does with a weapon, a flag, or a pen— *59.1.3*
Heaven (that sky level above the human head): *59.1.4*
must not—like the lost-in-the-bushes sinking sun, eh?— *59.1.5*
A Certain Someone compliantly combing their loose hair seems to be saying: 'this is as if...' *59.1.6*
thrifty as conserving wheat in a granary. *59.1.7*

---

304 From Chapters 22 and 45. This character is a sub-component of the glyph for *Dé*.
305 From Chapters 4, 52, and 56.
306 Also a key concept at the beginning of the previous chapter. This character is from Chapters 3, 8, 10, and 57.

That is to say, this particular grown man with a hairpin and public
courtesy name *59.2.8*
essentially and only—like the mouth of 'the short-tailed bird:' *59.2.9*
"thrifty as conserving wheat in a granary," *59.2.10*
the sun—walking across the sundial a while, stopping a while—sees indeed *59.2.11*
what it's called when speaking from the gut—words, like slaves or criminals
branded by a chisel emerging from a mouth: *59.2.12*
early, premature—like sunrise above an acorn on the jujube, that
thorny plant that's used for insomnia, contraception and causes
midterm miscarriages—[307] *59.2.13*
wearing clothes—like mourning dress as earthly and mortal
as commonplace plates—subdued like a kneeling person
by hand.[308] *59.2.14*

"Early, premature—like sunrise above an acorn on the jujube, that
thorny plant that's used for insomnia, contraception and causes
midterm miscarriages— *59.3.15*
wearing clothes—like mourning dress as earthly and mortal as commonplace
plates—subdued like a kneeling person by hand..." *59.3.16*
what it's called when speaking from the gut—words, like slaves or criminals
branded by a chisel emerging from a mouth.. *59.3.17*
what it has... *59.3.18*
a heavy load—a bag carried by a man—[309] *59.3.19*
storing and accumulating—amassing grain plants like cowry-riches under
a thorn tree *59.3.20*
Dé—the ethical, straight way of walking awhile and stopping awhile, eye
directed forward over the heart-core; *59.3.21*

---

[307] From Chapters 30 and 55.
[308] From Chapter 53.
[309] From Chapter 26.

"A heavy load—a bag carried by a man— *59.4.22*
storing and accumulating—amassing grain plants like cowry-riches under a thorn tree *59.4.23*
Dé—the ethical, straight way of walking awhile and stopping awhile, eye directed forward over the heart-core..." *59.4.24*
after following this sacrificial blade-and-cauldron-like ritual example or regulation... *59.4.25*
Not-Being—nobody trance-dancing with long tails flowing from her wrists— *59.4.26*
the husk of the initial protective bud casing—the sepal—but not really the true inner flower of *59.4.27*
prevailing like fire above the mouth of a kneeling person; *59.4.28*

"Not-Being—nobody trance-dancing with long tails flowing from her wrists— *59.5.29*
the husk of the initial protective bud casing—the sepal—but not really the true inner flower of *59.5.30*
prevailing like fire above the mouth of a kneeling person," *59.5.31*
after following this sacrificial blade-and-cauldron-like ritual example or regulation... *59.5.32*
must not—eh, like the lost-in-the-bushes , eh?— *59.5.33*
firing arrows from the mouth, sure *59.5.34*
what it holds a basket of... *59.5.35*
in the utmost—to the highest position of a double-beamed wooden ridgepole;[310] *59.5.36*

"Must not—eh, like the lost-in-the-bushes , eh?— *59.6.37*
firing arrows from the mouth, sure *59.6.38*
what it holds a basket of... *59.6.39*
in the utmost—to the highest position of a double-beamed wooden ridgepole" *59.6.40*
about which one can purse one's lips like a piece of cane and puff: 'Yup, that's it, definitely,' *59.6.41*
this carries like a plough—carries the meaning of... *59.6.42*
flesh-and-blood, meat-handling Being *59.6.43*
this nation—this particular territory, this enclave defended by a weapon on a pole plus its surroundings; *59.6.44*

[310] From Chapters 16, 28, and 58.

"Flesh-and-blood, meat-handling Being *59.7.45*
this nation—this particular territory, this enclave defended by a weapon on a pole plus its surroundings..." *59.7.46*
what it has... *59.7.47*
suckling—like being nursed by a woman—[311] *59.7.48*
about which one can purse one's lips like a piece of cane and puff: 'Yup, that's it, definitely,' *59.7.49*
this carries like a plough—carries the meaning of... *59.7.50*
"long as hair that has to be tied with a brooch[312] *59.7.51*
enduring through time—like someone receiving moxibustion treatments with mugwort used for cramps, turning a breech baby, or other health issues."[313] *59.7.52*

The sun—walking across the sundial a while, stopping a while—sees indeed *59.8.53*
what it's called when speaking from the gut—words, like slaves or criminals branded by a chisel emerging from a mouth: *59.8.54*
deep as far water,[314] *59.8.55*
the root of the family tree—a penis...[315] *59.8.56*
solidly, anciently—for ten generations of mouths, keeping as firm to what happened in the first place as this land surrounding and holding this nation since ancient times— *59.8.57*
rooted like a tree—a person standing on the ground bowing to their lineage; *59.8.58*

"long as hair that has to be tied with a brooch" *59.9.59*
birthing—a bud sprouting from the ground, *59.9.60*
"enduring through time—like someone receiving moxibustion treatments with mugwort used for cramps, turning a breech baby, or other health issues—" *59.9.61*
regarding like one big eye for a head seeing at an altar...[316] *59.9.62*
what it has... *59.9.63*
The Way of the loose-haired headperson—walking a while, stopping a while, and speaking of it all *59.9.64*

---

[311] From Chapters 1, 20, 25, and 52. This is its last appearance.
[312] From Chapters 2, 7, 9, 44, and 54.
[313] From Chapters 7, 15, 16, 23, 33, 44, and 58. This two-word phrase was also used in Chapter 44.
[314] From Chapter 15.
[315] From Chapters 6, 16, and 26. This is its last appearance.
[316] From Chapters 14 and 35.

60.

Governing—regulating by harnessing the river named Happy or speaking of turning oneself— *60.1.1*[317]
great giant *60.1.2*
this nation—this particular territory, this enclave defended by a weapon on a pole plus its surroundings... *60.1.3*
A Certain Someone compliantly combing their loose hair seems to be saying: 'this is as if...' *60.1.4*
boiling alive—a baby crying over the fire— *60.1.5*
very little—like three grains of sand—[318] *60.1.6*
delicacies like fresh fish or ram's head. *60.1.7*

This carries like a plough—carries the meaning of *60.2.8*
The Way of the loose-haired headperson—walking a while, stopping a while, and speaking of it all, *60.2.9*
arriving at an official ceremony, managing—like a person, a person standing on ground, drying up water in the grass— *60.2.10*
Heaven (that sky level above the human head)-Down Below
(lower level)... *60.2.11 & 12*

what it holds a basket of... *60.3.13*
a ghost... *60.3.14*
the husk of the initial protective bud casing—the sepal—but not really the true inner flower of *60.3.15*
a lightning god. *60.3.16*

Breaking the little wings off... *60.4.17*
"what it holds a basket of... *60.4.18*
a ghost... *60.4.19*
the husk of the initial protective bud casing—the sepal—but not really the true inner flower of *60.4.20*
a lightning god..."[319] *60.4.21*

---

[317] Also a key concept at the beginning of the previous two chaptera. This character is from Chapters 3, 8, 10, 57, and 59.
[318] From Chapters 32, 34, and 52.
[319] From Chapters 6, 29, and 39.

what it holds a basket of... *60.5.22*
"a lightning god" *60.5.23*
the husk of the initial protective bud casing—the sepal—but not really the true inner flower of *60.5.24*
wounded—a bent person with that male principle of sun shining on an altar like strands of hair, *60.5.25*
that person. *60.5.26*

Breaking the little wings off *60.6.27*
"what it holds a basket of... *60.6.28*
a lightning god *60.6.29*
the husk of the initial protective bud casing—the sepal—but not really the true inner flower of *60.6.30*
wounded—a bent person with that male principle of sun shining on an altar like strands of hair, *60.6.31*
that person..." *60.6.32*

a grounded sage—listening and speaking, standing connected to earth as well as the heavens, *60.7.33*
that person *60.7.34*
—both armpits sweat this too!— *60.7.35*
"the husk of the initial protective bud casing—the sepal—but not really the true inner flower of *60.7.36*
wounded—a bent person with that male principle of sun shining on an altar like strands of hair, *60.7.37*
that person." *60.7.38*

That is to say, this particular grown man with a hairpin and public courtesy name... *60.8.39*
a matched pair, like a harness of ox yokes...[320] *60.8.40*
the husk of the initial protective bud casing—the sepal—but not really the true inner flower of *60.8.41*
mutually—like a seen tree and the eye seeing it—[321] *60.8.42*
"wounded—a bent person with that male principle of sun shining on an altar like strands of hair." *60.8.43*

---

[320] From Chapter 1.
[321] From Chapters 2, 20, and 32.

Anciently, for ten generations, this lightly hits and leaves a mark of reason: *60.9.44*
Dé—the ethical, straight way of walking awhile and stopping awhile, eye directed forward over the heart-core— *60.9.45*
intersecting—making friends like someone with crossed legs— *60.9.46*
"returning after sweeping troops out of the hills to this[322] *60.9.47*
here—this place where that yellow bird lives around the Yangtze and Huai Rivers."[323] *60.9.48*

61.

"Great giant... *61.1.1*
this nation—this particular territory, this enclave defended by a weapon on a pole plus its surroundings—"[324] *61.1.2*
—now this is cooking with fire!— *61.1.3*
down below, lower level... *61.1.4*
flowing like a baby coming out head first in a river of watery waste. *61.1.5*

> Heaven (that sky level above the human head)-Down Below (lower level) *61.2.6 & 7*
> has this... *61.2.8*
> intersecting—making friends like someone with crossed legs;[325] *61.2.9*
>
> Heaven (that sky level above the human head)-Down Below (lower level) *61.3.10 & 11*
> has this... *61.3.12*
> of a mother's lap—a cow with an arrow... a vagina.[326] *61.3.13*

---

[322] From Chapters 14, 16, 20, 22, 28, 34, and 52.
[323] This two-character expression is from Chapter 34. The second character also appears in Chapters 2, 25, and 49. This is its last appearance.
[324] From Chapter 60.
[325] From Chapter 60.
[326] From Chapters 6 and 55.

"Of a mother's lap—a cow with an arrow... a vagina..." *61.4.14*
the ever-present square fabric—like that which our grown men wrap around the 'little bird' top knots on their heads after receiving their public courtesy-names—or what we know as the timeless, whole head-cloth 'ji' version of, *61.4.15*
this carries like a plough—carries the meaning of *61.4.16*
calm peace—when the clear blue-green growth of that sedative cinnabar plant quiets a dispute between two hands on a ploughshare—[327] *61.4.17*
forcing a victory over—using a blade to mend a boat or roll rice into a ball under moonlight—[328] *61.4.18*
a bull soil... male genitals.[329] *61.4.19*

> This carries like a plough—carries the meaning of *61.5.20*
> "calm peace—when the clear blue-green growth of that sedative cinnabar plant quiets a dispute between two hands on a ploughshare..." *61.5.21*
> efforting—like lifting up an elephant— *61.5.22*
> down below, lower level. *61.5.23*

Anciently, for ten generations, this lightly hits and leaves a mark of reason: *61.6.24*
"great giant *61.6.25*
this nation—this particular territory, this enclave defended by a weapon on a pole plus its surroundings," *61.6.26*
this carries like a plough—carries the meaning of *61.6.27*
"down below, lower level..." *61.6.28*
very little, like three grains of sand,[330] *61.6.29*
"this nation—this particular territory, this enclave defended by a weapon on a pole plus its surroundings..." *61.6.30*

> after following this sacrificial blade-and-cauldron-like ritual example or regulation... *61.7.31*
> grabbing the ear of—like marrying—[331] *61.7.32*
> "very little, like three grains of sand *61.7.33*
> this nation—this particular territory, this enclave defended by a weapon on a pole plus its surroundings;" *61.7.34*

---

[327] From Chapters 15, 16, 26, 37, 45, and 57.
[328] From Chapters 31, 33, 36, and 45 (in the last one it also appeared with the preceding character, "calm peace").
[329] From Chapter 55.
[330] From Chapters 32, 52, and 60.
[331] From Chapters 12, 29, 30, and 57.

"very little, like three grains of sand, *61.8.35*
this nation—this particular territory, this enclave defended by a weapon on a pole plus its surroundings," *61.8.36*
this carries like a plough—carries the meaning of *61.8.37*
"down below, lower level..." *61.8.38*
"great giant *61.8.39*
this nation—this particular territory, this enclave defended by a weapon on a pole plus its surroundings..." *61.8.40*

> "after following this sacrificial blade-and-cauldron-like ritual example or regulation... *61.9.41*
> grabbing the ear of—like marrying—" *61.9.42*
> "great giant *61.9.43*
> this nation—this particular territory, this enclave defended by a weapon on a pole plus its surroundings." *61.9.44*

Anciently, for ten generations, this lightly hits and leaves a mark of reason: *61.10.45*
this particular territory—this enclave, defended by a weapon on a pole, plus its surroundings— *61.10.46*
"down below, lower level..." *61.10.47*
> this carries like a plough—carries the meaning of *61.10.48*
> "grabbing the ear of—like marrying;" *61.10.49*

"this particular territory—this enclave, defended by a weapon on a pole, plus its surroundings— *61.11.50*
down below, lower level" *61.11.51*
> and yet now, bearded... *61.11.52*
> "grabbing the ear of—like marrying." *61.11.53*

"Great giant *61.12.54*
this nation—this particular territory, this enclave defended by a weapon on a pole plus its surroundings..." *61.12.55*
the husk of the initial protective bud casing—the sepal—but not really the true inner flower of *61.12.56*
this way of walking a while and stopping a while that's past and surpassing—like a slanting skull mouth speaking—[332] *61.12.57*
wanting—missing what's been eroded from this ravine... *61.12.58*
> that hand holding two stalks of grain—doing two things at once... *61.12.59*
> rearing animals—giving them feed from a bag tied with a rope,[333] *61.12.60*
> that person. *61.12.61*

---

[332] From Chapter 35.
[333] From Chapter 10.

"Very little, like three grains of sand *61.13.62*
this nation—this particular territory, this enclave defended by a weapon on a pole plus its surroundings..." *61.13.63*
"the husk of the initial protective bud casing—the sepal—but not really the true inner flower of *61.13.64*
this way of walking a while and stopping a while that's past and surpassing—like a slanting skull mouth speaking— *61.13.65*
wanting—missing what's been eroded from this ravine..." *61.13.66*
entering like an arrow...[334] *61.13.67*
one's personal, manual role—what one does with a weapon, a flag, or a pen, *61.13.68*
that person. *61.13.69*

"That is to say, this particular grown man with a hairpin and public courtesy name... *61.14.70*
a matched pair, like a harness of ox yokes..."[335] *61.14.71*
—now this is cooking with fire! *61.14.72*
each foot and mouth[336] *61.14.73*
hand-picking, like-cowry-shell-riches-along-the-road, *61.14.74*
what it holds a basket of... *61.14.75*
'place'—somewhere intentionally created, like a door chopped with an axe— *61.14.76*
"wanting—missing what's been eroded from this ravine." *61.14.77*

"Great giant" *61.15.78*
—now this is cooking with fire!— *61.15.79*
it's appropriate to be—like two pieces of meat in a sacrificial altar— *61.15.80*
"efforting—like lifting up an elephant— *61.15.81*
down below, lower level." *61.15.82*

---

[334] From Chapters 43 and 50. This is its last appearance.
[335] This character is from Chapters 1 and 60. It was used with the same preceding charcter in Chapter 60.
[336] From Chapter 16.

62.

The Way of the loose-haired headperson—walking a while, stopping a while, and speaking of it all... *62.1.1*
—now this is cooking with fire!— *62.1.2*
the myriad, scorpion-medicine-dancing Ten Thousand *62.1.3*
Things cut off—all matter external to oneself like seeds, cows etc. *62.1.4*
has this *62.1.5*
secret corner—a sanctuary like that backwater place on the city outskirts where grain's arriving and divided by a great giant; *62.1.6*

virtue—such as offering up a ram's head while back and forth speaking words that are emerging from a mouth like slaves or criminals branded by a chisel... *62.2.7*
that person *62.2.8*
has this *62.2.9*
treasure—like a house containing cowry-riches, jade, and a lidded pot; *62.2.10*

“the husk of the initial protective bud casing—the sepal—but not really the true inner flower of *62.3.11*
virtue—such as offering up a ram's head while back and forth speaking words that are emerging from a mouth like slaves or criminals branded by a chisel...”[337] *62.3.12*
that person *62.3.13*
has this *62.3.14*
'place'—somewhere intentionally created, like a door chopped with an axe— *62.3.15*
safeguarding—like carrying a child on one's back.[338] *62.3.16*

Admired beauty—picture someone wearing a ram's horn headdress—[339] *62.4.17*
speaking—words, like slaves or criminals branded by a chisel emerging from a mouth *62.4.18*
about which one can purse one's lips like a piece of cane and puff: 'Yup, that's it, definitely...' *62.4.19*
this carries like a plough—carries the meaning of *62.4.20*
market—a bustling city at the fork in a tree; *62.4.21*

---

[337] See Chapter 49.
[338] From Chpaters 9 and 15.
[339] From Chapters 2 and 31.

honoring—like offering by hand the yi ritual alcohol vessel with the chief charged with its preparation[340] *62.5.22*
on a public road, practicing—moving with— *62.5.23*
about which one can purse one's lips like a piece of cane and puff: 'Yup, that's it, definitely...' *62.5.24*

this carries like a plough—carries the meaning of *62.5.25*
putting on top of another like a mouth ordering a cow over a plough, *62.5.26*
that person. *62.5.27*

That person *62.6.28*
has this... *62.6.29*
"the husk of the initial protective bud casing—the sepal—but not really the true inner flower of *62.6.30*
virtue—such as offering up a ram's head while back and forth speaking words that are emerging from a mouth like slaves or criminals branded by a chisel..." *62.6.31*

that very one about whom you can purse your lips around a cane and puff, 'yup, that's the person,' *62.7.32*
abandoned—like hanging a baby upside down in three leaves on a branch or generation of a tree— [341] *62.7.33*
has this... *62.7.34*
flesh-and-blood, meat-handling Being. *62.7.35*

Anciently, for ten generations, this lightly hits and leaves a mark of reason: *62.8.36*
a person standing straight up on the ground... *62.8.37*
Heaven (that sky level above the human head) *62.8.38*
baby—arms wide open and legs swaddled [342] *62.8.39*

installing—like a net looking straight on, straight ahead *62.9.40*
three [times] *62.9.41*
as publicly fair and impartial as a high ranking old big-balled man—a duke... *62.9.42*

---

[340] From Chapter 51.
[341] From Chapters 19 and 27.
[342] From Chapters 4, 31, 52, 54, and 55. This is its last ppearance. It is the second part of Lǎo Zǐ's honorific name.

although—even if 'a venomous snake' has 'a short-tailed bird' right next to it— *62.10.43*
flesh-and-blood, meat-handling Being *62.10.44*
arching around and holding aloft like hands folded on the chest, sharing *62.10.45*
jade annulus—shaped like the backside of a kneeling slave or criminal being punished, marked with a chisel, *62.10.46*

this carries like a plough—carries the meaning of *62.11.47*
being long before—that is, an ancestor...[343] *62.11.48*
driving four horses—like to pull a chariot, *62.11.49*
horse,[344] *62.11.50*

the husk of the initial protective bud casing—the sepal—but not really the true inner flower of *62.12.51*
'as if'—like a woman just doing as told— *62.12.52*
sitting—two people staying there, on the ground... *62.12.53*
walking forward awhile and stopping awhile like a 'short-tailed bird,'[345] *62.12.54*
this here—the foot stops a person here on their footprint... *62.12.55*
The Way of the loose-haired headperson—walking a while, stopping a while, and speaking of it all. *62.12.56*

Ancient times—ten generations of mouths ago— *62.13.57*
has this *62.13.58*
'place'—somewhere intentionally created, like a door chopped with an axe, *62.13.59*
this carries like a plough—carries the meaning of... *62.13.60*
treasuring—as if as valuable as cowry-shell-riches—[346] *62.13.561*
this here—the foot stops a person here on their footprint: *62.13.62*
The Way of the loose-haired headperson—walking a while, stopping a while, and speaking of it all *62.13.63*
—now this is cooking with fire!— *62.13.64*
that very one about whom you can purse your lips around a cane and puff, 'yup, that's the person... *62.13.65*

343 From Chapters 4, 7, and 25.
344 From Chapter 46.
345 From Chapter 41.
346 From Chapters 3, 9, 13, 17, 20, 27, 31, 39, 51, and 56.

the husk of the initial protective bud casing—the sepal—but not really the true inner flower of *62.14.66*
what it's called when issued on a breath from the mouth... *62.14.67*
'seeking and requesting—like a coveted fur coat,' *62.15.68*
this carries like a plough—carries the meaning of... *62.15.69*
hand-picking, like-cowry-shell-riches-along-the-road; *62.15.70*

Flesh-and-blood, meat-handling Being... *62.16.71*
a sin or crime like a net breaking the little wings off something,[347] *62.16.72*
this carries like a plough—carries the meaning of... *62.16.73*
exempting—like a man taking off a hat— *62.16.74*
of disastrous nature—like that disease-causing environment around Tusk Town.[348] *62.16.75*

"*Anciently, for ten generations, this lightly hits and leaves a mark of reason: 62.17.76*
efforting—like lifting up an elephant— 62.17.77
Heaven (that sky level above the human head)-Down Below (lower level) 62.17.78 & 79
treasuring—as if as valuable as cowry-shell-riches."[349] *62.17.80*

63.

Efforting—like lifting up an elephant... *63.1.1*
"Not-Being—nobody trance-dancing with long tails flowing from her wrists— *63.1.2*
efforting—like lifting up an elephant..."[350] *63.1.3*

one's personal, manual role—what one does with a weapon, a flag, or a pen... *63.2.4*
Not-Being—nobody trance-dancing with long tails flowing from her wrists— *63.2.5*
one's personal, manual role—what one does with a weapon, a flag, or a pen... *63.2.6*

---

[347] From Chapter 46.
[348] From Chapters 7 and 39.
[349] This line is from Chapter 56. The last character also appears in Chapters 3, 9, 13, 17, 20, 27, 31, 39, and 51.
[350] From Chapters 38, 43 and 57.

tasting—reflecting on the flavor in your mouth which is still forming like a tree whose top branches aren't yet fully grown...[351] *63.3.7*
Not-Being—nobody trance-dancing with long tails flowing from her wrists— *63.3.8*
tasting—reflecting on the flavor in your mouth which is still forming like a tree whose top branches aren't yet fully grown... *63.3.9*

great giant... *63.4.10*
very little, like three grains of sand, *63.4.11*
much more—like a double serving of meat— *63.4.12*
reducing to few—four little dots...[352] *63.4.13*

judging and making someone answer for what's happened—handcuffing and subduing with a hand to the back— *63.5.14*
resenting—the heart sleeping like someone kneeling to lie down below the moon... *63.5.15*
this carries like a plough—carries the meaning of *63.5.16*
Dé—the ethical, straight way of walking awhile and stopping awhile, eye directed forward over the heart-core. *63.5.17*

Planning—plotting a chart like someone receiving by mouth from the grannies within a walled city— *63.6.18*
the solidly hard—as difficult as the dried yellow earth of Han where short-tailed birds can't find food—[353] *63.6.19*
here—oh, black, icy raven... *63.6.20*
what it holds a basket of... *63.6.21*
easily changeable to something else—going from saying 'don't' as seriously as blood on a blade to shining as sunny as the sun above.[354] *63.6.22*

Efforting—like lifting up an elephant— *63.7.23*
"great giant" *63.7.24*
here—oh, black, icy raven... *63.7.25*
what it holds a basket of... *63.7.26*
small, delicate, and young—a skein of silk fontanelle *63.7.27*

---

[351] From Chapters 12 and 35.
[352] From Chapters 19, 22, and 47.
[353] From Chapters 2, 3, and 12.
[354] From Chapter 2 where it and "hard" were mutually completing.

Heaven (that sky level above the human head)-Down Below
(lower level)... *63.8.28 & 29*
"the solidly hard—as difficult as the dried yellow earth of Han where short-tailed birds can't find food..." *63.8.30*
"one's personal, manual role—what one does with a weapon, a flag, or a pen," *63.8.31*

analytically—hands over heart-core— *63.9.32*
getting up and going to work[355] *63.9.33*
here—oh, black, icy raven... *63.9.34*
"easily changeable to something else—going from saying 'don't' as seriously as blood on a blade to shining as sunny as the sun above." *63.9.35*

Heaven (that sky level above the human head)-Down Below
(lower level)... *63.10.36 & 37*
"great giant..." *63.10.38*
"one's personal, manual role—what one does with a weapon, a flag, or a pen," *63.10.39*

"analytically—hands over heart-core— *63.11.40*
getting up and going to work *63.11.41*
here—oh, black, icy raven..." *63.11.42*
"small, delicate, and young—a skein of silk fontanelle." *63.11.43*

The sun—walking across the sundial a while, stopping a while—sees indeed *63.12.44*
this carries like a plough—carries the meaning of *63.12.45*
a grounded sage—listening and speaking, standing connected to earth as well as the heavens, *63.12.46*
that person *63.12.47*
ending—the knot at the end of a thick silk skein in winter...[356] *63.12.48*
the husk of the initial protective bud casing—the sepal—but not really the true inner flower of *63.12.49*
"efforting—like lifting up an elephant, *63.12.50*
great giant." *63.12.51*

---

[355] From Chapters 2, 16, 37, and 55.
[356] From Chapters 23, 26, 34, 52, and 55.

Anciently, for ten generations, this lightly hits and leaves a mark of reason: *63.13.52*
using a legendary capability—the hybrid power of that mythical bear with deer legs—for *63.13.53*
completing—that final nail in the weapon on a pole—[357] *63.13.54*
what it holds a basket of... *63.13.55*
"great giant." *63.13.56*

That is to say, this particular grown man with a hairpin and public courtesy name...[358] *63.14.57*
as if lightweight—as lightweight as using a bladed tool in a light carriage on an underground stream— *63.14.58*
promising like A Certain Someone compliantly combing their loose hair who seems to be speaking up and saying: 'this is as if... yeah, definitely', *63.14.59*
analytically—hands over heart-core... *63.14.60*
scant as one widowed, alone—separating them from the kneeling head of the household with a blade—[359] *63.14.61*
truth-speaking—speaking words like slaves or criminals, branded by a chisel, emerging from a mouth of good luck that's as empty and quiet as a mouth with a soldier's axe above it, speaking of grass; *63.14.62*

much more—like a double serving of meat— *63.15.63*
"easily changeable to something else—going from saying 'don't' as seriously as blood on a blade to shining as sunny as the sun above," *63.15.64*
analytically—hands over heart-core... *63.15.65*
much more—like a double serving of meat— *63.15.66*
"the solidly hard—as difficult as the dried yellow earth of Han where short-tailed birds can't find food." *63.15.67*

[357] From Chapter 2, 7, 15, 17, 25, 34, 41, 45, 47, and 51.
[358] Together, these last two characters *dà fú* (great giant, that is to say, this particular grown man) were a class of nobility in the Zhou era: "the gentlemen beuraaucrats."
[359] From Chapters 19, 39, and 42.

The sun—walking across the sundial a while, stopping a while—sees indeed *63.16.68*
this carries like a plough—carries the meaning of *63.16.69*
a grounded sage—listening and speaking, standing connected to earth as well as the heavens, *63.16.70*
that person, *63.16.71*
indeed, like a dog that rises to the top of the alcohol vat..[360] *63.16.72*
"the solidly hard—as difficult as the dried yellow earth of Han where short-tailed birds can't find food..." *63.16.73*
what it has; *63.16.74*

anciently, for ten generations, this lightly hits and leaves a mark of reason... *63.17.75*
"ending—the knot at the end of a thick silk skein in winter..." *63.17.76*
Not-Being—nobody trance-dancing with long tails flowing from her wrists... *63.17.77*
"the solidly hard—as difficult as the dried yellow earth of Han where short-tailed birds can't find food—" *63.17.79*
—swearing on an arrow revolving around oneself, that's it![361] *63.17.79*

64.

What it holds a basket of, *64.1.1*
calm like a woman sitting on her heels at home:[362] *64.1.2*
easily changeable to something else—going from saying 'don't' as seriously as blood on a blade to shining as sunny as the sun above...[363] *64.1.3*
holding on to something—like a patron from a temple or government office that's expert at stopping and giving a hand.[364] *64.1.4*

"What it holds a basket of, *64.2.5*
not yet—a tree whose top branches aren't yet fully grown— *64.2.6*
an omen like the cracks in a shell during divination:"[365] *64.2.7*
easily changeable to something else—going from saying 'don't' as seriously as blood on a blade to shining as sunny as the sun above... *64.2.8*
consulting on strategy—speaking with a tree, words like slaves or criminals, branded by a chisel, emerging from a mouth. *64.2.9*

[360] From Chapters 5, 15, and 32.
[361] From Chapters 31 and 46.
[362] From Chapters 15 and 35.
[363] From Chapters 2 and 63.
[364] From Chapter 9.
[365] From Chapter 20.

What it holds a basket of, *64.3.10*
fragile as crispy meat from a roof—precariously high above a kneeling person: *64.3.11*
easily changeable to something else—going from saying 'don't' as seriously as blood on a blade to shining as sunny as the sun above... *64.3.12*
dissolving as half a beef in the river—like the Zhou dynasty school of that name! *64.3.13*

What it holds a basket of, *64.4.14*
so triflingly small and humble as to almost not exist—as someone being followed from behind, stepping slowly with only the left leg leading around the left side of three high peaks where the foot of the mountains cuts off:[366] *64.4.15*
easily changeable to something else—going from saying 'don't' as seriously as blood on a blade to shining as sunny as the sun above...*64.4.16*
becoming free and loose—like bamboos lightly hit by the crescent moon, breaking apart.[367] *64.4.17*

Efforting—like lifting up an elephant...*64.5.18*
what it has *64.5.19*
here—oh, black, icy raven... *64.5.20*
not yet—a tree whose top branches aren't yet fully grown—[368] *64.5.21*
flesh-and-blood, meat-handling Being. *64.5.22*

Governing—regulating by harnessing the river named Happy or speaking of turning oneself... *64.6.23*
what it has *64.6.24*
here—oh, black, icy raven... *64.6.25*
"not yet—a tree whose top branches aren't yet fully grown—" *64.6.26*
confused anxiety—one's tongue is like twisted threads with one remnant string hanging out.[369] *64.6.27*

Joining together from three sides over a mouth—having sex—[370] *64.7.28*
bundling it all up together—in one's arms...[371] *64.7.29*
what it has *64.7.30*
tree with roots... *64.7.31*

---

[366] From Chapters 14, 15, and 36. This is its last appearance.
[367] From Chapter 28.
[368] From Chapters 20 and 55.
[369] From Chapters 3, 18, and 38. This is its last appearance.
[370] From Chapters 32 and 55, This is its last appearance.
[371] From Chapters 10, 19, 22, 42, and 54. This is its last appearance.

birthing—a bud sprouting from the ground— *64.8.32*
here—oh, black, icy raven...*64.8.33*
    as tiny as the fine hair covering below the mouth, *64.8.34*
    tip-top, tree-top. *64.8.35*

Nine (the elbow in that old way of counting) *64.9.36*
layers piling up—- someone bent like one who represents the dead in a rite flexing to step out of a cave has bent over the steam cooker previously many times... *64.9.37*
what it has *64.9.38*
as its place name—what it says, revolving around itself... *64.9.39*

coming up like a young man who will die young running from a snake or fetus[372] *64.10.40*
here—oh, black, icy raven... *64.10.41*
    piling up—like fatigue after work in the field, with a skein of silk— *64.10.42*
    clay soil. *64.10.43*

One thousand—where a person reaches when extending their counting— *64.11.44*
traditional miles—that village measurement of fields on the clay soil... *64.11.45*
what it has *64.11.46*
on a public road, practicing—moving with... *64.11.47*

beginning—like conception in and by a woman— *64.12.48*
here—oh, black, icy raven... *64.12.49*
    enough—the full leg-cut of the animal—[373] *64.12.50*
    down below, lower level. *64.12.51*

"Efforting—like lifting up an elephant... 64.13.52
—now this is cooking with fire!— 64.13.53
    being defeated—its riches hit lightly by hand, failing, decaying...[374] *64.13.54*
    what it has. 64.13.55

[372] From Chapter 57.
[373] From Chapters 17, 19, 23, 28, 33, 35, 41, 44, 46, and 48.
[374] From Chapter 29.

Holding tight in the hand—not letting go of, not dying young...[375] 64.14.56
—now this is cooking with fire!— 64.14.57
dropping something—losing[376]*...* 64.14.58
what it has."[377] 64.14.59

The sun—walking across the sundial a while, stopping a while—sees indeed *64.15.60*
this carries like a plough—carries the meaning of *64.15.61*
a grounded sage—listening and speaking, standing connected to earth as well as the heavens, *64.15.62*
that person: *64.15.63*
"Not-Being—nobody trance-dancing with long tails flowing from her wrists— *64.15.64*
efforting—like lifting up an elephant," *64.15.65*
anciently, for ten generations, this lightly hits and leaves a mark of reason... *64.15.66*
Not-Being—nobody trance-dancing with long tails flowing from her wrists— *64.15.67*
"being defeated—its riches hit lightly by hand, failing, decaying;" *64.15.68*

Not-Being—nobody trance-dancing with long tails flowing from her wrists— *64.16.69*
"holding tight in the hand—not letting go of, not dying young," *64.16.70*
anciently, for ten generations, this lightly hits and leaves a mark of reason... *64.16.71*
Not-Being—nobody trance-dancing with long tails flowing from her wrists— *64.16.72*
"dropping something—losing." *64.16.73*

---

[375] From Chapters 14, 29, and 35.
[376] From Chapters 13, 23, 26, 29, 33, and 38.
[377] These two lines together are from Chapter 29.

Civilians—like the Mín people enslaved by blinding with a dagger... *64.17.74*
what it has ... *64.17.75*
following in those footprints—stepping slowly with only the left leg leading the way, directly after another person, and stopping on one's footprint— *64.17.76*
one's personal, manual role—what one does with a weapon, a flag, or a pen, *64.17.77*
the ever-present square fabric—like that which our grown men wrap around the 'little bird' top knots on their heads after receiving their public courtesy-names—or what we know as the timeless, whole head-cloth 'ji' version— *64.17.78*
here—oh, black, icy raven... *64.17.79*
being as near as a border of fine, fine silk you'd guard with a blade to[378] *64.17.80*
completing—that final nail in the weapon on a pole,[379] *64.17.81*
and yet now, bearded... *64.17.82*
"being defeated—its riches hit lightly by hand, failing, decaying..." *64.17.83*
what it has. *64.17.84*

Prudent—your heart genuinely acting sincerely with care as with using your fork to get food right from the cauldron— *64.18.85*
ending—the knot at the end of a thick silk skein in winter—[380] *64.18.86*
'as if'—like a woman just doing as told— *64.18.87*
beginning—like conception in and by a woman... *64.18.88*

after following this sacrificial blade-and-cauldron-like ritual example or regulation: *64.19.89*
"Not-Being—nobody trance-dancing with long tails flowing from her wrists... *64.19.90*
being defeated—its riches hit lightly by hand, failing, decaying..." *64.19.91*
"one's personal, manual role—what one does with a weapon, a flag, or a pen." *64.19.92*

---

[378] From Chapters 8 and 20.
[379] From Chapters 2, 7, 15, 17, 2534, 41, 45, 47, 51, and 63.
[380] From Chapters 23, 26, 34, 52, 55, and 63. This is its last appearance.

The sun—walking across the sundial a while, stopping a while—sees indeed *64.20.93*
this carries like a plough—carries the meaning of *64.20.94*
a grounded sage—listening and speaking, standing connected to earth as well as the heavens, *64.20.95*
that person: *64.20.96*
wanting—missing what's been eroded from this ravine... *64.20.97*
the husk of the initial protective bud casing—the sepal—but not really the true inner flower of *64.20.98*
wanting—missing what's been eroded from this ravine... *64.20.99*
"the husk of the initial protective bud casing—the sepal—but not really the true inner flower of *64.20.100*
treasuring—as if as valuable as cowry-shell-riches... *64.20.101*
the solidly hard—as difficult as the dried yellow earth of Han where short-tailed birds can't find food— *64.20.102*
hand-picking, like-cowry-shell-riches-along-the-road *64.20.103*
what it has ... *64.20.104*
transformation of cowry-shell-riches—like from a right-side-up person to an upside down person;"[381] *64.20.105*

learning—like hands-on teaching a child gets in school—[382] *64.21.106*
the husk of the initial protective bud casing—the sepal—but not really the true inner flower of *64.21.107*
learning—like hands-on teaching a child gets in school... *64.21.108*
walking forth and then back again... *64.21.109*
the sun shining down like an eye on the people sees all this, sees *64.21.110*
that person, *64.21.111*
what it has ... *64.21.112*
'place'—somewhere intentionally created, like a door chopped with an axe... *64.21.113*
this way of walking a while and stopping a while that's past and surpassing—like a slanting skull mouth speaking.[383] *64.21.114*

---

[381] This entire phrase comes from Chapter 3. Without the first two characters (i.e. just "hard hand-picking's transformation of riches") the phrase appears in Chapter 12. This last character also appears in Chapter 44 and 53. This is its last appearance.
[382] From Chapters 19, 20, and 48.
[383] From Chapters 35 and 61. This is its last appearance.

This carries like a plough—carries the meaning of *64.22.115*
assisting—a man's courtesy name he gets when he replaces a bucket with a weapon on a pole, protecting like the wooden bars that help prevent a carriage from over-turning— *64.22.116*
the myriad, scorpion-medicine-dancing Ten Thousand *64.22.117*
Things cut off—all matter external to oneself like seeds, cows etc., *64.22.118*
what it has ... *64.22.119*
of course—one's self personally, right on one's nose, *64.22.120*
accomplished thus, in this manner: as naturally as dog meat over a fire, *64.22.121*
and yet now, bearded, *64.22.122*
"the husk of the initial protective bud casing—the sepal—but not really the true inner flower of *64.22.123*
daring—lightly hitting ears on both sides of the head— *64.22.124*
efforting—like lifting up an elephant."[384] *64.22.125*

65.

Ancient times—ten generations of mouths ago... *65.1.1*
what it has... *65.1.2*
"virtue—such as offering up a ram's head while back and forth speaking words that are emerging from a mouth like slaves or criminals branded by a chisel— *65.1.3*
efforting—like lifting up an elephant—"[385] *65.1.4*
The Way of the loose-haired headperson—walking a while, stopping a while, and speaking of it all: *65.1.5*
—now this is cooking with fire!— *65.1.6*

breaking the little wings off,[386] *65.2.7*
this carries like a plough—carries the meaning of, *65.2.8*
as bright as dawn rising on a crescent moon—enlightened—[387] *65.2.9*
civilians—like the Mín people enslaved by blinding with a dagger... *65.2.10*

---

[384] The whole phrase is from Chapter 3. "Not really daring" also appears in Chapter 30.
[385] Similar to the beginning of Chapter 15 where "ancient times had this.. traditional virtue efforting bachelor soldier-scholar-official."
[386] From Chapters 1, 7, 31, 39, 53, and 60. This is its last appearance.
[387] From Chapters 10, 16, 22, 24, 27, 33, 36, 41, 52, and 55. This is its last appearance.

soon will be—as if offering a meat tribute by hand on a table— *65.3.11*
this carries like a plough—carries the meaning of, *65.3.12*
having a heart-core as foolish as that trampling monkey with the head of a ghost...[388] *65.3.13*
what it has. *65.3.14*

Civilians—like the Mín people enslaved by blinding with a dagger... *65.4.15*
what it has... *65.4.16*
the solidly hard—as difficult as the dried yellow earth of Han where short-tailed birds can't find food—[389] *65.4.17*
governing—regulating by harnessing the river named Happy or speaking of turning oneself: *65.4.18*

this carries like a plough—carries the meaning of *65.5.19*
what it holds a basket of... *65.5.20*
firing arrows from the mouth—sure as the sun, on the daily[390] *65.5.21*
much more—like a double serving of meat.[391] *65.5.22*

Anciently, for ten generations, this lightly hits and leaves a mark of reason: *65.6.23*
this carries like a plough—carries the meaning of *65.6.24*
"firing arrows from the mouth—sure as the sun, on the daily—" *65.6.25*
"governing—regulating by harnessing the river named Happy or speaking of turning oneself—" *65.6.26*
this nation—this particular territory, this enclave defended by a weapon on a pole plus its surroundings— *65.6.27*

this nation—this particular territory, this enclave defended by a weapon on a pole plus its surroundings— *65.7.28*
what it has... *65.7.29*
using a weapon on a pole in a blade-and-cauldron ritual standard to damage or rob;[392] *65.7.30*

---

[388] From Chapters 20 and 38.
[389] From Chapters 2, 3, 12, and 63.
[390] From Chapters 3, 18, 19, 27, and 33, This is its last appearance.
[391] From Chapters 5, 22, 44, 57, and 63.
[392] From Chapters 19 and 57. This is its last appearance.

the husk of the initial protective bud casing—the sepal—but not really the true inner flower of, *65.8.31*
this carries like a plough—carries the meaning of, *65.8.32*
"firing arrows from the mouth—sure as the sun, on the daily— *65.8.33*
governing—regulating by harnessing the river named Happy or speaking of turning oneself— *65.8.34*
this nation—this particular territory, this enclave defended by a weapon on a pole plus its surroundings," *65.8.35*

> this nation—this particular territory, this enclave defended by a weapon on a pole plus its surroundings— *65.9.36*
> what it has... *65.9.37*
> blessings and good fortune—like a full vessel on display on an altar.[393] *65.9.38*

"Firing arrows from the mouth, sure..." *65.10.39*
this here—the foot stops a person here on their footprint— [394] *65.10.40*
a matched pair, like a harness of ox yokes...[395] *65.10.41*
—now this is cooking with fire!— *65.10.42*

—both armpits sweat this too!— *65.11.43*

> examining—like looking at a grain plant to check its deliciousness— *65.11.44*
> a model example—like a bladed tool is for work or a retrievable arrow attached to a string is for shooting and catching.[396] *65.11.45*

The ever-present square fabric—like that which our grown men wrap around the 'little bird' top knots on their heads after receiving their public courtesy-names—or what we know as the timeless, whole head-cloth 'ji' version of *65.12.46*
"firing arrows from the mouth, sure..." *65.12.47*
"examining—like looking at a grain plant to check its deliciousness *65.12.48*
a model example—like a bladed tool is for work or a retrievable arrow attached to a string is for shooting and catching..." *65.12.49*

[393] From Chapter 58. This is its last apperance.
[394] From Chapters 1, 12, 14, 19, 23, 38, 39, 54, 57, and 62.
[395] From Chapters 1, 60, and 61.
[396] From Chapters 22 and 28. This is its last appearance.

the sun—walking across the sundial a while, stopping a while—sees indeed *65.13.50*
what it's called when speaking from the gut—words, like slaves or criminals
branded by a chisel emerging from a mouth: *65.13.51*
hard-to-see dark structure—like a figure-eight skein of string-dyed-black[397] *65.13.52*
Dé—the ethical, straight way of walking awhile and stopping awhile, eye directed forward over the heart-core. *65.13.53*

"Hard-to-see dark structure—like a figure-eight skein of string-dyed-black *65.14.54*
Dé—the ethical, straight way of walking awhile and stopping awhile, eye directed forward over the heart-core..." *65.14.55*
deep as far water,[398] *65.14.56*
—swearing on an arrow revolving around oneself, that's it! [399] *65.14.57*
remote—not intimately close but a profound way in which you walk a while, stop a while, shaped like a big round spindle with a long robe, like the afterbirth hanging from a recently pregnant woman...[400] *65.14.58*
—swearing on an arrow revolving around oneself, that's it!— *65.14.59*

supporting—offering to carry on one's shoulders[401] *65.15.60*
Things cut off—all matter external to oneself like seeds, cows etc... *65.15.61*
... making someone return, with one's right hand, to the habitable cave in the cliff[402] *65.15.62*
—swearing on an arrow revolving around oneself, that's it! *65.15.63*

---

[397] From Chapters 1, 6, 10, 15, 51, and 56. It's also used with "*Dè*" in Chapter 10. This chapter is its last appearance.
[398] From Chapters 15 (where it described ancient times' traditional-virtue-efforting bachelor-soldier-official appointedby the emperor) and 59. This is its last appearance.
[399] From Chapters 31, 46, and 63.
[400] From Chapters 25 (where a breath issued on a mouth called it "making someone return to the cave") and 47 (where it described "stepping out of the cave)".
[401] From Chapters 8, 20, 22, 35, 36, and 44.
[402] From Chapters 25 and 40.

Accomplished thus, in this manner: as naturally as dog meat over a fire...[403] *65.16.64*

afterwards—what remains when stepping slowly with only one's left leg leading the way, leaving the tiniest of silk thread footprints, that is, one's descendants...[404] *65.16.65*

you, then, *65.16.66*

reaching the extreme—like an arrow straight into the clay soil—[405]*65.16.67*

great giant *65.16.68*

smoothly going along with -- like the loose-haired headperson kneeling at a river. *65.16.69*

66.

"The Yangtze River—the river that 'works like someone with a stone axe'—flows into *66.1.1*

the ocean—water lush with new life sprouting from a nursing mother"[406] *66.1.2*

'place'—somewhere intentionally created, like a door chopped with an axe... *66.1.3*

this carries like a plough—carries the meaning of *66.1.4*

using a legendary capability—the hybrid power of that mythical bear with deer legs—for *66.1.5*

efforting—like lifting up an elephant— *66.1.6*

a hundred *66.1.7*

within that valley mouth between two mountains[407] *66.1.8*

kings—connecting heaven, man, and earth *66.1.9*

—now this is cooking with fire! *66.1.10*

This carries like a plough—carries the meaning of *66.2.11*

what it holds a basket of... *66.2.12*

virtue—such as offering up a ram's head while back and forth speaking words that are emerging from a mouth like slaves or criminals branded by a chisel... *66.2.13*

down below, lower level... *66.2.14*

what it has, *66.2.15*

---

[403] From Chapters 17, 23, 2526, 51, 53, 54, 57, and 64.

[404] From Chapters 2, 7, 14, 30, and 38.

[405] From Chapters 43, 48, and 55.

[406] From Chapter 32 where it described The Way's existing sprouting here on earth.

[407] From Chapters 6, 15, 28, 32, and 39. This is its last appearance.

anciently, for ten generations, this lightly hits and leaves a mark of reason: *66.3.16*
"using a legendary capability—the hybrid power of that mythical bear with deer legs—for *66.3.17*
efforting—like lifting up an elephant— *66.3.18*
a hundred *66.3.19*
within that valley mouth between two mountains *66.3.20*
kings—connecting heaven, man, and earth." *66.3.21*

The sun—walking across the sundial a while, stopping a while—sees indeed *66.4.22*
this carries like a plough—carries the meaning of *66.4.23*
a grounded sage—listening and speaking, standing connected to earth as well as the heavens, *66.4.24*
that person: *66.4.25*
wanting—missing what's been eroded from this ravine— *66.4.26*
higher, ruling level *66.4.27*
civilians—like the Mín people enslaved by blinding with a dagger, *66.4.28*
analytically—hands over heart-core— *66.4.29*
this carries like a plough—carries the meaning of *66.4.30*
speaking—words, like slaves or criminals branded by a chisel emerging from a mouth *66.4.31*
"down below, lower level...*66.4.32*
what it has." *66.4.33*

wanting—missing what's been eroded from this ravine— *66.5.34*
being long before—that is, an ancestor—[408] *66.5.35*
civilians—like the Mín people enslaved by blinding with a dagger, *66.5.36*
analytically—hands over heart-core— *66.5.37*
this carries like a plough—carries the meaning of *66.5.38*
one's pregnant self *66.5.39*
afterwards—what remains when stepping slowly with only one's left leg leading the way, leaving the tiniest of silk thread footprints, that is, one's descendants...[409] *66.5.40*
what it has. *66.5.41*

---

[408] From Chapters 4, 7, 25, and 62.

[409] From Chapters 2, 7, 14, 30, 38, and 65. In Chapter 7 it's similarly associated with "one's pregnant self" and also with the "being long before" character from above.

The sun—walking across the sundial a while, stopping a while—sees indeed *66.6.42*
this carries like a plough—carries the meaning of *66.6.43*
a grounded sage—listening and speaking, standing connected to earth as well as
the heavens, *66.6.44*
that person *66.6.45*
dwelling here—staying, as someone at home at the tea table,
chaste and unmarried, someone being followed from behind
by a tiger-fur head,[410] *66.6.46*
"higher, ruling level," *66.6.47*
and yet now, bearded... *66.6.48*
civilians—like the Mín people enslaved by blinding
with a dagger— *66.6.49*
the husk of the initial protective bud casing—the sepal—but not
really the true inner flower of *66.6.50*
a heavy load—a bag carried by a man[411]; *66.6.51*

dwelling here—staying, as someone at home at the tea table,
chaste and unmarried, someone being followed from behind
by a tiger-fur head, *66.7.52*
forward—the front place in battle where a step could mean one's feet get
cut off as punishment,[412] *66.7.53*
and yet now, bearded... *66.7.54*
civilians—like the Mín people enslaved by blinding
with a dagger— *66.7.55*
the husk of the initial protective bud casing—the sepal—but not
really the true inner flower of *66.7.56*
being harmed, like speaking and tallying many lies within
the house.[413] *66.7.57*

---

[410] From Chapters 2, 8, 24, 26, 30, 31, and 38.
[411] From Chapter 26 and 59.
[412] From Chapters 2 and 38. This is its last appearance.
[413] From Chapters 35 and 56.

The sun—walking across the sundial a while, stopping a while—sees indeed *66.8.58*
this carries like a plough—carries the meaning of *66.8.59*
Heaven (that sky level above the human head)-Down Below (lower level) *66.8.60 & 61*
enjoying—like glad music played upon a wooden instrument's
    silk strings—[414] *66.8.62*
promoting along like hand-pushing that 'short-tailed bird,' *66.8.63*
and yet now, bearded... *66.8.64*
the husk of the initial protective bud casing—the sepal—but not really the true
    inner flower of *66.8.65*
sated like by some sweet dog meat in the mouth;[415] *66.8.66*

this carries like a plough—carries the meaning of *66.9.67*
what it holds a basket of... *66.9.68*

> "'*the husk of the initial protective bud casing—the sepal—but not really the true inner flower of* *66.9.69*
> *contending—two hands clawing over a ploughshare,'*[416] *66.9.70*
>
> *anciently, for ten generations, this lightly hits and leaves a mark of reason...* *66.10.71*
> *Heaven (that sky level above the human head)-Down Below (lower level)* *66.10.72 & 73*
> *must not—eh, like the lost-in-the-bushes, eh?—* *66.10.74*
> *using a legendary capability—the hybrid power of that mythical bear with deer legs—for* *66.10.75*
> *supporting—offering to carry on one's shoulders...* *66.10.76*
> *what it has...* *66.10.77*
> *contending—two hands clawing over a ploughshare."*[417] *66.10.78*

[414] From Chapters 23, 31, and 35.
[415] From Chapter 53.
[416] From Chapters 3, 8, and 22.
[417] This entire phrase comes from Chapter 22.

67.

"Heaven (that sky level above the human head)-Down Below (lower level) *67.1.1 & 2*
public opinion—that clear, plain back and forth between people..."[418] *67.1.3*
what it's called when speaking from the gut—words, like slaves or criminals branded by a chisel emerging from a mouth... *67.1.4*
I/we—holding a rake-like weapon to defend ourselves and our opinion... *67.1.5*
The Way of the loose-haired headperson—walking a while, stopping a while, and speaking of it all... *67.1.6*
great giant. *67.1.7*

It bears a side-by-side personal resemblance —like a person to a fetus—to[419] *67.2.8*
the husk of the initial protective bud casing—the sepal—but not really the true inner flower of *67.2.9*
resembling like how a small child—a tiny three-dot-meat—looks like their parents. *67.2.10*

That is to say, this particular grown man with a hairpin and public courtesy name... *67.3.11*
essentially and only—like the mouth of 'the short-tailed bird'— *67.3.12*
"great giant," *67.3.13*

anciently, for ten generations, this lightly hits and leaves a mark of reason: *67.4.14*
"it bears a side-by-side personal resemblance —like a person to a fetus—to *67.4.15*
the husk of the initial protective bud casing—the sepal—but not really the true inner flower of *67.4.16*
resembling like how a small child—a tiny three-dot-meat—looks like their parents." *67.4.17*

A Certain Someone compliantly combing their loose hair seems to be saying: 'this is as if...' *67.5.18*
"resembling like how a small child—a tiny three-dot-meat—looks like their parents..." *67.5.19*

---

[418] From Chapter 2
[419] From Chapters 4 and 20

enduring through time—like someone receiving moxibustion treatments with mugwort used for cramps, turning a breech baby, or other health issues...[420] *67.6.20*
—swearing on an arrow revolving around oneself, that's it!— *67.6.21*

what it holds a basket of... *67.7.22*
small, delicate, and young—a skein of silk fontanelle...[421] *67.7.23*
—yes, that too, vagina!— *67.7.24*
that is to say, this particular grown man with a hairpin and public courtesy name. *67.7.25*

"I/we—holding a rake-like weapon to defend ourselves and our opinion—" *67.8.26*
flesh-and-blood, meat-handling Being... *67.8.27*
three *67.8.28*
treasures—like a house containing cowry-riches, jade, and a lidded pot—[422] *67.8.29*

holding on to something—like a patron from a temple or government office that's expert at stopping and giving a hand,[423] *67.9.30*
and yet now, bearded, *67.9.31*
safeguarding—like carrying a child on one's back...[424] *67.9.32*
what it has: *67.9.33*

One, *67.10.34*
what it's called when issued on a breath from the mouth... *67.10.35*
'benevolent as doubly-profound parental love, mysterious as two loops of string dyed black over the heart-core;'[425] *67.10.36*

Two, *67.11.37*
what it's called when issued on a breath from the mouth... *67.11.38*
'frugal—like one modest person next to people all together speaking, gathering from three sides;' *67.11.39*

---

[420] From Chapters 7, 15, 16, 23, 33, 44, 58, and 59. This is its last appearance.
[421] From Chapter 63.
[422] From Chapter 62.
[423] From Chapters 9 and 64. This chapter is its last appearance.
[424] From Chapters 9, 15, and 62. This chapter is its last appearance.
[425] From Chapters 18 and 19. This chapter is its last appearance.

Three, *67.12.40*
what it's called when issued on a breath from the mouth... *67.12.41*
'"the husk of the initial protective bud casing—the sepal—but not really the true inner flower of *67.12.42*
daring—lightly hitting ears on both sides of the head— *67.12.43*
efforting—like lifting up an elephant—"[426] *67.12.44*
Heaven (that sky level above the human head)-Down Below (lower level) *67.12.45 & 46*
being long before—that is, an ancestor.'[427] *67.12.47*

"Benevolent as doubly-profound parental love, mysterious as two loops of string dyed black over the heart-core," *67.13.48*
anciently, for ten generations, this lightly hits and leaves a mark of reason: *67.13.49*
using a legendary capability—the hybrid power of that mythical bear with deer legs—for *67.13.50*
courageous and sturdy like a soldier, strong as an arm, bladed tool, or a plough—the handle of a bell. *67.13.51*

"Frugal—like one modest person next to people all together speaking, gathering from three sides," *67.14.52*
anciently, for ten generations, this lightly hits and leaves a mark of reason: *67.14.53*
using a legendary capability—the hybrid power of that mythical bear with deer legs—for *67.14.54*
wide like a person with a large belly in a habitable cave in a cliff.[428] *67.14.55*

---

[426] From Chapters 3 and 64. "Not really daring" also appears in Chapter 30.
[427] From Chapters 4, 7, 25, 62, and 66. This chapter is its last appearance.
[428] From Chapter 41. This chapter is its last appearance.

"The husk of the initial protective bud casing—the sepal—but not really the true inner flower of *67.15.56*
daring—lightly hitting ears on both sides of the head— *67.15.57*
efforting—like lifting up an elephant— *67.15.58*
Heaven (that sky level above the human head)-Down Below (lower level) *67.15.59 & 60*
being long before—that is, an ancestor," *67.15.61*
anciently, for ten generations, this lightly hits and leaves a mark of reason: *67.15.62*
using a legendary capability—the hybrid power of that mythical bear with deer legs—for *67.15.63*
completing—that final nail in the weapon on a pole— *67.15.64*
set of valuable vessels with lots of capacity—worthy of a guard dog—[429] *67.15.65*
long as hair that has to be tied with a brooch.[430] *67.15.66*

What's being said—in the mouth now, in modern times: *67.16.67*
handing over, like at a thatched inn—abandoning *67.16.68*
"benevolent as doubly-profound parental love, mysterious as two loops of string dyed black over the heart-core..." *67.16.69*
abiding for a long time—the erect penis of a male ancestor— *67.16.70*
"courageous and sturdy like a soldier, strong as an arm, bladed tool, or a plough—the handle of a bell;" *67.16.71*

handing over, like [at] a thatched inn—abandoning *67.17.72*
"frugal—like one modest person next to people all together speaking, gathering from three sides..." *67.17.73*
abiding for a long time—the erect penis of a male ancestor— *67.17.74*
"wide like a person with a large belly in a habitable cave in a cliff;" *67.17.75*

[429] From Chapters 11, 28, 29, 31, 36, 41, and 57.
[430] From Chapters 2, 7, 9, 44, 54, and 59. This chapter is its last appearance.

handing over, like [at] a thatched inn—abandoning *67.18.76*
afterwards—what remains when stepping slowly with only one's left leg leading the way, leaving the tiniest of silk thread footprints, that is, one's descendants...[431] *67.18.77*
abiding for a long time—the erect penis of a male ancestor— *67.18.78*
"being long before—that is, an ancestor;"[432] *67.18.79*

dying—going from a standing person to a pile of bones[433] *67.19.80*
—swearing on an arrow revolving around oneself, that's it! *67.19.81*

That is to say, this particular grown man with a hairpin and public courtesy name... *67.20.82*
"benevolent as doubly-profound parental love, mysterious as two loops of string dyed black over the heart-core," *67.20.83*
this carries like a plough—carries the meaning of *67.20.84*
battling—using a net for catching animals against a weapon on a pole...[434] *67.20.85*
after following this sacrificial blade-and-cauldron-like ritual example or regulation... *67.20.86*
forcing a victory over—using a blade to mend a boat or roll rice into a ball under moonlight;[435] *67.20.87*

this carries like a plough—carries the meaning of *67.21.88*
hand-defending this—one's building...[436] *67.21.89*
after following this sacrificial blade-and-cauldron-like ritual example or regulation... *67.21.90*
solidly, anciently—for ten generations of mouths, keeping as firm to what happened in the first place as this land surrounding and holding this nation since ancient times. [437] *67.21.91*

---

[431] From Chapters 2, 7, 14, 30, 38, 65, and 66. This chapter is its last appearance.
[432] From Chapter From Chapters 2, 7, 14, 30, 38, and 65. In Chapter 7 it's similarly associated with "one's pregnant self" and also with the "being long before" character from above s 4, 7, 25, 62, and 66. This chapter is its last appearance.
[433] From Chapters 6, 33, 42, and 50.
[434] From Chapter 31.
[435] From Chapters 31, 33, 36, 45, and 61.
[436] From Chapters 5, 9, 16, 28, 32, and 52. This chapter is its last appearance.
[437] From Chapters 36, 58, and 59. This chapter is its last appearance.

Heaven (that sky level above the human head)... *67.22.92*
soon will be—as if offering a meat tribute by hand on a table— *67.22.93*
rescuing—lightly hitting upon request someone in a fur coat...[438] *67.22.94*
what it has... *67.22.95*

this carries like a plough—carries the meaning of... *67.23.96*
"benevolent as doubly-profound parental love, mysterious as two loops of string dyed black over the heart-core..." *67.23.76*
guarding—footsteps around an enclosure at an intersection... *67.23.98*
what it has. *67.23.99*

68.

"Virtue—such as offering up a ram's head while back and forth speaking words that are emerging from a mouth like slaves or criminals branded by a chisel— *68.1.1*
efforting—like lifting up an elephant— *68.1.2*
bachelor soldier-scholar-official—a yeoman... *68.1.3*
—now this is cooking with fire!—"[439] *68.1.4*
the husk of the initial protective bud casing—the sepal—but not really the true inner flower of *68.1.5*
military—setting out by foot with spear as one for a long journey. *68.1.6*

Virtue—such as offering up a ram's head while back and forth speaking words that are emerging from a mouth like slaves or criminals branded by a chisel— *68.2.7*
battling—using a net for catching animals against a weapon on a pole...[440] *68.2.8*
—now this is cooking with fire!— *68.2.9*
the husk of the initial protective bud casing—the sepal—but not really the true inner flower of *68.2.10*
angry like the heart beneath a hand capturing a woman to be a slave. *68.2.11*

---

[438] From Chapters 27 and 52. This chapter is its last appearance.
[439] This whole phrase was used in Chapter 15. The bachelor-soldier-scholar-official also appeared in 41. This is its last appearance.
[440] From Chapters 31 and 67. This is its last appearance.

Virtue—such as offering up a ram's head while back and forth speaking words that are emerging from a mouth like slaves or criminals branded by a chisel— *68.3.12*
forcing a victory over—using a blade to mend a boat or roll rice into a ball under moonlight—[441] *68.3.13*
enemy—hostilely resisting, lightly hitting, merely speaking of 'God of Heaven,' (as we call our emperors, for they're like flower sepals connecting to above with their covering of that ever-present, timeless, whole-cloth 'ji' square fabric which our grown-men wrap around their 'little bird' top knots once they've received adult, public courtesy-names)... *68.3.14*
—now this is cooking with fire!— *68.3.15*
the husk of the initial protective bud casing—the sepal—but not really the true inner flower of *68.3.16*
supporting—offering to carry on one's shoulders.[442] *68.3.17*

Virtue—such as offering up a ram's head while back and forth speaking words that are emerging from a mouth like slaves or criminals branded by a chisel— *68.4.18*
doing truly useful work like a water bucket—by means of carrying-capacity, *68.4.19*
that person... *68.4.20*
—now this is cooking with fire!— *68.4.21*
efforting—like lifting up an elephant... *68.4.22*
has this... *68.4.23*
down below, lower level. *68.4.24*

The sun—walking across the sundial a while, stopping a while—sees indeed *68.5.25*
what it's called when speaking from the gut—words, like slaves or criminals branded by a chisel emerging from a mouth... *68.5.26*
"the husk of the initial protective bud casing—the sepal—but not really the true inner flower of *68.5.27*
contending—two hands clawing over a ploughshare..." [443] *68.5.28*
has this... *68.5.29*
Dé—the ethical, straight way of walking awhile and stopping awhile, eye directed forward over the heart-core. *68.5.30*

[441] From Chapters 31, 33, 36, 45, 61, and 67.
[442] From Chapters 8, 20, 22, 35, 36, 44, 65, and 66.
[443] From Chapters 3, 8, 22, and 66.

The sun—walking across the sundial a while, stopping a while—sees indeed *68.6.31*
what it's called when speaking from the gut—words, like slaves or criminals
branded by a chisel emerging from a mouth... *68.6.32*
"doing truly useful work like a water bucket—by means of carrying-capacity, *68.6.33*
that person..." *68.6.34*
has this... *68.6.35*
forceful—strong like an arm, a bladed tool, or a plough.[444] *68.6.36*

The sun—walking across the sundial a while, stopping a while—sees indeed *68.7.37*
what it's called when speaking from the gut—words, like slaves or criminals
branded by a chisel emerging from a mouth... *68.7.38*
matching—like an alcohol vat with a silk rope for binding oneself— *68.7.39*
Heaven (that sky level above the human head)... *68.7.40*

ancient times—ten generations of mouths ago—[445] *68.8.41*
has this... *68.8.42*
in the utmost—to the highest position of a double-beamed
wooden ridgepole.[446] *68.8.4*

69.

Doing truly useful work like a water bucket—by means of carrying-capacity *69.1.1*
carrying a short ax with two hands like a soldier or pawn...[447] *69.1.2*
flesh-and-blood, meat-handling Being *69.1.3*
speaking—words, like slaves or criminals branded by a chisel emerging from
a mouth: *69.1.4*

'I/we—our five mouths— *69.2.5*
"the husk of the initial protective bud casing—the sepal—but not really
the true inner flower of *69.2.6*
daring—lightly hitting ears on both sides of the head—"[448] *69.2.7*
efforting—like lifting up an elephant— *69.2.8*
master—the owner and host of the lamp's flame,[449] *69.2.9*

---

444 From Chapter 33.
445 From Chapters 14, 15, 21, 22, 62, and 65. This is its last appearance.
446 From Chapters 16, 28, 58, and 59. This is its last appearance.
447 From Chapters 30, 31, 50, and 57. It appears with the previous character ("doing truly useful work") in Chapter 57.
448 From Chapters 3, 30, 64, and 67. It appears with the following character ("efforting") in Chapter 3.
449 From Chapters 26, 30, and 34.

and yet now, bearded... *69.3.10*
efforting—like lifting up an elephant— *69.3.11*
a guest entering the mouth of your house under your roof
on foot[450]; *69.3.12*

"the husk of the initial protective bud casing—the sepal—but not really
the true inner flower of *69.4.13*
daring—lightly hitting ears on both sides of the head—" *69.4.14*
walking forward awhile and stopping awhile like a 'short-
tailed bird'[451] *69.4.15*
one short inch—that spot on the forearm where the pulse
beats strong, *69.4.16*

and yet now, bearded... *69.5.17*
withdrawing—walking awhile and stopping a while, retreating
from the sun—[452] *69.5.18*
one foot—measured with a bent person.' *69.5.19*

The sun—walking across the sundial a while, stopping a while—sees indeed *69.6.20*
what it's called when speaking from the gut—words, like slaves or criminals
branded by a chisel emerging from a mouth... *69.6.21*
on a public road, practicing—moving with... *69.6.22*
Not-Being—nobody trance-dancing with long tails flowing from
her wrists... *69.6.23*
on a public road, practicing—moving with; *69.6.24*

"their hand helping to undress, rolling up the sleeves, disturbs—throws
into disorder...[453] *69.7.25*
Not-Being—nobody trance-dancing with long tails flowing from
her wrists... *69.7.26*
their arm—like the meat of a ruler or dead husband who administered and
punished, marked a kneeling slave or criminal with a chisel; *69.7.27*

---

[450] From Chapters 15 and 35.
[451] From Chapters 41 and 62.
[452] From Chapters 9 and 41 (in the latter, it also was juxtaposed with walking forward).
[453] From Chapter 38.

your hand unexpectedly throwing away what it has..." [454] *69.8.28*
Not-Being—nobody trance-dancing with long tails flowing from her wrists... *69.8.29*
enemy—hostilely resisting, lightly hitting, merely speaking of 'God of Heaven,' (as we call our emperors, for they're like flower sepals connecting to above with their covering of that ever-present, timeless, whole-cloth 'ji' square fabric which our grown-men wrap around their 'little bird' top knots once they've received adult, public courtesy-names);[455] *69.8.30*

holding tight in the hand—not letting go of, not dying young...[456] *69.9.31*
Not-Being—nobody trance-dancing with long tails flowing from her wrists... *69.9.32*
"carrying a short ax with two hands like a soldier or pawn." *69.9.33*

Disaster—slanting mouth of a skull on a sacrifice altar...[457] *69.10.34*
must not—like the lost-in-the-bushes sinking sun, eh?— *69.10.35*
great giant *69.10.36*
here—oh, black, icy raven: *69.10.37*
as if lightweight—as lightweight as using a bladed tool in a light carriage on an underground stream— *69.10.38*
"enemy—hostilely resisting, lightly hitting, merely speaking of 'God of Heaven,' (as we call our emperors, for they're like flower sepals connecting to above with their covering of that ever-present, timeless, whole-cloth 'ji' square fabric which our grown-men wrap around their 'little bird' top knots once they've received adult, public courtesy-names);" *69.10.39*

---

[454] See Chapter 38.
[455] From Chapter 68.
[456] From Chapters 14, 29, 35, and 64.
[457] From Chapters 46 and 58.

"as if lightweight—as lightweight as using a bladed tool in a light carriage on an underground stream— *89.11.40*

enemy—hostilely resisting, lightly hitting, merely speaking of 'God of Heaven,' (as we call our emperors, for they're like flower sepals connecting to above with their covering of that ever-present, timeless, whole-cloth 'ji' square fabric which our grown-men wrap around their 'little bird' top knots once they've received adult, public courtesy-names)" *69.11.41*

being as near as a border of fine, fine silk you'd guard with a blade to[458] *69.11.42*

circumstances associated with a disappearance, with death,[459] *69.11.43*

I/we—our five mouths *69.11.44*

treasure—like a house containing cowry-riches, jade, and a lidded pot.[460] *69.11.45*

Anciently, for ten generations, this lightly hits and leaves a mark of reason: *69.12.46*

opposing—expertly by hand lifting a high, arrogant, extreme like the ridge of a roof... *69.12.47*

"carrying a short ax with two hands like a soldier or pawn..." *69.12.48*

mutually—like a seen tree and the eye seeing it—[461] *69.12.49*

putting on top of another like a mouth ordering a cow over a plough...[462] *69.12.50*

lamenting from the chest, under one's roof...[463] *69.13.51*

—now this is cooking with fire!— *69.13.52*

forcing a victory over—using a blade to mend a boat or roll rice into a ball under moonlight... *69.13.53*

—swearing on an arrow revolving around oneself, that's it! *69.13.54*

---

[458] From Chapters 8, 20, and 64.

[459] From Chapter 31.

[460] From Chapters 62 and 67.

[461] From Chapters 2, 20, 32, and 60.

[462] From Chapter 62.

[463] From Chapter 31.

70.

I/we—our five mouths— *70.1.1*
speaking—words, like slaves or criminals branded by a chisel emerging from
a mouth: *70.1.2*
'in the extreme—something pleasing in the mouth, matched so it's
doubly pleasing... *70.1.3*
easily changeable to something else—going from saying 'don't' as seriously
as blood on a blade to shining as sunny as the sun above...[464] *70.1.4*
firing arrows from the mouth, sure, *70.1.5*

in the extreme—something pleasing in the mouth, matched so it's
doubly pleasing... *70.2.6*
easily changeable to something else—going from saying 'don't' as seriously
as blood on a blade to shining as sunny as the sun above... *70.2.7*
on a public road, practicing—moving with.' *70.2.8*

Heaven (that sky level above the human head)-Down Below (lower level) *70.3.9 & 10*
must not—eh, like the lost-in-the-bushes , eh?— *70.2.11*
using a legendary capability—the hybrid power of that mythical bear with
deer legs—for *70.3.12*
"firing arrows from the mouth, sure,"*70.3.13*

must not—eh, like the lost-in-the-bushes , eh?— *70.4.14*
using a legendary capability—the hybrid power of that mythical bear with
deer legs—for *70.4.15*
"on a public road, practicing—moving with." *70.4.16*

"Speaking—words, like slaves or criminals branded by a chisel emerging from
a mouth..." *70.5.17*
flesh-and-blood, meat-handling Being *70.5.18*
ancestral shrine, *70.5.19*

one's personal, manual role—what one does with a weapon, a flag, or a pen... *70.6.20*
flesh-and-blood, meat-handling Being *70.6.21*
a lord prince administering—his hand holding a rod over a mouth; *70.6.22*

that is to say, this particular grown man with a hairpin and public
courtesy name *70.7.23*
essentially and only—like the mouth of 'the short-tailed bird'— *70.7.24*
Not-Being—nobody trance-dancing with long tails flowing from her wrists— *70.7.25*
firing arrows from the mouth, sure. *70.7.26*

---

[464] From Chapters 2 (where it was mutually competing with "hard"), 63, and 64.

The sun—walking across the sundial a while, stopping a while—
sees indeed *70.8.27*
this carries like a plough—carries the meaning of *70.8.28*
I/we—holding a rake-like weapon to defend ourselves and our opinion... *70.8.29*
the husk of the initial protective bud casing—the sepal—but not really the
true inner flower of *70.8.30*
firing arrows from the mouth, sure; *70.8.31*

firing arrows from the mouth, sure" *70.9.32*
I/we—holding a rake-like weapon to defend ourselves and
our opinion— *70.9.33*
—now this is cooking with fire!— *70.9.34*
sparse—as spare as the interconnecting threads in that square cloth men
wrap around their 'little bird' top knots and heads. *70.9.35*

After following this sacrificial blade-and-cauldron-like ritual example
or regulation *70.10.36*
I/we—holding a rake-like weapon to defend ourselves and
our opinion— *70.10.37*
—now this is cooking with fire!— *70.10.38*
treasuring—as if as valuable as cowry-shell-riches.[465] *70.10.39*

The sun—walking across the sundial a while, stopping a while—sees indeed *70.11.40*
this carries like a plough—carries the meaning of *70.11.41*
a grounded sage—listening and speaking, standing connected to earth as well as
the heavens, *70.11.42*
that person... *70.11.43*
wearing like clothing—especially like a robe on the torso, like the
placental afterbirth hanging from a recently pregnant woman—made
of fur stripped by hand from its pelt... *70.11.44*
dull brown like coarse clothing—especially like that robe on the torso, or
the placental afterbirth hanging from a recently pregnant woman—
we're speaking of that used to bundle up and hide; *70.11.45*

carrying in one's bosom—affectionately concealed in one's heart by
clothing that's like a net over water... *70.12.46*
jade totems. *70.12.47*[466]

[465] From Chapters 3, 9, 13, 17, 20, 27, 31, 39, 51, 56, 62, and 64.
[466] From Chapters 9 and 39.

71.

Firing arrows from the mouth, sure... *71.1.1*
the husk of the initial protective bud casing—the sepal—but not really the true inner flower of *71.1.2*
firing arrows from the mouth, sure: *71.1.3*
higher, ruling level. *71.1.4*

"The husk of the initial protective bud casing—the sepal—but not really the true inner flower of *71.2.5*
firing arrows from the mouth, sure..." *71.2.6*
"the husk of the initial protective bud casing—the sepal—but not really the true inner flower of *71.2.7*
firing arrows from the mouth, sure:" *71.2.8*
ill as one carried on a stretcher on the third heavenly stem.[467] *71.2.9*

That is to say, this particular grown man with a hairpin and public courtesy name *71.3.10*
essentially and only—like the mouth of 'the short-tailed bird'— *71.3.11*
ill as one carried on a stretcher on the third heavenly stem *71.3.12*
ill as one carried on a stretcher on the third heavenly stem... *71.3.13*

the sun—walking across the sundial a while, stopping a while—sees indeed *71.4.14*
this carries like a plough—carries the meaning of *71.4.15*
the husk of the initial protective bud casing—the sepal—but not really the true inner flower of *71.4.16*
ill as one carried on a stretcher on the third heavenly stem. *71.4.17*

A grounded sage—listening and speaking, standing connected to earth as well as the heavens, *71.5.18*
that person *71.5.19*
"the husk of the initial protective bud casing—the sepal—but not really the true inner flower of *71.5.20*
ill as one carried on a stretcher on the third heavenly stem," *71.5.21*

this carries like a plough—carries the meaning of *71.6.22*
what it holds a basket of... *71.6.23*
"ill as one carried on a stretcher on the third heavenly stem *71.6.24*
ill as one carried on a stretcher on the third heavenly stem." *71.6.25*

[467] From Chapter 44.

The sun—walking across the sundial a while, stopping a while—
sees indeed *71.7.26*
this carries like a plough—carries the meaning of *71.7.27*
"the husk of the initial protective bud casing—the sepal—but not really
the true inner flower of *71.7.28*
ill as one carried on a stretcher on the third heavenly stem." *71.7.29*

72.

Civilians—like the Mín people enslaved by blinding with a dagger— *72.1.1*
the husk of the initial protective bud casing—the sepal—but not really the true
inner flower of *72.1.2*
fearing—like when there's a ghost holding a stick or maybe part of a tiger with
its claw—[468] *72.1.3*
pomp and power—intimidating like an axe over a woman kneeling
with breasts... *72.1.4*

after following this sacrificial blade-and-cauldron-like ritual example
or regulation, *72.2.5*
great giant... *72.2.6*
higher, ruling level *72.2.7*
"pomp and power—intimidating like an axe over a woman kneeling
with breasts..." *72.2.8*
reaching the extreme—like an arrow straight into the clay soil.[469] *72.2.9*

Not-Being—nobody trance-dancing with long tails flowing from her wrists— *72.3.10*
intimate with—maybe improperly familiar with—like a dog with a
turtle shell... *72.3.11*
what it holds a basket of... *72.3.12*
'place'—somewhere intentionally created, like a door chopped with an axe— *72.3.13*
abiding—dwelling where birthed, sitting over ten mouths...[470] *72.3.14*

---

[468] From Chapters 15, 17, 20, and 53.
[469] From Chapters 43, 48, 55, and 65.
[470] From Chapters 2, 8, 25, 31, and 38.

Not-Being—nobody trance-dancing with long tails flowing from her wrists— *72.4.15*
sated by—like by some sweet dog meat in the mouth—[471] *72.4.18*
what it holds a basket of... *72.4.17*
'place'—somewhere intentionally created, like a door chopped with an axe— *72.4.18*
birthing—a bud sprouting from the ground; *72.4.19*

that is to say, this particular grown man with a hairpin and public courtesy name *72.5.20*
essentially and only—like the mouth of 'the short-tailed bird'— *72.5.21*
the husk of the initial protective bud casing—the sepal—but not really the true inner flower of *72.5.22*
"sated—like by some sweet dog meat in the mouth." *72.5.23*

The sun—walking across the sundial a while, stopping a while—sees indeed *72.6.24*
this carries like a plough—carries the meaning of... *72.6.25*
"the husk of the initial protective bud casing—the sepal—but not really the true inner flower of *72.6.26*
sated—like by some sweet dog meat in the mouth." *72.6.27*

The sun—walking across the sundial a while, stopping a while—sees indeed *72.7.28*
this carries like a plough—carries the meaning of *72.7.29*
a grounded sage—listening and speaking, standing connected to earth as well as the heavens, *72.7.30*
that person *72.7.31*
"of course—one's self personally, right on one's nose, *72.7.32*
firing arrows from the mouth, sure;"[472] *72.7.33*

the husk of the initial protective bud casing—the sepal—but not really the true inner flower of *72.8.34*
"of course—one's self personally, right on one's nose, *72.8.35*
seeing—one big eye for a head;"[473] *72.8.36*

of course—one's self personally, right on one's nose, *72.9.37*
loving—your heart-core stuck in your throat;[474] *72.9.38*

---

471 From Chapters 53 and 66.
472 From Chapter 35.
473 This phrase is used in Chapters 22 and 24. This second character also appears in Chapters 3, 14, 19, 29, 35, 47, and 52.
474 From Chapters 13, 27, and 44. It was also compared with treasuring in Chapters 13 and 27

the husk of the initial protective bud casing—the sepal—but not really the true inner flower of *72.10.39*
of course—one's self personally, right on one's nose, *72.10.40*
treasuring—as if as valuable as cowry-shell-riches.[475] *72.10.341*

Anciently, for ten generations, this lightly hits and leaves a mark of reason: *72.11.42*
"withdrawing—like a person with a mouth or cave between their legs leaving *72.11.42*
that—that fur stripped by hand from its pelt on the road where you stepped slowly, only the left leg leading the way; *72.11.42*
grabbing the ear of—like marrying— *72.11.42*
this here—the foot stops a person here on their footprint."[476] *72.11.42*

73.

Courageous and sturdy like a soldier, strong as an arm, bladed tool, or a plough—the handle of a bell—[477] *73.1.1*
here—oh, black, icy raven... *73.1.2*
daring—lightly hitting ears on both sides of the head: *73.1.3*
after following this sacrificial blade-and-cauldron-like ritual example or regulation... *73.1.4*
killing a man by impaling a spear into the hair on his head.[478] *73.1.5*

Courageous and sturdy like a soldier, strong as an arm, bladed tool, or a plough—the handle of a bell— *73.2.6*
here—oh, black, icy raven... *73.2.7*
"the husk of the initial protective bud casing—the sepal—but not really the true inner flower of *73.2.8*
daring—lightly hitting ears on both sides of the head:"[479] *73.2.9*
after following this sacrificial blade-and-cauldron-like ritual example or regulation... *73.2.10*
really living, like a tongue or 'clapper of a bell' licking the river water. *73.2.11*

---

[475] From Chapters 3, 9, 13, 17, 20, 27, 31, 39, 51, 56, 62, 64, and 70.
[476] From Chapters 12 and 38.
[477] From Chapter 67.
[478] From Chapter 31.
[479] From Chapters 3, 30, 64, 67, and 69.

This here—the foot stops a person here on their footprint— *73.3.12*
a matched pair, like a harness of ox yokes... *73.3.13*
—now this is cooking with fire!— *73.3.14*
this particular territory—this enclave, defended by a weapon on a pole, plus
its surroundings— *73.3.15*
benefiting, like by reaping grain with a sharp-edged blade...[480] *73.3.16*
this particular territory—this enclave, defended by a weapon on a pole, plus
its surroundings— *73.3.17*
being harmed, like speaking and tallying many lies within
the house.[481] *73.3.18*

Heaven (that sky level above the human head) *73.4.19*
has this... *73.4.20*
a 'place'—somewhere intentionally created, like a door chopped with an axe... *73.4.21*
a house's inferior-hearted evil—seen from overhead...[482] *73.4.22*

whoever—which person, like a baby with a slanting mouth of enjoyment
is this *73.5.23*
firing arrows from the mouth, sure *73.5.24*
what it holds a basket of... *73.5.25*
anciently, for ten generations, this lightly hits and leaves a
mark of reason? *73.5.26*

"The sun—walking across the sundial a while, stopping a while—sees
indeed 73.6.27
this carries like a plough—carries the meaning of 73.6.28
a grounded sage—listening and speaking, standing connected to earth as well as
the heavens, 73.6.29
that person 73.6.30
indeed, like a dog that rises to the top of the alcohol vat...73.6.31
the solidly hard—as difficult as the dried yellow earth of Han where short-tailed
birds can't find food...[483] *73.6.32*
has this."[484] *73.6.33*

[480] From Chapters 8, 11, 19, 36, 53, 56, and 57.
[481] From Chapters 35, 56, and 66.
[482] From Chapters 24, 31, and 42.
[483] From Chapters 2, 3, 12, 63, 64, and 65.
[484] This line is from Chapter 63.

Heaven (that sky level above the human head) *73.7.34*
has this... *73.7.35*
The Way of the loose-haired headperson—walking a while, stopping a while, and speaking of it all: *73.7.36*
"the husk of the initial protective bud casing—the sepal—but not really the true inner flower of *73.7.37*
contending—two hands clawing over a ploughshare,"[485] *73.7.38*
and yet now, bearded... *73.7.39*
virtue—such as offering up a ram's head while back and forth speaking words that are emerging from a mouth like slaves or criminals branded by a chisel... *73.7.40*
forcing a victory over—using a blade to mend a boat or roll rice into a ball under moonlight;[486] *73.7.41*

the husk of the initial protective bud casing—the sepal—but not really the true inner flower of *73.8.42*
speaking—words, like slaves or criminals branded by a chisel emerging from a mouth, *73.8.43*
and yet now, bearded... *73.8.44*
virtue—such as offering up a ram's head while back and forth speaking words that are emerging from a mouth like slaves or criminals branded by a chisel... *73.8.45*
as it ought to be—like the heart of a person as ugly as a short-tailed bird in a habitable cave in a cliff;[487] *73.8.46*

the husk of the initial protective bud casing—the sepal—but not really the true inner flower of *73.9.47*
imperial summons calling everyone together like a blade out of a mouth, *73.9.48*
and yet now, bearded... *73.9.49*
of course—one's self personally, right on one's nose, *73.9.50*
coming next like a stalk of wheat under foot; *73.9.51*

[485] From Chapters 3, 8, 22, 66, and 68.
[486] From Chapters 31, 33, 36, 45, 61, 67, 68, and 69.
[487] From Chapter 38.

easy-going as a solitary individual who uses a net of loose silk with weights to catch animals, *73.10.52*
accomplished thus, in this manner: as naturally as dog meat over a fire, *73.10.53*
and yet now, bearded, *73.10.54*
virtue—such as offering up a ram's head while back and forth speaking words that are emerging from a mouth like slaves or criminals branded by a chisel... *73.10.55*
consulting on strategy—speaking with a tree, words like slaves or criminals, branded by a chisel, emerging from a mouth.[488] *73.10.56*

Heaven (that sky level above the human head)... *73.11.57*
thin silk net... *73.11.58*
vast—like an expanded heart restored from fire that can be toughed by hand, that is disheartened gray ashes— *73.11.59*
vast—like an expanded heart restored from fire that can be toughed by hand, that is disheartened gray ashes, *73.11.60*

distant and sparse—picture a foot with a thigh above it and an upside-down baby with amniotic fluid streaming down below its head,[489] *73.12.61*
and yet now, bearded, *73.12.62*
the husk of the initial protective bud casing—the sepal—but not really the true inner flower of *73.12.63*
dropping something—losing.[490] *73.12.64*

74.

Civilians—like the Mín people enslaved by blinding with a dagger— *74.1.1*
the husk of the initial protective bud casing—the sepal—but not really the true inner flower of *74.1.2*
fearing—like when there's a ghost holding a stick or maybe part of a tiger with its claw—[491] *74.1.3*
dying—going from a standing person to a pile of bones...[492] *74.1.4*

---

[488] From Chapter 64.
[489] From Chapter 56.
[490] From Chapters 13, 23, 26, 29, 33, 38, and 64. "Not really dropping something" appears in Chapter 33.
[491] From Chapters 15, 17, 20, 53, and 72. In Chapters 20 and 72, it appears as part of this same phrase of "not really fearing."
[492] From Chapters 6, 33, 42, 50, and 67.

how, how, indeed—like a big man at an altar—[493] *74.2.5*
that very one about whom you can purse your lips around a cane and puff,
'yup, that's the person,' *74.2.6*
this carries like a plough—carries the meaning of, *74.2.7*
dying—going from a standing person to a pile of bones— *74.2.8*
frightening—two eyes over 'a short-tailed bird' scaring one's heart... *74.2.9*
what it has? *74.2.10*

A Certain Someone compliantly combing their loose hair seems to be saying: 'this is as if...' *74.3.11*
"breeding—like a gentleman holding a fountain pen making
something happen—[494] *74.3.12*
civilians—like the Mín people enslaved by blinding with a dagger..."[495] *74.3.13*
the ever-present square fabric—like that which our grown men wrap around the 'little bird' top knots on their heads after receiving their public courtesy-names—or what we know as the timeless, whole head-cloth 'ji' version of *74.3.14*
"fearing—like when there's a ghost holding a stick or maybe part of a tiger with its claw— *74.3.15*
dying—going from a standing person to a pile of bones—" *74.3.16*

and yet now, bearded... *74.4.17*
efforting—like lifting up an elephant— *74.4.18*
remarkably cunning like the great giant about which one can purse one's
lips like a piece of cane and puff: 'Yup, that's it, definitely...'[496] *74.4.19*
—now this is cooking with fire! *74.4.20*

I/we—our five mouths— *74.5.21*
hand-picking, like-cowry-shell-riches-along-the-road, *74.5.22*
holding tight in the hand—not letting go of, not
dying young,[497] *74.5.23*
and yet now, bearded... *74.5.24*
killing a man by impaling a spear into the hair on
his head... [498] *74.5.25*
what it has... *74.5.26*

---

[493] From Chapter 26.
[494] From Chapters 3, 53, and 55. In Chapter 3, it was also used with the next character ("civilians").
[495] See previous note.
[496] From Chapter 57 and 58.
[497] From Chapters 14, 29, 35, 64, and 69.
[498] From Chapters 31 and 73.

whoever—which person, like a baby with a slanting mouth of
enjoyment is this *74.6.27*
daring—lightly hitting ears on both sides of the head? *74.6.28*

"The ever-present square fabric—like that which our grown men wrap around the
'little bird' top knots on their heads after receiving their public courtesy-
names—or what we know as the timeless, whole head-cloth 'ji' version of" *74.7.29*
flesh-and-blood, meat-handling Being *74.7.30*
taking charge—like a flipped queen or king, that is, head speaker, *74.7.31*
"killing a man by impaling a spear into the hair on his head" *74.7.32*
—now this is cooking with fire!— *74.7.33*
"killing a man by impaling a spear into the hair on his head." *74.7.34*

That is to say, this particular grown man with a hairpin and public
courtesy name *74.8.35*
taking the place of, like a person with a retrievable arrow attached to a
string or an era or a dynasty lineage... *74.8.36*
"taking charge—like a flipped queen or king, that is, head speaker *74.8.37*
killing a man by impaling a spear into the hair on his head *74.8.38*
—now this is cooking with fire!— *74.8.39*
killing a man by impaling a spear into the hair on his head." *74.8.40*

The sun—walking across the sundial a while, stopping a while—sees indeed *74.9.41*
what it's called when speaking from the gut—words, like slaves or criminals
branded by a chisel emerging from a mouth... *74.9.42*
"taking the place of like a person with a retrievable arrow attached to a string or an
era or a dynasty lineage..." *74.9.43*
great giant *74.9.44*
master craftsmen who builds a box with axe *74.9.45*
chopping like a keen axe cutting a stone flagon. *74.9.46*

That is to say, this particular grown man with a hairpin and public
courtesy name *74.10.47*
"taking the place of like a person with a retrievable arrow attached to a
string or an era or a dynasty lineage... *74.10.48*
great giant *74.10.49*
master craftsmen who builds a box with axe *74.10.50*
chopping like a keen axe cutting a stone flagon..." *74.10.51*
—now this is cooking with fire!— *74.10.52*

sparse—as spare as the interconnecting threads in that square cloth men wrap around their 'little bird' top knots and heads—[499] *74.11.53*
flesh-and-blood, meat-handling Being *74.11.54*
the husk of the initial protective bud casing—the sepal—but not really the true inner flower of *74.11.55*
wounded—a bent person with that male principle of sun shining on an altar like strands of hair...[500] *74.11.56*
what it holds a basket of... *74.11.57*
their expert, convenient hand *74.11.58*
—swearing on an arrow revolving around oneself, that's it! *74.11.59*

75.

Civilians—like the Mín people enslaved by blinding with a dagger— *75.1.1*
has this... *75.1.2*
starving—having a meal with one's mouth over a bowl of rice on a stand is carefully watched over like the smallest things, tiny silk threads, under guard by a man with a spear, by a garrison, *75.1.3*

this carries like a plough—carries the meaning of *75.2.4*
what it holds a basket of... *75.2.5*
higher, ruling level... *75.2.6*
having a meal—mouth over a bowl of rice on a stand... *75.2.7*
grain tax—a rice plant to an open mouth like that of a smiling, breathy older brother— *75.2.8*
has this... *75.2.9*
much more—like a double serving of meat. *75.2.10*

The sun—walking across the sundial a while, stopping a while—sees indeed *75.3.11*
this carries like a plough—carries the meaning of *75.3.12*
"starving—having a meal with one's mouth over a bowl of rice on a stand is carefully watched over like the smallest things, tiny silk threads, under guard by a man with a spear, by a garrison." *75.3.13*

[499] From Chapters 14, 23, 41, 43, and 70.
[500] From Chapter 60.

"Civilians—like the Mín people enslaved by blinding with a dagger— *75.4.14*
has this... *75.4.15*
the solidly hard—as difficult as the dried yellow earth of Han where short-tailed birds can't find food— *75.4.16*
governing—regulating by harnessing the river named Happy or speaking of turning oneself,"[501] *75.4.17*

> this carries like a plough—carries the meaning of *75.5.178*
> what it holds a basket of... *75.5.19*
> higher, ruling level *75.5.20*
> has this... *75.5.10*
> flesh-and-blood, meat-handling Being *75.5.22*
> efforting—like lifting up an elephant. *75.5.23*
>
> The sun—walking across the sundial a while, stopping a while—sees indeed *75.6.24*
> this carries like a plough—carries the meaning of *75.6.25*
> "the solidly hard—as difficult as the dried yellow earth of Han where short-tailed birds can't find food— *75.6.26*
> governing—regulating by harnessing the river named Happy or speaking of turning oneself." *75.6.27*

Civilians—like the Mín people enslaved by blinding with a dagger— *75.7.28*
has this... *75.7.29*
as if lightweight—as lightweight as using a bladed tool in a light carriage on an underground stream—[502] *75.7.30*
dying—going from a standing person to a pile of bones, *75.7.31*

> this carries like a plough—carries the meaning of *75.8.32*
> what it holds a basket of... *75.8.33*
> higher, ruling level[503] *75.8.34*
> seeking and requesting—like a coveted fur coat—[504] *75.8.35*
> "birthing—a bud sprouting from the ground— *75.8.36*
> has this... *75.8.37*
> thick like a generous cliff with a habitable cave that opposes the flow of the river, housing a baby with a large head, spread arms and swaddled legs under the sun."[505] *75.8.38*

---

[501] From Chapter 65.
[502] From Chapters 26, 63, and 69.
[503] Some versions don't have this character, but most do.
[504] From Chapter 62.
[505] From Chapter 50. The final character also appears in Chapters 38, 44, 50, and 55.

The sun—walking across the sundial a while, stopping a while—
sees indeed *75.9.39*
this carries like a plough—carries the meaning of *75.9.40*
"as if lightweight—as lightweight as using a bladed tool in a light carriage
on an underground stream— *75.9.41*
dying—going from a standing person to a pile of bones." *75.9.42*

That is to say, this particular grown man with a hairpin and public
courtesy name *75.10.43*
essentially and only—like the mouth of 'the short-tailed bird'— *75.10.44*
Not-Being—nobody trance-dancing with long tails flowing from her wrists, *75.10.45*
this carries like a plough—carries the meaning of, *75.10.46*
"birthing—a bud sprouting from the ground—" *75.10.47*
efforting—like lifting up an elephant— *75.10.48*
—now this is cooking with fire! *75.10.49*

The sun—walking across the sundial a while, stopping a while—sees indeed *75.11.50*
important folks—their eye looking down, surrendering, with
cowry-like riches—[506] *75.11.51*
here—oh, black, icy raven... *75.11.52*
treasuring—as if as valuable as cowry-shell-riches—[507] *75.11.53*
"birthing—a bud sprouting from the ground." *75.11.54*

76.

That person *76.1.1*
has this *76.1.2*
birthing—a bud sprouting from the ground: *76.1.3*
—yes, that too, vagina!— *76.1.4*
softening—to be like a tree that can be cut with a spear,[508] *76.1.5*
to be as fragile as a matching pair of decorative bows or little wings;[509] *76.1.6*

---

[506] From Chapter 3.
[507] From Chapters 3, 9, 13, 17, 20, 27, 31, 39, 51, 56, 62, 64, 70, and 72. This is its last appearance.
[508] From Chapters 10, 36, 43, 52, and 55.
[509] From Chapters 3, 36, 40, and 55.

what it holds a basket of, *76.2.7*
dying—going from a standing person to a pile of bones:[510] *76.2.8*
—yes, that too, vagina!— *76.2.9*
hard and solid as a right hand through an eye cast down in surrender over solid clay soil[511] *76.2.10*
strengthening like an insect—revolving oneself as a venomous snake-like bow. *76.2.11*

The myriad, scorpion-medicine-dancing Ten Thousand *76.3.12*
Things cut off—all matter external to oneself like seeds, cows etc., *76.3.13*
grass that's early, premature—like sunrise above an acorn on the jujube, that thorny plant that's used for insomnia, contraception and causes midterm miscarriages—such as herbs, *76.3.14*
a tree with roots[512] *76.3.15*
"has this *76.3.16*
birthing—a bud sprouting from the ground: *76.3.17*
—yes, that too, vagina!— *76.3.18*
softening—to be like a tree that can be cut with a spear," *76.3.19*
fragile as crisp meat from a roof—precariously high above a kneeling person;[513] *76.3.20*

"what it holds a basket of, *76.4.21*
dying—going from a standing person to a pile of bones: *76.4.22*
—yes, that too, vagina!—" *76.4.23*
dried and withered like an ancient tree of ten generations, *76.4.24*
meagre and withered like a tree high above (a two-story building in the city outskirts). *76.4.25*

[510] From Chapters 6, 33, 4, 50, 67, 74, and 75.
[511] From Chapter 43.
[512] From Chapter 64.
[513] From Chapter 64.

Anciently, for ten generations, this lightly hits and leaves a mark of reason: *76.5.26*
"hard and solid as a right hand through an eye cast down in surrender over solid clay soil *76.5.27*
strengthening like an insect—revolving oneself as a venomous snake-like bow—" *76.5.28*
—now this is cooking with fire!— *76.5.29*
"dying—going from a standing person to a pile of bones..." *76.5.30*
has this *76.5.31*
follower—a foot soldier, walking awhile and stopping a while on the clay soil;[514] *76.5.32*

"softening—to be like a tree that can be cut with a spear *76.6.33*
to be as fragile as a matching pair of decorative bows or little wings" *76.6.34*
—now this is cooking with fire!— *76.6.35*
"birthing—a bud sprouting from the ground..."[515] *76.6.36*
"has this *76.6.37*
follower—a foot soldier, walking awhile and stopping a while on the clay soil." *76.6.38*

The sun—walking across the sundial a while, stopping a while—sees indeed *76.7.39*
this carries like a plough—carries the meaning of: *76.7.40*
carrying a short ax with two hands like a soldier or pawn *76.7.41*
"strengthening like an insect—revolving oneself as a venomous snake-like bow..." *76.7.42*
after following this sacrificial blade-and-cauldron-like ritual example or regulation... *76.7.43*
the husk of the initial protective bud casing—the sepal—but not really the true inner flower of *76.7.44*
forcing a victory over—using a blade to mend a boat or roll rice into a ball under moonlight; *76.7.45*

"a tree with roots" *76.8.46*
"strengthening like an insect—revolving oneself as a venomous snake-like bow..." *76.8.47*
after following this sacrificial blade-and-cauldron-like ritual example or regulation... *76.8.48*
breaking off—cutting a tree in half with an axe; *76.8.49*

---

[514] From Chapter 50.
[515] This charactrer's final appearance.

"strengthening like an insect—revolving oneself as a venomous
snake-like bow," *76.9.50*
great giant... *76.9.51*
dwelling here—staying, as someone at home at the tea table, chaste and unmarried, someone being followed from behind by a tiger-fur head— *76.9.52*
down below, lower level; *76.9.53*

"softening—to be like a tree that can be cut with a spear— *76.10.54*
to be as fragile as a matching pair of decorative bows or little wings..." *76.10.54*
dwelling here—staying, as someone at home at the tea table, chaste and unmarried, someone being followed from behind by a tiger-fur head—[516] *76.10.54*
higher, ruling level. *76.10.54*

77.

Heaven (that sky level above the human head), *77.1.1*
what it has... *77.1.2*
The Way of the loose-haired headperson—walking a while, stopping a while, and speaking of it all... *77.1.3*

what it holds a basket of... *77.2.4*
indeed, like a dog that rises to the top of the alcohol vat...[517] *77.2.5*
stretching—lengthening the bow string—[518] *77.2.6*
like a bow *77.2.7*
supporting—offering to carry on one's shoulders: *77.2.8*

high above (a two-story building in the city outskirts)...[519] *77.3.9*
—now this is cooking with fire!— *77.3.10*
suppressing like a hand pushing down on a kneeling person... *77.3.11*
what it has; *77.3.12*

---

[516] From Chapters 2, 8, 24, 26, 30, 31, 38, and 66.
[517] From Chapters 5, 15, 32, 63, and 73.
[518] From Chapter 36
[519] From Chapters 2 and 39.

down below, lower level... *77.4.13*
—now this is cooking with fire!— *77.4.14*
lifting up—supporting, offering to hand-carry on one's shoulders above a fang... *77.4.15*
what it has; *77.4.16*

flesh-and-blood, meat-handling Being *77.5.17*
having leftovers—excess food remains in one's house...[520] *77.5.18*
—now this is cooking with fire!— *77.5.19*
diminishing like hands and fingers injured by the top edge of the cauldron that is the monarchy government...[521] *77.5.20*
what it has; *77.5.21*

"the husk of the initial protective bud casing—the sepal—but not really the true inner flower of *77.6.22*
enough—the full leg-cut of the animal..."[522] *77.6.23*
—now this is cooking with fire!— *77.6.24*
mending—clothing such as a robe, especially that worn on the torso, like the placental afterbirth hanging from a recently pregnant woman being fixed by the courtesy name of a man after he replaces a water bucket with a weapon on a pole... *77.6.25*
what it has; *77.6.26*

"Heaven (that sky level above the human head), *77.7.27*
what it has... *77.7.28*
The Way of the loose-haired headperson—walking a while, stopping a while, and speaking of it all..." *77.7.29*
"diminishing like hands and fingers injured by the top edge of the cauldron that is the monarchy government" *77.7.30*
flesh-and-blood, meat-handling Being *77.7.31*
"having leftovers—excess food remains in one's house—" *77.7.32*

---

[520] From Chapters 20, 24, 52, and 54.
[521] From Chapters 42 and 48.
[522] From Chapters 17, 19, 23, 28, 33, 35, 41, 44, 46, 48, and 64.

and yet now, bearded, *77.8.33*

"mending—clothing such as a robe, especially that worn on the torso, like the placental afterbirth hanging from a recently pregnant woman being fixed by the courtesy name of a man after he replaces a water bucket with a weapon on a pole..." *77.8.34*

"the husk of the initial protective bud casing—the sepal—but not really the true inner flower of *77.8.35*

enough—the full leg-cut of the animal." *77.8.36*

That person, *77.9.37*

what it has... *77.9.38*

The Way of the loose-haired headperson—walking a while, stopping a while, and speaking of it all... *77.9.39*

after following this sacrificial blade-and-cauldron-like ritual example or regulation... *77.9.40*

the husk of the initial protective bud casing—the sepal—but not really the true inner flower of *77.9.41*

accomplished thus, in this manner: as naturally as dog meat over a fire:[523] *77.9.42*

"diminishing like hands and fingers injured by the top edge of the cauldron that is the monarchy government..." *77.10.43*

"the husk of the initial protective bud casing—the sepal—but not really the true inner flower of *77.10.44*

enough—the full leg-cut of the animal..." *77.10.45*

this carries like a plough—carries the meaning of *77.10.46*

offering a lush growth of plants with two hands *77.10.47*

"flesh-and-blood, meat-handling Being *77.10.48*

having leftovers—excess food remains in one's house." *77.10.49*

Whoever—which person, like a baby with a slanting mouth of enjoyment is this *77.11.50 & 51*

using a legendary capability—the hybrid power of that mythical bear with deer legs—for *77.11.52*

"flesh-and-blood, meat-handling Being *77.11.53*

having leftovers—excess food remains in one's house..." *77.11.54*

this carries like a plough—carries the meaning of *77.11.505*

"offering a lush growth of plants with two hands" *77.11.56*

Heaven (that sky level above the human head)-Down Below (lower level)? *77.11.57*

[523] From Chapters 17, 23, 25, 26, 51, 53, 54, 57, 64, 65, and 73.

Essentially and only—like the mouth of 'the short-tailed bird'— 77.12.58
flesh-and-blood, meat-handling Being 77.12.59
The Way of the loose-haired headperson—walking a while, stopping a while, and speaking of it all 77.12.60
—now this is cooking with fire! 77.12.61

The sun—walking across the sundial a while, stopping a while—sees indeed 77.13.62
this carries like a plough—carries the meaning of 77.13.63
a grounded sage—listening and speaking, standing connected to earth as well as the heavens, 77.13.64
that person... 77.13.65
"efforting—like lifting up an elephant— 77.13.66
and yet now, bearded, 77.13.67
the husk of the initial protective bud casing—the sepal—but not really the true inner flower of 77.13.68
expecting that will be holding one's heart-core like a mother;"[524] 77.13.69

"real work—laboring with the force from a bladed tool, one's arm, or a plough— 77.14.70
completing—that final nail in the weapon on a pole— 77.14.71
and yet now, bearded, 77.14.72
the husk of the initial protective bud casing—the sepal—but not really the true inner flower of 77.14.73
dwelling here—staying, as someone at home at the tea table, chaste and unmarried, someone being followed from behind by a tiger-fur head;"[525] 77.14.74

what it holds a basket of... 77.15.75
the husk of the initial protective bud casing—the sepal—but not really the true inner flower of 77.15.76
wanting—missing what's been eroded from this ravine— 77.15.77
seeing—one big eye for a head—[526] 77.15.78
important folks—their eye looking down, surrendering, with cowry-like riches.[527] 77.15.79

---

[524] This whole phrase is from Chapters 2, 10, and 51. The last character also appears in Chapter 34

[525] This whole phrase is from Chapter 2 except the last character there is a slightly different character for dwelling. In Chapter 17, the first two characters appear together ("real work completing"). The character "completing" aso appears in Chapters 7, 15, 25, 34, 41, 45, 47, 51, 63, 64, and 67. This is its last appearance. The last character ("dwelling") also appears in Chapters 8, 24, 26, 30, 31, 38, 66, and 76. This is its last appearance.

[526] From Chapters 3, 14, 19, 22, 24, 29, 35, 47, and 72. This is its last appearance.

[527] From Chapters 3 and 75.

78.

Heaven (that sky level above the human head)-Down Below (lower level): *78.1.1 & 2*
must not—eh, like the lost-in-the-bushes , eh?— *78.1.3*
"*softening—to be like a tree that can be cut with a spear,*[528] *78.1.4*
to be as fragile as a matching pair of decorative bows or little wings"[529]*78.1.5*
here—oh, black, icy raven... *78.1.6*
water, flowing right in the center of the Han River and spraying up on
both sides,[530] *78.1.7*

and yet now, bearded, ...*78.2.8*
attacking—hitting lightly with a bladed tool, being on top, *78.2.9*
"*hard and solid as a right hand through an eye cast down in surrender over solid*
clay soil[531]*78.2.10*
strengthening like an insect—revolving oneself as a venomous snake-like bow—"[532]*78.2.11*
—now this is cooking with fire! *78.2.12*

Must not—eh, like the lost-in-the-bushes , eh?— *78.3.13*
what it has... *78.3.14*
using a legendary capability—the hybrid power of that mythical bear with deer
legs—for *78.3.15*
forcing a victory over—using a blade to mend a boat or roll rice into a ball
under moonlight. *78.3.16*

What it holds a basket of... *78.4.17*
Not-Being—nobody trance-dancing with long tails flowing from her wrists, *78.4.18*
this carries like a plough—carries the meaning of... *78.4.19*
easily changeable to something else—going from saying 'don't' as seriously
as blood on a blade to shining as sunny as the sun above...[533] *78.4.20*
what it has. *78.4.21*

---

[528] From Chapters 10, 36, 43, 52, 55, and 76.
[529] From Chapters 3, 36, 40, 55, and 76. This two-word phrase appears in Chapter 76 describing someone's birthing.
[530] From Chapter 8 where it's used to describe "higher, ruling level traditional virtue."
[531] From Chapters 43 and 76.
[532] First used in Chapter 3 where it appears in the same paragraph as "strengthening." This two-word phrase appears in Chapter 76 regarding dying.
[533] From Chapters 2, 63, 64, and 70.

"To be as fragile as a matching pair of decorative bows or little wings..." *78.5.22*
what it has... *78.5.23*
"forcing a victory over—using a blade to mend a boat or roll rice into a ball under moonlight— *78.5.24*
strengthening like an insect—revolving oneself as a venomous snake-like bow."[534] *78.5.25*

"Softening—to be like a tree that can be cut with a spear..." *78.6.26*
what it has... *78.6.27*
"forcing a victory over—using a blade to mend a boat or roll rice into a ball under moonlight—" *78.6.28*
firmly—just exactly, barely, recently cutting grass on mountains within the city outskirts with a blade.[535] *78.6.29*

"Heaven (that sky level above the human head)-Down Below (lower level), 78.7.30 & 31
must not—eh, like the lost-in-the-bushes, eh?—" 78.7.32
'the husk of the initial protective bud casing—the sepal—but not really the true inner flower of 78.7.33
firing arrows from the mouth, sure...'[536] 78.7.34

must not—eh, like the lost-in-the-bushes, eh?— 78.8.35
using a legendary capability—the hybrid power of that mythical bear with deer legs—for 78.8.36
on a public road, practicing—moving with.[537] 78.8.37

The sun—walking across the sundial a while, stopping a while—sees indeed *78.9.38*
this carries like a plough—carries the meaning of *78.9.39*
a grounded sage—listening and speaking, standing connected to earth as well as the heavens, *78.9.40*
that person, *78.9.41*
saying like a cloud:[538] *78.9.42*

---

[534] These two characters were used together in Chapter 33.
[535] From Chapter 36 where it was also used with "softening" as well as "fragile."
[536] From 46, 56, and 70.
[537] These two lines are from Chapter 70. The last character was first used in Chapter 3.
[538] From Chapter 57.

'Receiving and bearing—a hand over a commonplace plate with a hand below, on bottom— *78.10.43*
this nation—this particular territory, this enclave defended by a weapon on a pole plus its surroundings... *78.10.44*
what it has... *78.10.45*
humiliated like filth—clay soil next to a queen or king, the head speaker... *78.10.46*

> the sun—walking across the sundial a while, stopping a while—sees indeed *78.11.47*
> what it's called when speaking from the gut—words, like slaves or criminals branded by a chisel emerging from a mouth: *78.11.48*
> the god of the soil to whom we build altars, *78.11.49*
> the god of plants -- a plant stalk in a farmland field divided from something coming up behind as with the knot at the end of a cord... *78.11.50*
> master—the owner and host of the lamp's flame. *78.11.51*

Receiving and bearing—a hand over a commonplace plate with a hand below, on bottom *78.12.52*
this nation—this particular territory, this enclave defended by a weapon on a pole plus its surroundings... *78.12.3*
the husk of the initial protective bud casing—the sepal—but not really the true inner flower of *78.12.54*
"a good omen—a ram's head at an altar..."[539] *78.12.55*

> the sun—walking across the sundial a while, stopping a while—sees indeed *78.13.56*
> what it's called when speaking from the gut—words, like slaves or criminals branded by a chisel emerging from a mouth: *78.13.57*
> Heaven (that sky level above the human head)-Down Below (lower level) *78.13.58 & 59*
> king—connecting heaven, man, and earth...' *78.13.60*

[539] From Chapters 31 and 55. In Chapter 31, it appeared with the preceding character ("not really).

Straight—upright as a nail in a footprint—[540] *78.14.62*
speaking—words, like slaves or criminals branded by a chisel emerging from a mouth... *78.13.60*
A Certain Someone compliantly combing their loose hair seems to be saying: 'this is as if...' *78.13.63*
making someone return, with one's right hand, to the habitable cave in the cliff.[541] *78.13.64*

79.

Harmonizing as a mouth organ...[542] *79.1.1*
great giant *79.1.2*
resenting—the heart sleeping like someone kneeling to lie down below the moon...[543] *79.1.3*

analytically—hands over heart-core: *79.2.4*
"flesh-and-blood, meat-handling Being... *79.2.15*
having leftovers—excess food remains in one's house—"[544] *79.2.6*
"resenting—the heart sleeping like someone kneeling to lie down below the moon." *79.2.7*

Calm like a woman sitting on her heels at home *79.3.8*
about which one can purse one's lips like a piece of cane and puff: 'Yup, that's it, definitely'... *79.3.9*
this carries like a plough—carries the meaning of *79.3.10*
efforting—like lifting up an elephant— *79.3.11*
virtue—such as offering up a ram's head while back and forth speaking words that are emerging from a mouth like slaves or criminals branded by a chisel. *79.3.12*

[540] From Chapters 8, 45, 57, and 58.
[541] From Chapters 25, 40, and 65.
[542] From Chapters 2, 4, 18, 42, 55, and 56.
[543] From Chapter 63.
[544] From Chapters 20, 24, 53, 54, and 77. The two-word phrase appears in 53 and 77.

The sun—walking across the sundial a while, stopping a while—sees indeed *79.4.13*
this carries like a plough—carries the meaning of *79.4.14*
a grounded sage—listening and speaking, standing connected to earth as well as the heavens, *79.4.15*
that person... *79.4.16*
holding tight in the hand—not letting go of, not dying young—[545] *79.4.17*
inferior position—left-handed work—[546] *79.4.18*
written contract—a great giant engraving like a blade in weeds dense as three strands of hair through, up and down, *79.4.19*

and yet now, bearded... *79.5.20*
the husk of the initial protective bud casing—the sepal—but not really the true inner flower of *79.5.21*
blaming—a tree with thorns over cowry-riches *79.5.22*
here—oh, black, icy raven... *79.5.23*
that person. *79.5.24*

Flesh-and-blood, meat-handling Being *79.6.25*
Dé—the ethical, straight way of walking awhile and stopping awhile, eye directed forward over the heart-core— *79.6.26*
taking charge—like a flipped queen or king, that is, head speaker...[547] *79.6.27*
"written contract—a great giant engraving like a blade in weeds dense as three strands of hair through, up and down;" *79.6.28*

Not-Being—nobody trance-dancing with long tails flowing from her wrists— *79.7.29*
Dé—the ethical, straight way of walking awhile and stopping awhile, eye directed forward over the heart-core— *79.7.30*
"taking charge—like a flipped queen or king, that is, head speaker..." *79.7.31*
thoroughly penetrating like a hand breaking a pot—that taxation system that was like walking slowly, hitting lightly an inverted baby being birthed. *79.7.32*

[545] From Chapters 14, 29, 35, 64, 69, and 74.
[546] From Chapters 30, 31, and 34.
[547] From Chapter 74.

Heaven (that sky level above the human head) *79.8.33*
The Way of the loose-haired headperson—walking a while, stopping a while, and speaking of it all: *79.8.34*
Not-Being—nobody trance-dancing with long tails flowing from her wrists... *79.8.35*
intimates—like a beloved that one sees closely even in suffering like from that chisel used to mark slaves and criminals;[548] *79.8.36*

the ever-present square fabric—like that which our grown men wrap around the 'little bird' top knots on their heads after receiving their public courtesy-names—or what we know as the timeless, whole head-cloth 'ji' version... *79.9.37*
supporting—offering to carry on one's shoulders— *79.9.38*
"virtue—such as offering up a ram's head while back and forth speaking words that are emerging from a mouth like slaves or criminals branded by a chisel," *79.9.39*
that person. *79.9.40*

80.

Very little, like three grains of sand,[549] *80.1.1*
this nation—this particular territory, this enclave defended by a weapon on a pole plus its surroundings... *80.1.2*
scant as one widowed, alone—separating them from the kneeling head of the household with a blade—[550] *80.1.3*
civilians—like the Mín people enslaved by blinding with a dagger: *80.1.4*

breeding—like a gentleman holding a fountain pen making something happen—[551] *80.2.5*
flesh-and-blood, meat-handling Being... *80.2.6*
ten people *80.2.7*
counts—people as clear as an acorn like an eldest brother or paternal uncle... *80.2.8*
what it has... *80.2.9*
set of valuable vessels with lots of capacity—worthy of a guard dog, *80.2.10*

---

[548] From Chapters 17, 18, 44, and 56.
[549] From Chapters 32, 34, 52, 60, 61, and 63.
[550] From Chapters 19, 39, 42, and 63.
[551] From Chapters 3, 55, and 74.

and yet now, bearded... *80.3.11*
the husk of the initial protective bud casing—the sepal—but not really the true inner flower of *80.3.12*
doing truly useful work like a water bucket—by means of carrying-capacity; *80.3.13*

"breeding—like a gentleman holding a fountain pen making something happen— *80.4.14*
civilians—like the Mín people enslaved by blinding with a dagger..."[552] *80.4.15*
a heavy load—a bag carried by a man—[553] *80.4.16*
dying—going from a standing person to a pile of bones, *80.4.17*

and yet now, bearded... *80.5.18*
the husk of the initial protective bud casing—the sepal—but not really the true inner flower of *80.5.19*
remote—not intimately close but a profound way in which you walk a while, stop a while, shaped like a big round spindle with a long robe, like the afterbirth hanging from a recently pregnant woman—[554] *80.5.20*
moving, shifting, migrating like feces leaving a living person representing the dead in a rite. *80.5.21*

Although—even if 'a venomous snake' has 'a short-tailed bird' right next to it— *80.6.22*
flesh-and-blood, meat-handling Being... *80.6.23*
a boat—a dugout canoe, *80.6.24*
a carriage's sedan chair surrounded by a mortar, upheld by two hands—the masses... *80.6.25*

Not-Being—nobody trance-dancing with long tails flowing from her wrists— *80.7.26*
'place'—somewhere intentionally created, like a door chopped with an axe... *80.7.27*
four-horse military carriage... *80.7.28*
what it has; *80.7.29*

---

[552] From Chapters 3 and 74.
[553] From Chapters 26, 59, and 66.
[554] From Chapters 25, 47, and 65.

although—even if 'a venomous snake' has 'a short-tailed bird' right next to it— *80.8.30*
flesh-and-blood, meat-handling Being... *80.8.31*
"shield—a turtle shell, *80.8.32*
carrying a short ax with two hands like a soldier or pawn..."[555] *80.8.33*

Not-Being—nobody trance-dancing with long tails flowing from her wrists— *80.9.34*
'place'—somewhere intentionally created, like a door chopped with an axe... *80.9.35*
displaying like the sun rising behind a tree in the east near a big mound of soil—ancient—like the vassal state of Chen... *80.9.36*
what it has; *80.9.37*

"breeding—like a gentleman holding a fountain pen making something happen— *80.10.38*
'civilians—like the Mín people enslaved by blinding with a dagger..." *80.10.39*
walking forth and then back again,'[556] *80.10.40*
tying up with a knot of a skein of silk, auspiciously unused,[557] *80.10.41*
a skein of silk around a striving toad,[558] *80.10.42*

and yet now, bearded... *80.11.43*
"doing truly useful work like a water bucket—by means of carrying-capacity..." *80.11.44*
what it has. *80.11.45*

Sweet in the mouth...[559] *80.12.46*
what it holds a basket of... *80.12.47*
having a meal—mouth over a bowl of rice on a stand;[560] *80.12.48*

---

[555] From Chapter 50.
[556] "Civilians walking forth and then back again" is from Chapter 19. The second character also appears in Chapters 14, 16, 19, 28, 52, 58, and 64.
[557] From Chapter 27 where "traditional virtue" was doing this while "Not-Being... a skein of silk around a striving toad, binding."
[558] From Chapters 14 and 27.
[559] From Chapter 32.
[560] From Chapters 20, 24, 53, and 75.

admired beauty—picture someone wearing a ram's horn headdress...[561] *80.13.49*
what it holds a basket of... *80.13.50*
wearing clothes—like mourning dress as earthly and mortal as commonplace plates—subdued like a kneeling person by hand;[562] *80.13.51*

calm like a woman sitting on her heels at home...[563] *80.14.52*
what it holds a basket of... *80.14.53*
abiding—dwelling where birthed, sitting over ten mouths;[564] *80.14.54*

enjoying—like glad music played upon a wooden instrument's silk strings...[565] *80.15.55*
what it holds a basket of... *80.15.56*
in the common practices of the people from that difficult position in the valley between two mountains.[566] *80.15.57*

The neighboring countries that are attracting like will o' wisp light emanating from a corpse attracting a kneeling person to a grave...[567] *80.16.58*
this nation—this particular territory, this enclave defended by a weapon on a pole plus its surroundings... *80.16.59*
mutually—like a seen tree and the eye seeing it— *80.16.60*
gazing from a distance like a good human standing on soil below the cutting edge of a knife and the crescent moon... *80.16.61*

a rooster—a 'short-tailed bird' a great giant whose tiniest silk thread child is grabbed by a hand from above like a female prostitute... *80.17.62*
a dog... *80.17.63*
what it has... *80.17.64*
many sounds—hitting chimes with one's right hand and hearing them—[568] *80.17.65*
mutually—like a seen tree and the eye seeing it— *80.17.66*
hearing at the double-winged gateway...[569] *80.17.67*

[561] From Chapters 2, 31, and 62.
[562] From Chapters 53 and 59.
[563] From Chapters 15, 35, 64, and 79.
[564] From Chapters 2, 8, 25, 31, 38, and 72.
[565] From Chapters 23, 31, 35, and 66.
[566] From Chapters 20 and 41.
[567] From Chapter 15.
[568] From Chapters 2 and 41.
[569] From Chapters 14, 35, 41, and 50.

civilians—like the Mín people enslaved by blinding with a dagger— *80.18.68*
reaching the extreme—like an arrow straight into the clay soil—[570] *80.18.69*
an old man with long hair and a cane...[571] *80.18.70*
dying—going from a standing person to a pile of bones— *80.18.71*

the husk of the initial protective bud casing—the sepal—but not really the true inner flower of *80.19.72*
mutually—like a seen tree and the eye seeing it— *80.19.73*
walking slowly toward you—like a host with a lamp, only the left leg leading the way...[572] *80.19.74*
coming next like a stalk of wheat under foot.[573] *80.19.75*

81.

Truth-speaking—speaking words like slaves or criminals, branded by a chisel, emerging from a mouth of good luck that's as empty and quiet as a mouth with a soldier's axe above it, speaking of grass—[574] *81.1.1*
speaking—words, like slaves or criminals branded by a chisel emerging from a mouth... *81.1.2*
the husk of the initial protective bud casing—the sepal—but not really the true inner flower of *81.1.3*
admired beauty—picture someone wearing a ram's horn headdress;[575] *81.1.4*

"admired beauty—picture someone wearing a ram's horn headdress— *81.2.5*
speaking—words, like slaves or criminals branded by a chisel emerging from a mouth..."[576] *81.2.6*
the husk of the initial protective bud casing—the sepal—but not really the true inner flower of *81.2.7*
"truth-speaking—speaking words like slaves or criminals, branded by a chisel, emerging from a mouth of good luck that's as empty and quiet as a mouth with a soldier's axe above it, speaking of grass." *81.2.8*

---

[570] From Chapters 43, 48, 55, 65, and 72.
[571] This character is the first part of Lǎo Zǐ's name.
[572] From Chapter 35.
[573] From Chapter 73.
[574] From Chapters 8, 17, 21, 23, 38, 49, and 63.
[575] From Chapters 2, 31, 62, and 80.
[576] From Chapter 62.

Virtue—such as offering up a ram's head while back and forth speaking words that are emerging from a mouth like slaves or criminals branded by a chisel... *81.3.9*
—now this is cooking with fire!— *81.3.10*
the husk of the initial protective bud casing—the sepal—but not really the true inner flower of *81.3.11*
debating—speaking words that are emerging from a mouth like slaves or criminals branded by a chisel while surrounded by more chisels on each side;[577] *81.3.12*

> "debating—speaking words that are emerging from a mouth like slaves or criminals branded by a chisel while surrounded by more chisels on each side..." *81.4.13*
> —now this is cooking with fire!— *81.4.14*
> the husk of the initial protective bud casing—the sepal—but not really the true inner flower of *81.4.15*
> "virtue—such as offering up a ram's head while back and forth speaking words that are emerging from a mouth like slaves or criminals branded by a chisel." *81.4.16*

Firing arrows from the mouth, sure... *81.5.17*
—now this is cooking with fire!— *81.5.18*
the husk of the initial protective bud casing—the sepal—but not really the true inner flower of *81.5.19*
widely winning like ten times scattered—a courtesy name a man takes, when the moon is covered by a weapon on a pole, that's as small as that an inch-sized spot where you measure the radial artery pulse in your wrist... *81.5.20*

> "widely winning like ten times scattered—a courtesy name a man takes, when the moon is covered by a weapon on a pole, that's as small as that an inch-sized spot where you measure the radial artery pulse in your wrist..." *81.6.21*
> —now this is cooking with fire!— *81.6.22*
> "the husk of the initial protective bud casing—the sepal—but not really the true inner flower of *81.6.23*
> firing arrows from the mouth, sure."[578] *81.6.24*

[577] From Chapter 45.
[578] From 46, 46, 71, and 78.

A grounded sage—listening and speaking, standing connected to earth as well as the heavens, *81.7.25*
that person... *81.7.26*
the husk of the initial protective bud casing—the sepal—but not really the true inner flower of *81.7.27*
storing and accumulating—amassing grain plants like cowry-riches under a thorn tree:[579] *81.7.28*

'done'—as de facto as a kneeling person turning away after eating a bowl of rice, done,[580] *81.8.29*
this carries like a plough—carries the meaning of, *81.8.30*
efforting—like lifting up an elephant— *81.8.31*
that person... *81.8.32*
binding oneself with a silk rope *81.8.33*
more and even more—like someone gathering themselves together from three sides by moonlight over their heart-core after a blade cut off their foot as punishment and now they've recovered from that illness—[581] *81.8.34*
flesh-and-blood, meat-handling Being; *81.8.35*

"'done'—as de facto as a kneeling person turning away after eating a bowl of rice, done, *81.9.36*
this carries like a plough—carries the meaning of," *81.9.37*
supporting—offering to carry on one's shoulders— *81.9.38*
"that person... *81.9.39*
binding oneself with a silk rope *81.9.40*
more and even more—like someone gathering themselves together from three sides by moonlight over their heart-core after a blade cut off their foot as punishment and now they've recovered from that illness—" *81.9.41*
much more—like a double serving of meat.[582] *81.9.42*

---

[579] From Chapter 59.
[580] From Chapters 32, 35, and 52.
[581] From Chapter 5.
[582] From Chapters 5, 22, 44, 57, 63, 65, and 75.

"Heaven (that sky level above the human head) *81.10.43*
has this... *81.10.44*
The Way of the loose-haired headperson—walking a while, stopping a while, and speaking of it all..."[583] *81.10.45*
benefiting, like by reaping grain with a sharp-edged blade,[584] *81.10.46*
"and yet now, bearded... 81.10.47
the husk of the initial protective bud casing—the sepal—but not really the true inner flower of 81.10.48
being harmed, like speaking and tallying many lies within the house."[585] *81.10.49*

A grounded sage—listening and speaking, standing connected to earth as well as the heavens, *81.11.50*
that person *81.11.51*
has this... *81.11.52*
The Way of the loose-haired headperson—walking a while, stopping a while, and speaking of it all... *81.11.53*
efforting—like lifting up an elephant, *81.11.54*
and yet now, bearded, *81.11.55*
"the husk of the initial protective bud casing—the sepal—but not really the true inner flower of 81.11.56
contending—two hands clawing over a ploughshare."[586] *81.11.57.*

[583] This phrase is from Chapter 77.
[584] From Chapters 8, 11, 19, 36, 53, 56, 57, and 73.
[585] This phrase is from Chapter 35. The final character also appears in Chapters 56, 66, and 73.
[586] From Chapters 3, 8, 22, 66, 68, and 73. The second character ("contending") also appears on its own in Chapters 22 and 66.

INDEX

Spot in the text	Modern Chinese	Pinyin
38.1.1	上	shàng
38.1.2	德	dé
38.1.3	不	bù
38.1.4	德	dé
38.2.5	是	shì
38.2.6	以	yǐ
38.2.7	有	yǒu
38.2.8	德	dé
38.3.9	下	xià
38.3.10	德	dé
38.3.11	不	bù
38.3.12	失	shī
38.3.13	德	dé
38.4.14	是	shì
38.4.15	以	yǐ
38.4.16	無	wú
38.4.17	德	dé
38.5.18	上	shàng
38.5.19	德	dé
38.5.20	無	wú
38.5.21	為	wéi
38.5.22	而	ér
38.5.23	無	wú
38.5.24	不	bù
38.5.25	為	wéi
38.6.26	下	xià
38.6.27	德	dé
38.6.28	為	wéi

38.6.29	之	zhī
38.6.30	而	ér
38.6.31	有	yǒu
38.6.32	以	yǐ
38.6.33	為	wéi
38.7.34	上	shàng
38.7.35	仁	rén
38.7.36	為	wéi
38.7.37	之	zhī
38.7.38	而	ér
38.7.39	無	wú
38.7.40	以	yǐ
38.7.41	為	wéi
38.8.42	上	shàng
38.8.43	義	yì
38.8.44	為	wéi
38.8.45	之	zhī
38.8.46	而	ér
38.8.47	有	yǒu
38.8.48	以	yǐ
38.8.49	為	wéi
38.9.50	上	shàng
38.9.51	禮	lǐ
38.9.52	為	wéi
38.9.53	之	zhī
38.9.54	而	ér
38.9.55	莫	mò
38.9.56	之	zhī
38.9.57	應	yīng
38.10.58	則	zé
38.10.59	攘	râng
38.10.60	臂	bì
38.10.61	而	ér
38.10.62	扔	réng
38.10.63	之	zhī

38.11.64	故	gù
38.11.65	失	shī
38.11.66	道	dào
38.11.67	而	ér
38.11.68	後	hòu
38.11.69	德	dé
38.12.70	失	shī
38.12.71	德	dé
38.12.72	而	ér
38.12.73	後	hòu
38.12.74	仁	rén
38.13.75	失	shī
38.13.76	仁	rén
38.13.77	而	ér
38.13.78	後	hòu
38.13.79	義	yì
38.14.80	失	shī
38.14.81	義	yì
38.14.82	而	ér
38.14.83	後	hòu
38.14.84	禮	lĭ
38.15.85	夫	fú
38.15.86	禮	lĭ
38.15.87	者	zhê
38.15.88	忠	zhōng
38.15.89	信	xìn
38.15.90	之	zhī
38.15.91	薄	bó
38.16.92	而	ér
38.16.93	亂	luàn
38.16.94	之	zhī
38.16.95	首	shǒu
38.17.96	前	qián
38.17.97	識	shí
38.17.98	者	zhê

38.17.99	道	dào
38.17.100	之	zhī
38.17.101	華	huá
38.18.102	而	ér
38.18.103	愚	yú
38.18.104	之	zhī
38.18.105	始	shǐ
38.19.106	是	shì
38.19.107	以	yǐ
38.19.108	大	dà
38.19.109	丈	zhàng
38.19.110	夫	fú
38.20.111	處	chù
38.20.112	其	qí
38.20.113	厚	hòu
38.21.114	不	bù
38.21.115	居	jū
38.21.116	其	qí
38.21.117	薄	bó
38.22.118	處	chù
38.22.119	其	qí
38.22.120	實	shí
38.23.121	不	bù
38.23.122	居	jū
38.23.123	其	qí
38.23.124	華	huá
38.24.125	故	gù
38.24.126	去	qù
38.24.127	彼	bǐ
38.24.128	取	qù
38.24.129	此	cǐ
39.1.1	昔	xī
39.1.2	之	zhī
39.1.3	得	dé
39.1.4	一	yī

39.1.5	者	zhê
39.2.6	天	tiān
39.2.7	得	dé
39.2.8	一	yī
39.2.9	以	yǐ
39.2.10	清	qīng
39.3.11	地	dì
39.3.12	得	dé
39.3.13	一	yī
39.3.14	以	yǐ
39.3.15	寧	níng
39.4.16	神	shén
39.4.17	得	dé
39.4.18	一	yī
39.4.19	以	yǐ
39.4.20	靈	líng
39.5.21	谷	gǔ
39.5.22	得	dé
39.5.23	一	yī
39.5.24	以	yǐ
39.5.25	盈	yíng
39.6.26	萬	wàn
39.6.27	物	wù
39.6.28	得	dé
39.6.29	一	yī
39.6.30	以	yǐ
39.6.31	生	shēng
39.7.32	侯	hóu
39.7.33	王	wáng
39.7.34	得	dé
39.7.35	一	yī
39.7.36	以	yǐ
39.7.37	為	wéi
39.7.38	天	tiān
39.7.39	下	xià

39.7.40	貞	zhēn
39.8.41	其	qī
39.8.42	致	zhì
39.8.43	之	zhí
39.9.44	天	tiān
39.9.45	無	wú
39.9.46	以	yǐ
39.9.47	清	qīng
39.9.48	將	jiāng
39.9.49	恐	kǒng
39.9.50	裂	liè
39.10.51	地	dì
39.10.52	無	wú
39.10.53	以	yǐ
39.10.54	寧	níng
39.10.55	將	jiāng
39.10.56	恐	kǒng
39.10.57	發	fā
39.11.58	神	shēn
39.11.59	無	wú
39.11.60	以	yǐ
39.11.61	靈	líng
39.11.62	將	jiāng
39.11.63	恐	kǒng
39.11.64	歇	xié
39.12.65	谷	gǔ
39.12.66	無	wú
39.12.67	以	yǐ
39.12.68	盈	yíng
39.12.69	將	jiāng
39.12.70	恐	kǒng
39.12.71	竭	jiē
39.13.72	萬	wàn
39.13.73	物	wù
39.13.74	無	wú

39.13.75	以	yǐ
39.13.76	生	shēng
39.13.77	將	jiāng
39.13.78	恐	kǒng
39.13.79	滅	miè
39.14.80	侯	hóu
39.14.81	王	wáng
39.14.82	無	wú
39.14.83	以	yǐ
39.14.84	貴	guì
39.14.85	高	gāo
39.14.86	將	jiāng
39.14.87	恐	kǒng
39.14.88	蹶	jué
39.15.89	故	gù
39.15.90	貴	guì
39.15.91	以	yǐ
39.15.92	賤	jiàn
39.15.93	為	wéi
39.15.94	本	bên
39.16.95	高	gāo
39.16.96	以	yǐ
39.16.97	下	xià
39.16.98	為	wéi
39.16.99	基	jī
39.17.100	是	shì
39.17.101	以	yǐ
39.17.102	侯	hóu
39.17.103	王	wáng
39.17.104	自	zì
39.17.105	謂	wèi
39.17.106	孤	gū
39.17.107	寡	guâ
39.17.108	不	bù
39.17.109	穀	gǔ

39.18.110	此	cǐ
39.18.111	非	fēi
39.18.112	以	yǐ
39.18.113	賤	jiàn
39.18.114	為	wéi
39.18.115	本	bên
39.18.116	邪	yé
39.19.117	非	fēi
39.19.118	乎	hū
39.20.119	故	gù
39.20.120	致	zhì
39.20.121	數	shǔ
39.20.122	譽	yù
39.20.123	無	wú
39.20.124	譽	yù
39.21.125	不	bù
39.21.126	欲	yù
39.21.127	琭	lù
39.21.128	琭	lù
39.21.129	如	rú
39.21.130	玉	yù
39.22.131	珞	luò
39.22.132	珞	luò
39.22.133	如	rú
39.22.134	石	shí
40.1.1	反	fân
40.1.2	者	zhê
40.1.3	道	dào
40.1.4	之	zhī
40.1.5	動	dòng
40.2.6	弱	ruò
40.2.7	者	zhê
40.2.8	道	dào
40.2.9	之	zhī
40.2.10	用	yòng

40.3.11	天	tiān
40.3.12	下	xià
40.3.13	萬	wàn
40.3.14	物	wù
40.3.15	生	shēng
40.3.16	於	yú
40.3.17	有	yǒu
40.4.18	有	yǒu
40.4.19	生	shēng
40.4.20	於	yú
40.4.21	無	wú
41.1.1	上	shàng
41.1.2	士	shì
41.1.3	聞	wén
41.1.4	道	dào
41.1.5	勤	qín
41.1.6	而	ér
41.1.7	行	xíng
41.1.8	之	zhī
41.2.9	中	zhōng
41.2.10	士	shì
41.2.11	聞	wén
41.2.12	道	dào
41.2.13	若	ruò
41.2.14	存	cún
41.2.15	若	ruò
41.2.16	亡	wáng
41.3.17	下	xià
41.3.18	士	shì
41.3.19	聞	wén
41.3.20	道	dào
41.3.21	大	dà
41.3.22	笑	xiào
41.3.23	之	zhī
41.4.24	不	bù

41.4.25 笑 xiào
41.4.26 不 bù
41.4.27 足 zú
41.4.28 以 yĭ
41.4.29 為 wéi
41.4.30 道 dào
41.5.31 故 gù
41.5.32 建 jiàn
41.5.33 言 yán
41.5.34 有 yŏu
41.5.35 之 zhī
41.6.36 明 míng
41.6.37 道 dào
41.6.38 若 ruò
41.6.39 昧 mèi
41.7.40 進 jìn
41.7.41 道 dào
41.7.42 若 ruò
41.7.43 退 tuì
41.8.44 夷 yí
41.8.45 道 dào
41.8.46 若 ruò
41.8.47 纇 lèi
41.9.48 上 shàng
41.9.49 德 dé
41.9.50 若 ruò
41.9.51 俗 sú
41.10.52 大 dà
41.10.53 白 bái
41.10.54 若 ruò
41.10.55 辱 rŭ
41.11.56 廣 guâng
41.11.57 德 dé
41.11.58 若 ruò
41.11.59 不 bù

41.11.60	足	zú
41.12.61	建	jiàn
41.12.62	德	dé
41.12.63	若	ruò
41.12.64	偷	tōu
41.13.65	質	zhì
41.13.66	真	zhēn
41.13.67	若	ruò
41.13.68	渝	yū
41.14.69	大	dà
41.14.70	方	fāng
41.14.71	無	wú
41.14.72	隅	yú
41.15.73	大	dà
41.15.74	器	qì
41.15.75	晚	wân
41.15.76	成	chéng
41.16.77	大	dà
41.16.78	音	yīn
41.16.79	希	xī
41.16.80	聲	shēng
41.17.81	大	dà
41.17.82	象	xiàng
41.17.83	無	wú
41.17.84	形	xíng
41.18.85	道	dào
41.18.86	隱	yīn
41.18.87	無	wú
41.18.88	名	míng
41.19.89	夫	fú
41.19.90	唯	wéi
41.19.91	道	dào
41.19.92	善	shàn
41.19.93	貸	dài
41.19.94	且	qiê

41.19.95	成	chéng
42.1.1	道	dào
42.1.2	生	shēng
42.1.3	一	yī
42.2.4	一	yī
42.2.5	生	shēng
42.2.6	二	èr
42.3.7	二	èr
42.3.8	生	shēng
42.3.9	三	sān
42.4.10	三	sān
42.4.11	生	shēng
42.4.12	萬	wàn
42.4.13	物	wù
42.5.14	萬	wàn
42.5.15	物	wù
42.5.16	負	fù
42.5.17	陰	yīn
42.5.18	而	ér
42.5.19	抱	bào
42.5.20	陽	yáng
42.6.21	沖	chōng
42.6.22	氣	qì
42.6.23	以	yǐ
42.6.24	為	wéi
42.6.25	和	hé
42.7.26	人	rén
42.7.27	之	zhī
42.7.28	所	suǒ
42.7.29	惡	wù
42.8.30	唯	wéi
42.8.31	孤	gū
42.8.32	寡	guâ
42.8.33	不	bù
42.8.34	轂	gǔ

42.9.35	而	ér
42.9.36	王	wáng
42.9.37	公	gōng
42.9.38	以	yǐ
42.9.39	為	wéi
42.9.40	稱	chēng
42.10.41	故	gù
42.10.42	物	wù
42.10.43	或	huò
42.10.44	損	sǔn
42.10.45	之	zhī
42.10.46	而	ér
42.10.47	益	yì
42.11.48	或	huò
42.11.49	益	yì
42.11.50	之	zhī
42.11.51	而	ér
42.11.52	損	sǔn
42.12.53	人	rén
42.12.54	之	zhī
42.12.55	所	suǒ
42.12.56	教	jiào
42.13.57	我	wǒ
42.13.58	亦	yì
42.13.59	教	jiào
42.13.60	之	zhī
42.14.61	強	qiáng
42.14.62	梁	liáng
42.14.63	者	zhê
42.14.64	不	bù
42.14.65	得	dé
42.14.66	其	qí
42.14.67	死	sǐ
42.15.68	吾	wǔ
42.15.69	將	jiāng

42.15.70 以 yǐ
42.15.71 為 wéi
42.15.72 教 jiào
42.15.73 父 fǔ
43.1.1 天 tiān
43.1.2 下 xià
43.1.3 之 zhī
43.1.4 至 zhì
43.1.5 柔 róu
43.2.6 馳 chī
43.2.7 騁 chêng
43.2.8 天 tiān
43.2.9 下 xià
43.2.10 之 zhī
43.2.11 至 zhì
43.2.12 堅 jiān
43.3.13 無 wú
43.3.14 有 yǒu
43.3.15 入 rù
43.3.16 無 wú
43.3.17 間 jiān
43.4.18 吾 wǔ
43.4.18 是 shì
43.4.20 以 yǐ
43.4.21 知 zhī
43.4.22 無 wú
43.4.23 為 wéi
43.4.24 之 zhī
43.4.25 有 yǒu
43.4.26 益 yì
43.5.27 不 bù
43.5.28 言 yán
43.5.29 之 zhī
43.5.30 教 jiào
43.6.31 無 wú

43.6.32	為	wéi
43.6.33	之	zhī
43.6.34	益	yì
43.7.35	天	tiān
43.7.36	下	xià
43.7.37	希	xī
43.7.38	及	jí
43.7.39	之	zhī
44.1.1	名	míng
44.1.2	與	yǔ
44.1.3	身	shēn
44.1.4	孰	shú
44.1.5	親	qīn
44.2.6	身	shēn
44.2.7	與	yǔ
44.2.8	貨	huò
44.2.9	孰	shú
44.2.10	多	duō
44.3.11	得	dé
44.3.12	與	yǔ
44.3.13	亡	wáng
44.3.14	孰	shú
44.3.15	病	bìng
44.4.16	是	shì
44.4.17	故	gù
44.4.18	甚	shèn
44.4.19	愛	ài
44.4.20	必	bì
44.4.21	大	dà
44.4.22	費	fèi
44.5.23	多	duō
44.5.24	藏	cáng
44.5.25	必	bì
44.5.26	厚	hòu
44.5.27	亡	wáng

44.6.28	知	zhī
44.6.29	足	zú
44.6.30	不	bù
44.6.31	辱	rǔ
44.7.32	知	zhī
44.7.33	止	zhǐ
44.7.34	不	bù
44.7.35	殆	dài
44.8.36	可	kê
44.8.37	以	yǐ
44.8.38	長	cháng
44.8.39	久	jiǔ
45.1.1	大	dà
45.1.2	成	chéng
45.1.3	若	ruò
45.1.4	缺	quē
45.2.5	其	qí
45.2.6	用	yòng
45.2.7	不	bù
45.2.8	弊	bì
45.3.9	大	dà
45.3.10	盈	yí
45.3.11	若	ruò
45.3.12	沖	chōng
45.4.13	其	qí
45.4.14	用	yòng
45.4.15	不	bù
45.4.16	窮	qióng
45.5.17	大	dà
45.5.18	直	zhí
45.5.19	若	ruò
45.5.20	屈	qū
45.6.21	大	dà
45.6.22	巧	qiâo
45.6.23	若	ruò

45.6.24	拙	zhuō
45.7.25	大	dà
45.7.26	辯	biàn
45.7.27	若	ruò
45.7.28	訥	nè
45.8.29	躁	zào
45.8.30	勝	shèng
45.8.31	寒	hán
45.9.32	靜	jìng
45.9.33	勝	shèng
45.9.34	熱	rè
45.10.35	清	qīng
45.10.36	靜	jìng
45.10.37	為	wéi
45.10.38	天	tiān
45.10.39	下	xià
45.10.40	正	zhèng
46.1.1	天	tiān
46.1.2	下	xià
46.1.3	有	yǒu
46.1.4	道	dào
46.1.5	卻	què
46.1.6	走	zǒu
46.1.7	馬	mâ
46.1.8	以	yǐ
46.1.9	糞	fèn
46.2.10	天	tiān
46.2.11	下	xià
46.2.12	無	wú
46.2.13	道	dào
46.2.14	戎	róng
46.2.15	馬	mâ
46.2.16	生	shēng
46.2.17	於	yú
46.2.18	郊	jiāo

46.3.19 罪 zuì
46.3.20 莫 mò
46.3.21 大 dà
46.3.22 於 yú
46.3.23 可 kê
46.3.24 欲 yù
46.4.25 禍 huò
46.4.26 莫 mò
46.4.27 大 dà
46.4.28 於 yú
46.4.29 不 bù
46.4.30 知 zhī
46.4.31 足 zú
46.5.32 咎 jiŭ
46.5.33 莫 mò
46.5.34 大 dà
46.5.35 於 yú
46.5.36 欲 yù
46.5.37 得 dé
46.6.38 故 gù
46.6.39 知 zhī
46.6.40 足 zú
46.6.41 之 zhī
46.6.42 足 zú
46.7.43 常 cháng
46.7.44 足 zú
46.7.45 矣 yĭ
47.1.1 不 bù
47.1.2 出 chū
47.1.3 戶 hù
47.1.4 知 zhī
47.1.5 天 tiān
47.1.6 下 xià
47.2.7 不 bù
47.2.8 闚 kuī

47.2.9 牖 yǒu
47.2.10 見 jiàn
47.2.11 天 tiān
47.2.12 道 dào
47.3.13 其 qí
47.3.14 出 chū
47.3.15 彌 mí
47.3.16 遠 yuân
47.4.17 其 qí
47.4.18 知 zhī
47.4.19 彌 mí
47.4.20 少 shâo
47.5.21 是 shì
47.5.22 以 yǐ
47.5.23 聖 shèng
47.5.24 人 rén
47.5.25 不 bù
47.5.26 行 xíng
47.5.27 而 ér
47.5.28 知 zhī
47.6.29 不 bù
47.6.30 見 jiàn
47.6.31 而 ér
47.6.32 名 míng
47.7.33 不 bù
47.7.34 為 wéi
47.7.35 而 ér
47.7.36 成 chéng
48.1.1 為 wéi
48.1.2 學 xué
48.1.3 日 rì
48.1.4 益 yì
48.2.5 為 wéi
48.2.6 道 dào
48.2.7 日 rì

48.2.8	損	sǔn
48.3.9	損	sǔn
48.3.10	之	zhī
48.3.11	又	yòu
48.3.12	損	sǔn
48.4.13	以	yǐ
48.4.14	至	zhì
48.4.15	於	yú
48.4.16	無	wú
48.4.17	為	wéi
48.5.18	無	wú
48.5.19	為	wéi
48.5.20	而	ér
48.5.21	無	wú
48.5.22	不	bù
48.5.23	為	wéi
48.6.24	取	qǔ
48.6.25	天	tiān
48.6.26	下	xià
48.6.27	常	cháng
48.6.28	以	yǐ
48.6.29	無	wú
48.6.30	事	shì
48.7.31	及	jí
48.7.32	其	qí
48.7.33	有	yǒu
48.7.34	事	shì
48.8.35	不	bù
48.8.36	足	zú
48.8.37	以	yǐ
48.8.38	取	qǔ
48.8.39	天	tiān
48.8.40	下	xià
49.1.1	聖	shèng
49.1.2	人	rén

49.1.3	無	wú
49.1.4	常	cháng
49.1.5	心	xīn
49.2.6	以	yǐ
49.2.7	百	bâi
49.2.8	姓	xìng
49.2.9	心	xīn
49.2.10	為	wéi
49.2.11	心	xīn
49.3.12	善	shàn
49.3.13	者	zhê
49.3.14	吾	wú
49.3.15	善	shàn
49.3.16	之	zhī
49.4.17	不	bù
49.4.18	善	shàn
49.4.19	者	zhê
49.4.20	吾	wú
49.4.21	亦	yì
49.4.22	善	shàn
49.4.23	之	zhī
49.5.24	德	dé
49.5.25	善	shàn
49.6.26	信	xìn
49.6.27	者	zhê
49.6.28	吾	wú
49.6.29	信	xìn
49.6.30	之	zhī
49.7.31	不	bù
49.7.32	信	xìn
49.7.33	者	zhê
49.7.34	吾	wú
49.7.35	亦	yì
49.7.36	信	xìn
49.7.37	之	zhī

49.8.38	德	dé
49.8.39	信	xìn
49.9.40	聖	shèng
49.9.41	人	rén
49.9.42	在	zài
49.9.43	天	tiān
49.9.44	下	xià
49.10.45	歙	xī
49.10.46	歙	xī
49.10.47	焉	yān
49.10.48	為	wéi
49.10.49	天	tiān
49.10.50	下	xià
49.11.51	渾	hún
49.11.52	其	qí
49.11.53	心	xīn
49.12.54	百	bâi
49.12.55	姓	xìng
49.12.56	皆	jiē
49.12.57	注	zhù
49.12.58	其	qí
49.12.59	耳	êr
49.12.60	目	mù
49.13.61	聖	shèng
49.13.62	人	rén
49.13.63	皆	jiē
49.13.64	孩	hái
49.13.65	之	zhī
50.1.1	出	chū
50.1.2	生	shēng
50.1.3	入	rù
50.1.4	死	sǐ
50.2.5	生	shēng
50.2.6	之	zhī
50.2.7	徒	tú

50.2.8	十	shí
50.2.9	有	yǒu
50.2.10	三	sān
50.3.11	死	sǐ
50.3.12	之	zhī
50.3.13	徒	tú
50.3.14	十	shí
50.3.15	有	yǒu
50.3.16	三	sān
50.4.17	人	rén
50.4.18	之	zhī
50.4.19	生	shēng
50.4.20	動	dòng
50.4.21	之	zhī
50.4.22	死	sǐ
50.4.23	地	dì
50.5.24	亦	yì
50.5.25	十	shí
50.5.26	有	yǒu
50.5.27	三	sān
50.6.28	夫	fú
50.6.29	何	hé
50.6.30	故	gù
50.7.31	以	yǐ
50.7.32	其	qí
50.7.33	生	shēng
50.7.34	生	shēng
50.7.35	之	zhī
50.7.36	厚	hòu
50.8.37	蓋	gài
50.8.38	聞	wén
50.8.39	善	shàn
50.8.40	攝	shè
50.8.41	生	shēng
50.8.42	者	zhê

50.9.43	陸	lù
50.9.44	行	xíng
50.9.45	不	bù
50.9.46	遇	yù
50.9.47	兕	sì
50.9.48	虎	hǔ
50.10.49	入	rù
50.10.50	軍	jūn
50.10.51	不	bù
50.10.52	被	bèi
50.10.53	甲	jiâ
50.10.54	兵	bīng
50.11.55	兕	sì
50.11.56	無	wú
50.11.57	所	suǒ
50.11.58	投	tóu
50.11.59	其	qí
50.11.60	角	jiâo
50.12.61	虎	hǔ
50.12.62	無	wú
50.12.63	所	suǒ
50.12.64	措	cuò
50.12.65	其	qí
50.12.66	爪	zhâo
50.13.67	兵	bīng
50.13.68	無	wú
50.13.69	所	suǒ
50.13.70	容	róng
50.13.71	其	qí
50.13.72	刃	rèn
50.14.73	夫	fú
50.14.74	何	hé
50.14.75	故	gù
50.15.76	以	yǐ
50.15.77	其	qí

50.15.78	無	wú
50.15.79	死	sǐ
50.15.80	地	dì
51.1.1	道	dào
51.1.2	生	shēng
51.1.3	之	zhī
51.2.4	德	dé
51.2.5	畜	xù
51.2.6	之	zhī
51.3.7	物	wù
51.3.8	形	xíng
51.3.9	之	zhī
51.4.10	勢	shì
51.4.11	成	chéng
51.4.12	之	zhī
51.5.13	是	shì
51.5.14	以	yǐ
51.5.15	萬	wàn
51.5.16	物	wù
51.5.17	莫	mò
51.6.18	不	bù
51.6.19	尊	zūn
51.6.20	道	dào
51.6.21	而	ér
51.6.22	貴	guì
51.6.23	德	dé
51.7.24	道	dào
51.7.25	之	zhī
51.7.26	尊	zūn
51.8.27	德	dé
51.8.28	之	zhī
51.8.29	貴	guì
51.9.30	夫	fú
51.9.31	莫	mò
51.9.32	之	zhī

51.9.33 命 mìng
51.9.34 而 ér
51.9.35 常 cháng
51.9.36 自 zì
51.9.37 然 rán
51.10.38 故 gù
51.10.39 道 dào
51.10.40 生 shēng
51.10.41 之 zhī
51.11.42 德 dé
51.11.43 畜 xù
51.11.44 之 zhī
51.12.45 長 zháng
51.12.46 之 zhī
51.12.47 育 yù
51.12.48 之 zhī
51.13.49 亭 tíng
51.13.50 之 zhī
51.13.51 毒 dú
51.13.52 之 zhī
51.14.53 養 yâng
51.14.54 之 zhī
51.14.55 覆 fù
51.14.56 之 zhī
51.15.57 生 shēng
51.15.58 而 ér
51.15.59 不 bù
51.15.60 有 yǒu
51.16.61 為 wéi
51.16.62 而 ér
51.16.63 不 bù
51.16.64 恃 shì
51.17.65 長 zháng
51.17.66 而 ér
51.17.67 不 bù

51.17.68	宰	zâi
51.18.69	是	shì
51.18.70	謂	wèi
51.18.71	玄	xuán
51.18.72	德	dé
52.1.1	天	tiān
52.1.2	下	xià
52.1.3	有	yǒu
52.1.4	始	shǐ
52.2.5	以	yǐ
52.2.6	為	wéi
52.2.7	天	tiān
52.2.8	下	xià
52.2.9	母	mǔ
52.3.10	既	jì
52.3.11	得	dé
52.3.12	其	qí
52.3.13	母	mǔ
52.3.14	以	yǐ
52.3.15	知	zhī
52.3.16	其	qí
52.3.17	子	zī
52.4.18	既	jì
52.4.19	知	zhī
52.4.20	其	qí
52.4.21	子	zī
52.4.22	復	fù
52.4.23	守	shǒu
52.4.24	其	qí
52.4.25	母	mǔ
52.4.26	沒	mò
52.4.27	身	shēn
52.4.28	不	bù
52.4.29	殆	dài
52.5.30	塞	sāi

52.5.31	其	qí
52.5.32	兌	duì
52.6.33	閉	bì
52.6.34	其	qí
52.6.35	門	mén
52.7.36	終	zhōng
52.7.37	身	shēn
52.7.38	不	bù
52.7.39	勤	qín
52.8.40	開	kāi
52.8.41	其	qí
52.8.42	兌	duì
52.9.43	濟	jì
52.9.44	其	qí
52.9.45	事	shì
52.10.46	終	zhōng
52.10.47	身	shēn
52.10.48	不	bù
52.10.49	救	jiù
52.11.50	見	jiàn
52.11.51	小	xiâo
52.11.52	曰	yuē
52.11.53	明	míng
52.12.54	守	shǒu
52.12.55	柔	róu
52.12.56	曰	yuē
52.12.57	強	qiáng
52.13.58	用	yòng
52.13.59	其	qí
52.13.60	光	guāng
52.13.61	復	fù
52.13.62	歸	guī
52.13.63	其	qí
52.13.64	明	míng
52.14.65	無	wú

52.14.66	遺	yí
52.14.67	身	shēn
52.14.68	殃	yáng
52.15.69	是	shì
52.15.70	為	wéi
52.15.71	習	xí
52.15.72	常	cháng
53.1.1	使	shǐ
53.1.2	我	wǒ
53.1.3	介	jiè
53.1.4	然	rán
53.1.5	有	yǒu
53.1.6	知	zhī
53.2.7	行	xíng
53.2.8	於	yú
53.2.9	大	dà
53.2.10	道	dào
53.3.11	唯	wéi
53.3.12	施	shī
53.3.13	是	shì
53.3.14	畏	wèi
53.4.15	大	dà
53.4.16	道	dào
53.4.17	甚	shèn
53.4.18	夷	yí
53.5.19	而	ér
53.5.20	民	mín
53.5.21	好	hâo
53.5.22	徑	jìng
53.6.23	朝	cháo
53.6.24	甚	shèn
53.6.25	除	chú
53.7.26	田	tián
53.7.27	甚	shèn
53.7.28	蕪	wú

53.8.29	倉	cāng
53.8.30	甚	shèn
53.8.31	虛	xū
53.9.32	服	fú
53.9.33	文	wén
53.9.34	綵	câi
53.10.35	帶	dài
53.10.36	利	lì
53.10.37	劍	jiàn
53.11.38	厭	yàn
53.11.39	飲	yǐn
53.11.40	食	shí
53.12.41	財	cái
53.12.42	貨	huò
53.12.43	有	yǒu
53.12.44	餘	yú
53.13.45	是	shì
53.13.46	謂	wèi
53.13.47	盜	dào
53.13.48	夸	kuā
53.14.49	非	fēi
53.14.50	道	dào
53.14.51	也	yê
53.14.52	哉	zāi
54.1.1	善	shàn
54.1.2	建	jiàn
54.1.3	者	zhê
54.1.4	不	bù
54.1.5	拔	bá
54.2.6	善	shàn
54.2.7	抱	bào
54.2.8	者	zhê
54.2.9	不	bù
54.2.10	脫	tuō
54.3.11	子	zī

54.3.12	孫	sūn
54.3.13	以	yǐ
54.3.14	祭	jì
54.3.15	祀	sì
54.3.16	不	bù
54.3.17	輟	chuò
54.4.18	修	xiū
54.4.19	之	zhī
54.4.20	於	yú
54.4.21	身	shēn
54.4.22	其	qí
54.4.23	德	dé
54.4.24	乃	nâi
54.4.25	真	zhēn
54.5.26	修	xiū
54.5.27	之	zhī
54.5.28	於	yú
54.5.29	家	jiā
54.5.30	其	qí
54.5.31	德	dé
54.5.32	乃	nâi
54.5.33	餘	yú
54.6.34	修	xiū
54.6.35	之	zhī
54.6.36	於	yú
54.6.37	鄉	xiāng
54.6.38	其	qí
54.6.39	德	dé
54.6.40	乃	nâi
54.6.41	長	cháng
54.7.42	修	xiū
54.7.43	之	zhī
54.7.44	於	yú
54.7.45	國	guó
54.7.46	其	qí

54.7.47	德	dé
54.7.48	乃	nâi
54.7.49	豐	fēng
54.8.50	修	xiū
54.8.51	之	zhī
54.8.52	於	yú
54.8.53	天	tiān
54.8.54	下	xià
54.8.55	其	qí
54.8.56	德	dé
54.8.57	乃	nâi
54.8.58	普	pǔ
54.9.59	故	gù
54.9.60	以	yǐ
54.9.61	身	shēn
54.9.62	觀	guān
54.9.63	身	shēn
54.10.64	以	yǐ
54.10.65	家	jiā
54.10.66	觀	guān
54.10.67	家	jiā
54.11.68	以	yǐ
54.11.69	鄉	xiāng
54.11.70	觀	guān
54.11.71	鄉	xiāng
54.12.72	以	yǐ
54.12.73	國	guó
54.12.74	觀	guān
54.12.75	國	guó
54.13.76	以	yǐ
54.13.77	天	tiān
54.13.78	下	xià
54.13.79	觀	guān
54.13.80	天	tiān
54.13.81	下	xià

54.14.82	吾	wú
54.14.83	何	hé
54.14.84	以	yǐ
54.14.85	知	zhī
54.14.86	天	tiān
54.14.87	下	xià
54.14.88	然	rán
54.14.89	哉	zāi
54.15.90	以	yǐ
54.15.91	此	cǐ
55.1.1	含	hán
55.1.2	德	dé
55.1.3	之	zhī
55.1.4	厚	hòu
55.2.5	比	bǐ
55.2.6	於	yú
55.2.7	赤	chì
55.2.8	子	zī
55.3.9	蜂	féng
55.3.10	蠆	chài
55.3.11	虺	huǐ
55.3.12	蛇	shé
55.3.13	不	bù
55.3.14	螫	shì
55.4.15	猛	mêng
55.4.16	獸	shòu
55.4.17	不	bù
55.4.18	據	jù
55.4.19	攫	juē
55.4.20	鳥	niâo
55.4.21	不	bù
55.4.22	搏	bó
55.5.23	骨	gǔ
55.5.24	弱	ruò
55.5.25	筋	jīn

55.5.26	柔	róu
55.5.27	而	ér
55.5.28	握	wò
55.5.29	固	gù
55.6.30	未	wèi
55.6.31	知	zhī
55.6.32	牝	pìn
55.6.33	牡	mǔ
55.6.34	之	zhī
55.6.35	合	hé
55.6.36	而	ér
55.6.37	全	quán
55.6.38	作	zuò
55.7.39	精	jīng
55.7.40	之	zhī
55.7.41	至	zhì
55.7.42	也	yê
55.8.43	終	zhōng
55.8.44	日	rì
55.8.45	號	háo
55.8.46	而	ér
55.8.47	不	bù
55.8.48	嗄	shà
55.9.49	和	hé
55.9.50	之	zhī
55.9.51	至	zhì
55.9.52	也	yê
55.10.53	知	zhī
55.10.54	和	hé
55.10.55	曰	yuē
55.10.56	常	cháng
55.11.57	知	zhī
55.11.58	常	cháng
55.11.59	曰	yuē
55.11.60	明	míng

55.12.61 益 yì
55.12.62 生 shēng
55.12.63 曰 yuē
55.12.64 祥 xiáng
55.13.65 心 xīn
55.13.66 使 shǐ
55.13.67 氣 qì
55.13.68 曰 yuē
55.13.69 強 qiáng
55.14.70 物 wù
55.14.71 壯 zhuàng
55.14.72 則 zé
55.14.73 老 lâo
55.15.74 謂 wèi
55.15.75 之 zhī
55.15.76 不 bù
55.15.77 道 dào
55.16.78 不 bù
55.16.79 道 dào
55.16.80 早 zâo
55.16.81 已 yǐ
56.1.1. 知 zhī
56.1.2 者 zhê
56.1.3 不 bù
56.1.4 言 yán
56.1.5 言 yán
56.1.6 者 zhê
56.1.7 不 bù
56.1.8 知 zhī
56.2.9 塞 sāi
56.2.10 其 qí
56.2.11 兌 duì
56.3.12 閉 bì
56.3.13 其 qí
56.3.14 門 mén

56.4.15	挫	cuó
56.4.16	其	qí
56.4.17	銳	ruì
56.5.18	解	jiê
56.5.19	其	qí
56.5.20	紛	fēn
56.6.21	和	hé
56.6.22	其	qí
56.6.23	光	guāng
56.7.24	同	tóng
56.7.25	其	qí
56.7.26	塵	chén
56.8.27	是	shì
56.8.28	謂	wèi
56.8.29	玄	xuán
56.8.30	同	tóng
56.9.31	故	gù
56.9.32	不	bù
56.9.33	可	kê
56.9.34	得	dé
56.9.35	而	ér
56.9.36	親	qīn
56.10.37	不	bù
56.10.38	可	kê
56.10.39	得	dé
56.10.40	而	ér
56.10.41	疏	shū
56.11.42	不	bù
56.11.43	可	kê
56.11.44	得	dé
56.11.45	而	ér
56.11.46	利	lì
56.12.47	不	bù
56.12.48	可	kê
56.12.49	得	dé

56.12.50	而	ér
56.12.51	害	hài
56.13.52	不	bù
56.13.53	可	kê
56.13.54	得	dé
56.13.55	而	ér
56.13.56	貴	guì
56.14.57	不	bù
56.14.58	可	kê
56.14.59	得	dé
56.14.60	而	ér
56.14.61	賤	jiàn
56.15.62	故	gù
56.15.63	為	wéi
56.15.64	天	tiān
56.15.65	下	xià
56.15.66	貴	guì
57.1.1	以	yǐ
57.1.2	正	zhèng
57.1.3	治	zhì
57.1.4	國	guó
57.2.5	以	yǐ
57.2.6	奇	qí
57.2.7	用	yòng
57.2.8	兵	bīng
57.3.9	以	yǐ
57.3.10	無	wú
57.3.11	事	shì
57.3.12	取	qù
57.3.13	天	tiān
57.3.14	下	xià
57.4.15	吾	wú
57.4.16	何	hé
57.4.17	以	yǐ
57.4.18	知	zhī

57.4.19	其	qí
57.4.20	然	rán
57.4.21	哉	zāi
57.5.22	以	yǐ
57.5.23	此	cǐ
57.6.24	天	tiān
57.6.25	下	xià
57.6.26	多	duō
57.6.27	忌	jì
57.6.28	諱	huì
57.6.29	而	ér
57.6.30	民	mín
57.6.31	彌	mí
57.6.32	貧	pín
57.7.33	民	mín
57.7.34	多	duō
57.7.35	利	lì
57.7.36	器	qì
57.7.37	國	guó
57.7.38	家	jiā
57.7.39	滋	zī
57.7.40	昏	hūn
57.8.41	人	rén
57.8.42	多	duō
57.8.43	伎	jì
57.8.44	巧	qiâo
57.8.45	奇	qí
57.8.46	物	wù
57.8.47	泫	zí
57.8.48	起	qǐ
57.9.49	法	fâ
57.9.50	令	lìng
57.9.51	滋	zī
57.9.52	彰	zhāng
57.9.53	盜	dào

57.9.54 賊 zéi
57.9.55 多 duō
57.9.56 有 yǒu
57.10.57 故 gù
57.10.58 聖 shèng
57.10.59 人 rén
57.10.60 云 yún
57.11.61 我 wǒ
57.11.62 無 wú
57.11.63 為 wéi
57.11.64 而 ér
57.11.65 民 mín
57.11.66 自 zì
57.11.67 化 huà
57.12.68 我 wǒ
57.12.69 好 hâo
57.12.70 靜 jìng
57.12.71 而 ér
57.12.72 民 mín
57.12.73 自 zì
57.12.74 正 zhèng
57.13.75 我 wǒ
57.13.76 無 wú
57.13.77 事 shì
57.13.78 而 ér
57.13.79 民 mín
57.13.80 自 zì
57.13.81 富 fù
57.14.82 我 wǒ
57.14.83 無 wú
57.14.84 欲 yù
57.14.85 而 ér
57.14.86 民 mín
57.14.87 自 zì
57.14.88 樸 pǔ

58.1.1	其	qí
58.1.2	政	zhèng
58.1.3	悶	mèn
58.1.4	悶	mèn
58.2.5	其	qí
58.2.6	民	mín
58.2.7	淳	chún
58.2.8	淳	chún
58.3.9	其	qí
58.3.10	政	zhèng
58.3.11	察	chá
58.3.12	察	chá
58.4.13	其	qí
58.4.14	民	mín
58.4.15	缺	quē
58.4.16	缺	quē
58.5.17	禍	huò
58.5.18	兮	xī
58.5.19	福	fú
58.5.20	之	zhī
58.5.21	所	suǒ
58.5.22	倚	yǐ
58.6.23	福	fú
58.6.24	兮	xī
58.6.25	禍	huò
58.6.26	之	zhī
58.6.27	所	suǒ
58.6.28	伏	fú
58.7.29	孰	shú
58.7.30	知	zhī
58.7.31	其	qí
58.7.32	極	jí
58.8.33	其	qí
58.8.34	無	wú
58.8.35	正	zhèng

58.9.36	正	zhèng
58.9.37	復	fù
58.9.38	為	wéi
58.9.39	奇	qí
58.10.40	善	shàn
58.10.41	復	fù
58.10.42	為	wéi
58.10.43	妖	yāo
58.11.44	人	rén
58.11.45	之	zhī
58.11.46	迷	mí
58.12.47	其	qí
58.12.48	日	rì
58.12.49	固	gù
58.12.50	久	jiǔ
58.13.51	是	shì
58.13.52	以	yǐ
58.13.53	聖	shèng
58.13.54	人	rén
58.14.55	方	fāng
58.14.56	而	ér
58.14.57	不	bù
58.14.58	割	gē
58.15.59	廉	lián
58.15.60	而	ér
58.15.61	不	bù
58.15.62	劌	guì
58.16.63	直	zhí
58.16.64	而	ér
58.16.65	不	bù
58.16.66	肆	sì
58.17.67	光	guāng
58.17.68	而	ér
58.17.69	不	bù
58.17.70	燿	yào

59.1.1 治 zhì
59.1.2 人 rén
59.1.3 事 shì
59.1.4 天 tiān
59.1.5 莫 mò
59.1.6 若 ruò
59.1.7 嗇 sè
59.2.8 夫 fú
59.2.9 唯 wéi
59.2.10 嗇 sè
59.2.11 是 shì
59.2.12 謂 wèi
59.2.13 早 zâo
59.2.14 服 fú
59.3.15 早 zâo
59.3.16 服 fú
59.3.17 謂 wèi
59.3.18 之 zhī
59.3.19 重 zhòng
59.3.20 積 jī
59.3.21 德 dé
59.4.22 重 zhòng
59.4.23 積 jī
59.4.24 德 dé
59.4.25 則 zé
59.4.26 無 wú
59.4.27 不 bù
59.4.28 克 kè
59.5.29 無 wú
59.5.30 不 bù
59.5.31 克 kè
59.5.32 則 zé
59.5.33 莫 mò
59.5.34 知 zhī
59.5.35 其 qí

59.5.36	極	jí
59.6.37	莫	mò
59.6.38	知	zhī
59.6.39	其	qí
59.6.40	極	jí
59.6.41	可	kê
59.6.42	以	yĭ
59.6.43	有	yǒu
59.6.44	國	guó
59.7.45	有	yǒu
59.7.46	國	guó
59.7.47	之	zhī
59.7.48	母	mǔ
59.7.49	可	kê
59.7.50	以	yĭ
59.7.51	長	cháng
59.7.52	久	jiŭ
59.8.53	是	shì
59.8.54	謂	wèi
59.8.55	深	shēn
59.8.56	根	gēn
59.8.57	固	gù
59.8.58	柢	dĭ
59.9.59	長	cháng
59.9.60	生	shēng
59.9.61	久	jiŭ
59.9.62	視	shì
59.9.63	之	zhī
59.9.64	道	dào
60.1.1	治	zhì
60.1.2	大	dà
60.1.3	國	guó
60.1.4	若	ruò
60.1.5	烹	pēng
60.1.6	小	xiâo

60.1.7	鮮	xiān
60.2.8	以	yĭ
60.2.9	道	dào
60.2.10	蒞	lì
60.2.11	天	tiān
60.2.12	下	xià
60.3.13	其	qí
60.3.14	鬼	guĭ
60.3.15	不	bù
60.3.16	神	shén
60.4.17	非	fēi
60.4.18	其	qí
60.4.19	鬼	guĭ
60.4.20	不	bù
60.4.21	神	shēn
60.5.22	其	qí
60.5.23	神	shén
60.5.24	不	bù
60.5.25	傷	shāng
60.5.26	人	rén
60.6.27	非	fēi
60.6.28	其	qí
60.6.29	神	shén
60.6.30	不	bù
60.6.31	傷	shāng
60.6.32	人	rén
60.7.33	聖	shèng
60.7.34	人	rén
60.7.35	亦	yì
60.7.36	不	bù
60.7.37	傷	shāng
60.7.38	人	rén
60.8.39	夫	fú
60.8.40	兩	liâng
60.8.41	不	bù

60.8.42	相	xiāng
60.8.43	傷	shāng
60.9.44	故	gù
60.9.45	德	dé
60.9.46	交	jiāo
60.9.47	歸	guī
60.9.48	焉	yān
61.1.1	大	dà
61.1.2	國	guó
61.1.3	者	zhê
61.1.4	下	xià
61.1.5	流	liú
61.2.6	天	tiān
61.2.7	下	xià
61.2.8	之	zhī
61.2.9	交	jiāo
61.3.10	天	tiān
61.3.11	下	xià
61.3.12	之	zhī
61.3.13	牝	pìn
61.4.14	牝	pìn
61.4.15	常	cháng
61.4.16	以	yĭ
61.4.17	靜	jìng
61.4.18	勝	shèng
61.4.19	牡	mŭ
61.5.20	以	yĭ
61.5.21	靜	jìng
61.5.22	為	wéi
61.5.23	下	xià
61.6.24	故	gù
61.6.25	大	dà
61.6.26	國	guó
61.6.27	以	yĭ
61.6.28	下	xià

61.6.29	小	xiâo
61.6.30	國	guó
61.7.31	則	zé
61.7.32	取	qù
61.7.33	小	xiâo
61.7.34	國	guó
61.8.35	小	xiâo
61.8.36	國	guó
61.8.37	以	yǐ
61.8.38	下	xià
61.8.39	大	dà
61.8.40	國	guó
61.9.41	則	zé
61.9.42	取	qù
61.9.43	大	dà
61.9.44	國	guó
61.10.45	故	gù
61.10.46	或	huò
61.10.47	下	xià
61.10.48	以	yǐ
61.10.49	取	qù
61.11.50	或	huò
61.11.51	下	xià
61.11.52	而	ér
61.11.53	取	qù
61.12.54	大	dà
61.12.55	國	guó
61.12.56	不	bù
61.12.57	過	guò
61.12.58	欲	yù
61.12.59	兼	jiān
61.12.60	畜	chù
61.12.61	人	rén
61.13.62	小	xiâo
61.13.63	國	guó

61.13.64	不	bù
61.13.65	過	guò
61.13.66	欲	yù
61.13.67	入	rù
61.13.68	事	shì
61.13.69	人	rén
61.14.70	夫	fú
61.14.71	兩	liâng
61.14.72	者	zhê
61.14.73	各	gè
61.14.74	得	dé
61.14.75	其	qí
61.14.76	所	suǒ
61.14.77	欲	yù
61.15.78	大	dà
61.15.79	者	zhê
61.15.80	宜	yí
61.15.81	為	wéi
61.15.82	下	xià
62.1.1	道	dào
62.1.2	者	zhê
62.1.3	萬	wàn
62.1.4	物	wù
62.1.5	之	zhī
62.1.6	奧	ào
62.2.7	善	shàn
62.2.8	人	rén
62.2.9	之	zhī
62.2.10	寶	bâo
62.3.11	不	bù
62.3.12	善	shàn
62.3.13	人	rén
62.3.14	之	zhī
62.3.15	所	suǒ
62.3.16	保	bâo

62.4.17	美	mêi
62.4.18	言	yán
62.4.19	可	kê
62.4.20	以	yǐ
62.4.21	市	shì
62.5.22	尊	zūn
62.5.23	行	xíng
62.5.24	可	kê
62.5.25	以	yǐ
62.5.26	加	jiā
62.5.27	人	rén
62.6.28	人	rén
62.6.29	之	zhī
62.6.30	不	bù
62.6.31	善	shàn
62.7.32	何	hé
62.7.33	棄	qì
62.7.34	之	zhī
62.7.35	有	yǒu
62.8.36	故	gù
62.8.37	立	lì
62.8.38	天	tiān
62.8.39	子	zī
62.9.40	置	zhì
62.9.41	三	sān
62.9.42	公	gōng
62.10.43	雖	suī
62.10.44	有	yǒu
62.10.45	拱	gǒng
62.10.46	璧	bì
62.11.47	以	yǐ
62.11.48	先	xiān
62.11.49	駟	sì
62.11.50	馬	mâ
62.12.51	不	bù

62.12.52	如	rú
62.12.53	坐	zuò
62.12.54	進	jìn
62.12.55	此	cǐ
62.12.56	道	dào
62.13.57	古	gǔ
62.13.58	之	zhī
62.13.59	所	suǒ
62.13.60	以	yǐ
62.13.61	貴	guì
62.13.62	此	cǐ
62.13.63	道	dào
62.13.64	者	zhê
62.13.65	何	hé
62.14.66	不	bù
62.14.67	曰	yuē
62.15.68	求	qiú
62.15.69	以	yǐ
62.15.70	得	dé
62.16.71	有	yǒu
62.16.72	罪	zuì
62.16.73	以	yǐ
62.16.74	免	miàn
62.16.75	邪	yé
62.17.76	故	gù
62.17.77	為	wéi
62.17.78	天	tiān
62.17.79	下	xià
62.17.80	貴	guì
63.1.1	為	wéi
63.1.2	無	wú
63.1.3	為	wéi
63.2.4	事	shì
63.2.5	無	wú
63.2.6	事	shì

63.3.7 味 wèi
63.3.8 無 wú
63.3.9 味 wèi
63.4.10 大 dà
63.4.11 小 xiâo
63.4.12 多 duō
63.4.13 少 shâo
63.5.14 報 bào
63.5.15 怨 yuàn
63.5.16 以 yĭ
63.5.17 德 dé
63.6.18 圖 tú
63.6.19 難 nán
63.6.20 於 yú
63.6.21 其 qí
63.6.22 易 yì
63.7.23 為 wéi
63.7.24 大 dà
63.7.25 於 yú
63.7.26 其 qí
63.7.27 細 xì
63.8.28 天 tiān
63.8.29 下 xià
63.8.30 難 nán
63.8.31 事 shì
63.9.32 必 bì
63.9.33 作 zuò
63.9.34 於 yú
63.9.35 易 yì
63.10.36 天 tiān
63.10.37 下 xià
63.10.38 大 dà
63.10.39 事 shì
63.11.40 必 bì
63.11.41 作 zuò

63.11.42	於	yú
63.11.43	細	xì
63.12.44	是	shì
63.12.45	以	yǐ
63.12.46	聖	shèng
63.12.47	人	rén
63.12.48	終	zhōng
63.12.49	不	bù
63.12.50	為	wéi
63.12.51	大	dà
63.13.52	故	gù
63.13.53	能	néng
63.13.54	成	chéng
63.13.55	其	qí
63.13.56	大	dà
63.14.57	夫	fú
63.14.58	輕	qīng
63.14.59	諾	nuò
63.14.60	必	bì
63.14.61	寡	guâ
63.14.62	信	xìn
63.15.63	多	duō
63.15.64	易	yì
63.15.65	必	bì
63.15.66	多	duō
63.15.67	難	nán
63.16.68	是	shì
63.16.69	以	yǐ
63.16.70	聖	shèng
63.16.71	人	rén
63.16.72	猶	yóu
63.16.73	難	nán
63.16.74	之	zhī
63.17.75	故	gù
63.17.76	終	zhōng

63.17.77	無	wú
63.17.78	難	nán
63.17.79	矣	yĭ
64.1.1	其	qí
64.1.2	妄	ān
64.1.3	易	yì
64.1.4	持	chí =
64.2.5	其	qí
64.2.6	未	wèi
64.2.7	兆	zhâo
64.2.8	易	yì
64.2.9	謀	móu
64.3.10	其	qí
64.3.11	脆	cuì
64.3.12	易	yì
64.3.13	泮	pàn
64.4.14	其	qí
64.4.15	微	wēi
64.4.16	易	yì
64.4.17	散	sàn
64.5.18	為	wéi
64.5.19	之	zhī
64.5.20	於	yú
64.5.21	未	wèi
64.5.22	有	yǒu
64.6.23	治	zhì
64.6.24	之	zhī
64.6.25	於	yú
64.6.26	未	wèi
64.6.27	亂	luàn
64.7.28	合	hé
64.7.29	抱	bào
64.7.30	之	zhī
64.7.31	木	mù
64.8.32	生	shēng

64.8.33	於	yú
64.8.34	毫	háo
64.8.35	末	mò
64.9.36	九	jiǔ
64.9.37	層	céng
64.9.38	之	zhī
64.9.39	台	tái
64.10.40	起	qǐ
64.10.41	於	yú
64.10.42	累	lêi
64.10.43	土	tǔ
64.11.44	千	qiān
64.11.45	里	lǐ
64.11.46	之	zhī
64.11.47	行	xíng
64.12.48	始	shǐ
64.12.49	於	yú
64.12.50	足	zú
64.12.51	下	xià
64.13.52	為	wéi
64.13.53	者	zhê
64.13.54	敗	bài
64.13.55	之	zhī
64.14.56	執	zhí
64.14.57	者	zhê
64.14.58	失	shī
64.14.59	之	zhī
64.15.60	是	shì
64.15.61	以	yǐ
64.15.62	聖	shèng
64.15.63	人	rén
64.15.64	無	wú
64.15.65	為	wéi
64.15.66	故	gù
64.15.67	無	wú

64.15.68	敗	bài
64.16.69	無	wú
64.16.70	執	zhí
64.16.71	故	gù
64.16.72	無	wú
64.16.73	失	shī
64.17.74	民	mín
64.17.75	之	zhī
64.17.76	從	cóng
64.17.77	事	shì
64.17.78	常	cháng
64.17.79	於	yú
64.17.80	幾	jĭ
64.17.81	成	chéng
64.17.82	而	ér
64.17.83	敗	bài
64.17.84	之	zhī
64.18.85	慎	shèn
64.18.86	終	zhōng
64.18.87	如	rú
64.18.88	始	shĭ
64.19.89	則	zé
64.19.90	無	wú
64.19.91	敗	bài
64.19.92	事	shì
64.20.93	是	shì
64.20.94	以	yĭ
64.20.95	聖	shèng
64.20.96	人	rén
64.20.97	欲	yù
64.20.98	不	bù
64.20.99	欲	yù
64.20.100	不	bù
64.20.101	貴	guì
64.20.102	難	nán

64.20.103	得	dé
64.20.104	之	zhī
64.20.105	貨	huò
64.21.106	學	xué
64.21.107	不	bù
64.21.108	學	xué
64.21.109	復	fù
64.21.110	眾	zhòng
64.21.111	人	rén
64.21.112	之	zhī
64.21.113	所	suǒ
64.21.114	過	guò
64.22.115	以	yǐ
64.22.116	輔	fǔ
64.22.117	萬	wàn
64.22.118	物	wù
64.22.119	之	zhí
64.22.120	自	zì
64.22.121	然	rán
64.22.122	而	ér
64.22.123	不	bù
64.22.124	敢	gân
64.22.125	為	wéi
65.1.1	古	gǔ
65.1.2	之	zhī
65.1.3	善	shàn
65.1.4	為	wéi
65.1.5	道	dào
65.1.6	者	zhê
65.2.7	非	fēi
65.2.8	以	yǐ
65.2.9	明	míng
65.2.10	民	mín
65.3.11	將	jiāng
65.3.12	以	yǐ

65.3.13	愚	yú
65.3.14	之	zhī
65.4.15	民	mín
65.4.16	之	zhī
65.4.17	難	nán
65.4.18	治	zhì
65.5.19	以	yǐ
65.5.20	其	qí
65.5.21	智	zhì
65.5.22	多	duō
65.6.23	故	gù
65.6.24	以	yǐ
65.6.25	智	zhì
65.6.26	治	zhì
65.6.27	國	guó
65.7.28	國	guó
65.7.29	之	zhī
65.7.30	賊	zéi
65.8.31	不	bù
65.8.32	以	yǐ
65.8.33	智	zhì
65.8.34	治	zhì
65.8.35	國	guó
65.9.36	國	guó
65.9.37	之	zhī
65.9.38	福	fú
65.10.39	知	zhī
65.10.40	此	cǐ
65.10.41	兩	liâng
65.10.42	者	zhê
65.11.43	亦	yì
65.11.44	稽	jī
65.11.45	式	shì
65.12.46	常	cháng
65.12.47	知	zhī

65.12.48	稽	jī
65.12.49	式	shì
65.13.50	是	shì
65.13.51	謂	wèi
65.13.52	玄	xuán
65.13.53	德	dé
65.14.54	玄	xuán
65.14.55	德	dé
65.14.56	深	shēn
65.14.57	矣	yǐ
65.14.58	遠	yuân
65.14.59	矣	yǐ
65.15.60	與	yǔ
65.15.61	物	wù
65.15.62	反	fân
65.15.63	矣	yǐ
65.16.64	然	rán
65.16.65	後	hòu
65.16.66	乃	nâi
65.16.67	至	zhì
65.16.68	大	dà
65.16.69	順	shùn
66.1.1	江	jiāng
66.1.2	海	hâi
66.1.3	所	suǒ
66.1.4	以	yǐ
66.1.5	能	néng
66.1.6	為	wéi
66.1.7	百	bâi
66.1.8	谷	gǔ
66.1.9	王	wáng
66.1.10	者	zhê
66.2.11	以	yǐ
66.2.12	其	qí
66.2.13	善	shàn

66.2.14 下 xià
66.2.15 之 zhī
66.3.16 故 gù
66.3.17 能 néng
66.3.18 為 wéi
66.3.19 百 bâi
66.3.20 谷 gŭ
66.3.21 王 wáng
66.4.22 是 shì
66.4.23 以 yĭ
66.4.24 聖 shèng
66.4.25 人 rén
66.4.26 欲 yù
66.4.27 上 shàng
66.4.28 民 mín
66.4.29 必 bì
66.4.30 以 yĭ
66.4.31 言 yán
66.4.32 下 xià
66.4.33 之 zhī
66.5.34 欲 yù
66.5.35 先 xiān
66.5.36 民 mín
66.5.37 必 bì
66.5.38 以 yĭ
66.5.39 身 shēn
66.5.40 後 hòu
66.5.41 之 zhī
66.6.42 是 shì
66.6.43 以 yĭ
66.6.44 聖 shèng
66.6.45 人 rén
66.6.46 處 chù
66.6.47 上 shàng
66.6.48 而 ér

66.6.49	民	mín
66.6.50	不	bù
66.6.51	重	zhòng
66.7.52	處	chù
66.7.53	前	qián
66.7.54	而	ér
66.7.55	民	mín
66.7.56	不	bù
66.7.57	害	hài
66.8.58	是	shì
66.8.59	以	yǐ
66.8.60	天	tiān
66.8.61	下	xià
66.8.62	樂	lè
66.8.63	推	tuī
66.8.64	而	ér
66.8.65	不	bù
66.8.66	厭	yàn
66.9.67	以	yǐ
66.9.68	其	qí
66.9.69	不	bù
66.9.70	爭	zhēng
66.10.71	故	gù
66.10.72	天	tiān
66.10.73	下	xià
66.10.74	莫	mò
66.10.75	能	néng
66.10.76	與	yǔ
66.10.77	之	zhī
66.10.78	爭	zhēng
67.1.1	天	tiān
67.1.2	下	xià
67.1.3	皆	jiē
67.1.4	謂	wèi
67.1.5	我	wǒ

67.1.6	道	dào
67.1.7	大	dà
67.2.8	似	sì
67.2.9	不	bù
67.2.10	肖	xiào
67.3.11	夫	fú
67.3.12	唯	wéi
67.3.13	大	dà
67.4.14	故	gù
67.4.15	似	sì
67.4.16	不	bù
67.4.17	肖	xiào
67.5.18	若	ruò
67.5.19	肖	xiào
67.6.20	久	jiǔ
67.6.21	矣	yǐ
67.7.22	其	qí
67.7.23	細	xì
67.7.24	也	yê
67.7.25	夫	fú
67.8.26	我	wǒ
67.8.27	有	yǒu
67.8.28	三	sān
67.8.29	寶	bâo
67.9.30	持	chí =
67.9.31	而	ér
67.9.32	保	bâo
67.9.33	之	zhī
67.10.34	一	yī
67.10.35	曰	yuē
67.10.36	慈	cí
67.11.37	二	èr
67.11.38	曰	yuē
67.11.39	儉	jiân
67.12.40	三	sān

67.12.41	曰	yuē
67.12.42	不	bù
67.12.43	敢	gân
67.12.44	為	wéi
67.12.45	天	tiān
67.12.46	下	xià
67.12.47	先	xiān
67.13.48	慈	cí
67.13.49	故	gù
67.13.50	能	néng
67.13.51	勇	yǒng
67.14.52	儉	jiân
67.14.53	故	gù
67.14.54	能	néng
67.14.55	廣	guâng
67.15.56	不	bù
67.15.57	敢	gân
67.15.58	為	wéi
67.15.59	天	tiān
67.15.60	下	xià
67.15.61	先	xiān
67.15.62	故	gù
67.15.63	能	néng
67.15.64	成	chéng
67.15.65	器	qì
67.15.66	長	cháng
67.16.67	今	jīn
67.16.68	舍	shê
67.16.69	慈	cí
67.16.70	且	qiê
67.16.71	勇	yǒng
67.17.72	舍	shê
67.17.73	儉	jiân
67.17.74	且	qiê
67.17.75	廣	guâng

67.18.76	舍	shê
67.18.77	後	hòu
67.18.78	且	qiê
67.18.79	先	xiān
67.19.80	死	sǐ
67.19.81	矣	yǐ
67.20.82	夫	fú
67.20.83	慈	cí
67.20.84	以	yǐ
67.20.85	戰	zhàn
67.20.86	則	zé
67.20.87	勝	shèng
67.21.88	以	yǐ
67.21.89	守	shǒu
67.21.90	則	zé
67.21.91	固	gù
67.22.92	天	tiān
67.22.93	將	jiāng
67.22.94	救	jiù
67.22.95	之	zhī
67.23.96	以	yǐ
67.23.97	慈	cí
67.23.98	衛	wèi
67.23.99	之	zhī
68.1.1	善	shàn
68.1.2	為	wéi
68.1.3	士	shì
68.1.4	者	zhê
68.1.5	不	bù
68.1.6	武	wǔ
68.2.7	善	shàn
68.2.8	戰	zhàn
68.2.9	者	zhê
68.2.10	不	bù
68.2.11	怒	nù

68.3.12	善	shàn
68.3.13	勝	shèng
68.3.14	敵	dí
68.3.15	者	zhê
68.3.16	不	bù
68.3.17	與	yǔ
68.4.18	善	shàn
68.4.19	用	yòng
68.4.20	人	rén
68.4.21	者	zhê
68.4.22	為	wéi
68.4.23	之	zhī
68.4.24	下	xià
68.5.25	是	shì
68.5.26	謂	wèi
68.5.27	不	bù
68.5.28	爭	zhēng
68.5.29	之	zhī
68.5.30	德	dé
68.6.31	是	shì
68.6.32	謂	wèi
68.6.33	用	yòng
68.6.34	人	rén
68.6.35	之	zhī
68.6.36	力	lì
68.7.37	是	shì
68.7.38	謂	wèi
68.7.39	配	pèi
68.7.40	天	tiān
68.8.41	古	gǔ
68.8.42	之	zhī
68.8.43	極	jí
69.1.1	用	yòng
69.1.2	兵	bīng
69.1.3	有	yǒu

69.1.4	言	yán
69.2.5	吾	wú
69.2.6	不	bù
69.2.7	敢	gân
69.2.8	為	wéi
69.2.9	主	zhŭ
69.3.10	而	ér
69.3.11	為	wéi
69.3.12	客	kè
69.4.13	不	bù
69.4.14	敢	gân
69.4.15	進	jìn
69.4.16	寸	cùn
69.5.17	而	ér
69.5.18	退	tuì
69.5.19	尺	chĭ
69.6.20	是	shì
69.6.21	謂	wèi
69.6.22	行	xíng
69.6.23	無	wú
69.6.24	行	xíng
69.7.25	攘	râng
69.7.26	無	wú
69.7.27	臂	bì
69.8.28	扔	réng
69.8.29	無	wú
69.8.30	敵	dí
69.9.31	執	zhí
69.9.32	無	wú
69.9.33	兵	bīng
69.10.34	禍	huò
69.10.35	莫	mò
69.10.36	大	dà
69.10.37	於	yú
69.10.38	輕	qīng

69.10.39	敵	dí
69.11.40	輕	qīng
69.11.41	敵	dí
69.11.42	幾	jĭ
69.11.43	喪	sāng
69.11.44	吾	wú
69.11.45	寶	bâo
69.12.46	故	gù
69.12.47	抗	kàng
69.12.48	兵	bīng
69.12.49	相	xiāng
69.12.50	加	jiā
69.13.51	哀	āi
69.13.52	者	zhê
69.13.53	勝	shèng
69.13.54	矣	yĭ
70.1.1	吾	wú
70.1.2	言	yán
70.1.3	甚	shèn
70.1.4	易	yì
70.1.5	知	zhī
70.2.6	甚	shèn
70.2.7	易	yì
70.2.8	行	xíng
70.3.9	天	tiān
70.3.10	下	xià
70.3.11	莫	mò
70.3.12	能	néng
70.3.13	知	zhī
70.4.14	莫	mò
70.4.15	能	néng
70.4.16	行	xíng
70.5.17	言	yán
70.5.18	有	yŏu
70.5.19	宗	zōng

70.6.20 事 shì
70.6.21 有 yǒu
70.6.22 君 jūn
70.7.23 夫 fú
70.7.24 唯 wéi
70.7.25 無 wú
70.7.26 知 zhī
70.8.27 是 shì
70.8.28 以 yǐ
70.8.29 我 wǒ
70.8.30 不 bù
70.8.31 知 zhī
70.9.32 知 zhī
70.9.33 我 wǒ
70.9.34 者 zhê
70.9.35 希 xī
70.10.36 則 zé
70.10.37 我 wǒ
70.10.38 者 zhê
70.10.39 貴 guì
70.11.40 是 shì
70.11.41 以 yǐ
70.11.42 聖 shèng
70.11.43 人 rén
70.11.44 被 bèi
70.11.45 褐 hè
70.12.46 懷 huái
70.12.47 玉 yù
71.1.1 知 zhī
71.1.2 不 bù
71.1.3 知 zhī
71.1.4 上 shàng
71.2.5 不 bù
71.2.6 知 zhī
71.2.7 不 bù

71.2.8	知	zhī
71.2.9	病	bìng
71.3.10	夫	fú
71.3.11	唯	wéi
71.3.12	病	bìng
71.3.13	病	bìng
71.4.14	是	shì
71.4.15	以	yǐ
71.4.16	不	bù
71.4.17	病	bìng
71.5.18	聖	shèng
71.5.19	人	rén
71.5.20	不	bù
71.5.21	病	bìng
71.6.22	以	yǐ
71.6.23	其	qí
71.6.24	病	bìng
71.6.25	病	bìng
71.7.26	是	shì
71.7.27	以	yǐ
71.7.28	不	bù
71.7.29	病	bìng
72.1.1	民	mín
72.1.2	不	bù
72.1.3	畏	wèi
72.1.4	威	wēi
72.2.5	則	zé
72.2.6	大	dà
72.2.7	威	wēi
72.2.8	上	shàng
72.2.9	至	zhì
72.3.10	無	wú
72.3.11	狎	xiá
72.3.12	其	qí
72.3.13	所	suǒ

72.3.14	居	jū
72.4.15	無	wú
72.4.16	厭	yàn
72.4.17	其	qí
72.4.18	所	suǒ
72.4.19	生	shēng
72.5.20	夫	fú
72.5.21	不	bù
72.5.22	唯	wéi
72.5.23	厭	yàn
72.6.24	是	shì
72.6.25	以	yǐ
72.6.26	不	bù
72.6.27	厭	yàn
72.7.28	是	shì
72.7.29	以	yǐ
72.7.30	聖	shèng
72.7.31	人	rén
72.7.32	自	zì
72.7.33	知	zhī
72.8.34	不	bù
72.8.35	自	zì
72.8.36	見	jiàn
72.9.37	自	zì
72.9.38	愛	ài
72.10.39	不	bù
72.10.40	自	zì
72.10.41	貴	guì
72.11.42	故	gù
72.11.43	去	qù
72.11.44	彼	bǐ
72.11.45	取	qù
72.11.46	此	cǐ
73.1.1	勇	yǒng
73.1.2	於	yú

73.1.3	敢	gân
73.1.4	則	zé
73.1.5	殺	shā
73.2.6	勇	yǒng
73.2.7	於	yú
73.2.8	不	bù
73.2.9	敢	gân
73.2.10	則	zé
73.2.11	活	huó
73.3.12	此	cǐ
73.3.13	兩	liâng
73.3.14	者	zhê
73.3.15	或	huò
73.3.16	利	lì
73.3.17	或	huò
73.3.18	害	hài
73.4.19	天	tiān
73.4.20	之	zhī
73.4.21	所	suǒ
73.4.22	惡	wù
73.5.23	孰	shú
73.5.24	知	zhī
73.5.25	其	qí
73.5.26	故	gù
73.6.27	是	shì
73.6.28	以	yǐ
73.6.29	聖	shèng
73.6.30	人	rén
73.6.31	猶	yóu
73.6.32	難	nán
73.6.33	之	zhī
73.7.34	天	tiān
73.7.35	之	zhī
73.7.36	道	dào
73.7.37	不	bù

73.7.38	爭	zhēng
73.7.39	而	ér
73.7.40	善	shàn
73.7.41	勝	shèng
73.8.42	不	bù
73.8.43	言	yán
73.8.44	而	ér
73.8.45	善	shàn
73.8.46	應	yīng
73.9.47	不	bù
73.9.48	召	zhāo
73.9.49	而	ér
73.9.50	自	zì
73.9.51	來	lái
73.10.52	繟	chân
73.10.53	然	rán
73.10.54	而	ér
73.10.55	善	shàn
73.10.56	謀	móu
73.11.57	天	tiān
73.11.58	網	wâng
73.11.59	恢	huī
73.11.60	恢	huī
73.12.61	疏	shū
73.12.62	而	ér
73.12.63	不	bù
73.12.64	失	shī
74.1.1	民	mín
74.1.2	不	bù
74.1.3	畏	wèi
74.1.4	死	sǐ
74.2.5	奈	nài
74.2.6	何	hé
74.2.7	以	yǐ
74.2.8	死	sǐ

74.2.9	懼	jù
74.2.10	之	zhī
74.3.11	若	ruò
74.3.12	使	shǐ
74.3.13	民	mín
74.3.14	常	cháng
74.3.15	畏	wèi
74.3.16	死	sǐ
74.4.17	而	ér
74.4.18	為	wéi
74.4.19	奇	qí
74.4.20	者	zhê
74.5.21	吾	wú
74.5.22	得	dé
74.5.23	執	zhí
74.5.24	而	ér
74.5.25	殺	shā
74.5.26	之	zhī
74.6.27	孰	shú
74.6.28	敢	gân
74.7.29	常	cháng
74.7.30	有	yǒu
74.7.31	司	sī
74.7.32	殺	shā
74.7.33	者	zhê
74.7.34	殺	shā
74.8.35	夫	fú
74.8.36	代	dài
74.8.37	司	sī
74.8.38	殺	shā
74.8.39	者	zhê
74.8.40	殺	shā
74.9.41	是	shì
74.9.42	謂	wèi
74.9.43	代	dài

74.9.44	大	dà
74.9.45	匠	jiàng
74.9.46	斲	zhuō
74.10.47	夫	fú
74.10.48	代	dài
74.10.49	大	dà
74.10.50	匠	jiàng
74.10.51	斲	zhuō
74.10.52	者	zhê
74.11.53	希	xī
74.11.54	有	yǒu
74.11.55	不	bù
74.11.56	傷	shāng
74.11.57	其	qí
74.11.58	手	shǒu
74.11.59	矣	yǐ
75.1.1	民	mín
75.1.2	之	zhī
75.1.3	饑	jī
75.2.4	以	yǐ
75.2.5	其	qí
75.2.6	上	shàng
75.2.7	食	shí
75.2.8	稅	shuì
75.2.9	之	zhī
75.2.10	多	duō
75.3.11	是	shì
75.3.12	以	yǐ
75.3.13	饑	jī
75.4.14	民	mín
75.4.15	之	zhī
75.4.16	難	nán
75.4.17	治	zhì
75.5.18	以	yǐ
75.5.19	其	qí

75.5.20	上	shàng
75.5.21	之	zhī
75.5.22	有	yǒu
75.5.23	為	wéi
75.6.24	是	shì
75.6.25	以	yǐ
75.6.26	難	nán
75.6.27	治	zhì
75.7.28	民	mín
75.7.29	之	zhī
75.7.30	輕	qīng
75.7.31	死	sǐ
75.8.32	以	yǐ
75.8.33	其	qí
75.8.34	上	shàng
75.8.35	求	qiú
75.8.36	生	shēng
75.8.37	之	zhī
75.8.38	厚	hòu
75.9.39	是	shì
75.9.40	以	yǐ
75.9.41	輕	qīng
75.9.42	死	sǐ
75.10.43	夫	fú
75.10.44	唯	wéi
75.10.45	無	wú
75.10.46	以	yǐ
75.10.47	生	shēng
75.10.48	為	wéi
75.10.49	者	zhê
75.11.50	是	shì
75.11.51	賢	xián
75.11.52	於	yú
75.11.53	貴	guì
75.11.54	生	shēng

76.1.1	人	rén
76.1.2	之	zhī
76.1.3	生	shēng
76.1.4	也	yê
76.1.5	柔	róu
76.1.6	弱	ruò
76.2.7	其	qí
76.2.8	死	sĭ
76.2.9	也	yê
76.2.10	堅	jiān
76.2.11	強	qiáng
76.3.12	萬	wàn
76.3.13	物	wù
76.3.14	草	câo
76.3.15	木	mù
76.3.16	之	zhī
76.3.17	生	shēng
76.3.18	也	yê
76.3.19	柔	róu
76.3.20	脆	cuì
76.4.21	其	qí
76.4.22	死	sĭ
76.4.23	也	yê
76.4.24	枯	kū
76.4.25	槁	gâo
76.5.26	故	gù
76.5.27	堅	jiān
76.5.28	強	qiáng
76.5.29	者	zhê
76.5.30	死	sĭ
76.5.31	之	zhī
76.5.32	徒	tú
76.6.33	柔	róu
76.6.34	弱	ruò
76.6.35	者	zhê

76.6.36	生	shēng
76.6.37	之	zhī
76.6.38	徒	tú
76.7.39	是	shì
76.7.40	以	yǐ
76.7.41	兵	bīng
76.7.42	強	qiáng
76.7.43	則	zé
76.7.44	不	bù
76.7.45	勝	shèng
76.8.46	木	mù
76.8.47	強	qiáng
76.8.48	則	zé
76.8.49	折	zhé
76.9.50	強	qiáng
76.9.51	大	dà
76.9.52	處	chù
76.9.53	下	xià
76.10.54	柔	róu
76.10.55	弱	ruò
76.10.56	處	chù
76.10.57	上	shàng
77.1.1	天	tiān
77.1.2	之	zhī
77.1.3	道	dào
77.2.4	其	qí
77.2.5	猶	yóu
77.2.6	張	zhāng
77.2.7	弓	gōng
77.2.8	與	yǔ
77.3.9	高	gāo
77.3.10	者	zhê
77.3.11	抑	yì
77.3.12	之	zhī
77.4.13	下	xià

77.4.14	者	zhê
77.4.15	舉	jǔ
77.4.16	之	zhī
77.5.17	有	yǒu
77.5.18	餘	yú
77.5.19	者	zhê
77.5.20	損	sǔn
77.5.21	之	zhī
77.6.22	不	bù
77.6.23	足	zú
77.6.24	者	zhê
77.6.25	補	bǔ
77.6.26	之	zhī
77.7.27	天	tiān
77.7.28	之	zhī
77.7.29	道	dào
77.7.30	損	sǔn
77.7.31	有	yǒu
77.7.32	餘	yú
77.8.33	而	ér
77.8.34	補	bǔ
77.8.35	不	bù
77.8.36	足	zú
77.9.37	人	rén
77.9.38	之	zhī
77.9.39	道	dào
77.9.40	則	zé
77.9.41	不	bù
77.9.42	然	rán
77.10.43	損	sǔn
77.10.44	不	bù
77.10.45	足	zú
77.10.46	以	yǐ
77.10.47	奉	fèng
77.10.48	有	yǒu

77.10.49	餘	yú
77.11.50	孰	shú
77.11.51	能	néng
77.11.52	有	yǒu
77.11.53	餘	yú
77.11.54	以	yǐ
77.11.55	奉	fèng
77.11.56	天	tiān
77.11.57	下	xià
77.12.58	唯	wéi
77.12.59	有	yǒu
77.12.60	道	dào
77.12.61	者	zhê
77.13.62	是	shì
77.13.63	以	yǐ
77.13.64	聖	shèng
77.13.65	人	rén
77.13.66	為	wéi
77.13.67	而	ér
77.13.68	不	bù
77.13.69	恃	shì
77.14.70	功	gōng
77.14.71	成	chéng
77.14.72	而	ér
77.14.73	不	bù
77.14.74	處	chù
77.15.75	其	qí
77.15.76	不	bù
77.15.77	欲	yù
77.15.78	見	jiàn
77.15.79	賢	xián
78.1.1	天	tiān
78.1.2	下	xià
78.1.3	莫	mò
78.1.4	柔	róu

78.1.5	弱	ruò
78.1.6	於	yú
78.1.7	水	shuĭ
78.2.8	而	ér
78.2.9	攻	gōng
78.2.10	堅	jiān
78.2.11	強	qiáng
78.2.12	者	zhê
78.3.13	莫	mò
78.3.14	之	zhī
78.3.15	能	néng
78.3.16	勝	shèng
78.4.17	其	qí
78.4.18	無	wú
78.4.19	以	yĭ
78.4.20	易	yì
78.4.21	之	zhī
78.5.22	弱	ruò
78.5.23	之	zhī
78.5.24	勝	shèng
78.5.25	強	qiáng
78.6.26	柔	róu
78.6.27	之	zhī
78.6.28	勝	shèng
78.6.29	剛	gāng
78.7.30	天	tiān
78.7.31	下	xià
78.7.32	莫	mò
78.7.33	不	bù
78.7.34	知	zhī
78.8.35	莫	mò
78.8.36	能	néng
78.8.37	行	xíng
78.9.38	是	shì
78.9.39	以	yĭ

78.9.40	聖	shèng
78.9.41	人	rén
78.9.42	云	yún
78.10.43	受	shòu
78.10.44	國	guó
78.10.45	之	zhī
78.10.46	垢	gòu
78.11.47	是	shì
78.11.48	謂	wèi
78.11.49	社	shè
78.11.50	稷	jì
78.11.51	主	zhǔ
78.12.52	受	shòu
78.12.53	國	guó
78.12.54	不	bù
78.12.55	祥	xiáng
78.13.56	是	shì
78.13.57	謂	wèi
78.13.58	天	tiān
78.13.59	下	xià
78.13.60	王	wáng
78.14.61	正	zhèng
78.14.62	言	yán
78.14.63	若	ruò
78.14.64	反	fân
79.1.1	和	hé
79.1.2	大	dà
79.1.3	怨	yuàn
79.2.4	必	bì
79.2.5	有	yǒu
79.2.6	餘	yú
79.2.7	怨	yuàn
79.3.8	安	ān
79.3.9	可	kê
79.3.10	以	yǐ

79.3.11	為	wéi
79.3.12	善	shàn
79.4.13	是	shì
79.4.14	以	yĭ
79.4.15	聖	shèng
79.4.16	人	rén
79.4.17	執	zhí
79.4.18	佐	zuŏ
79.4.19	契	qì
79.5.20	而	ér
79.5.21	不	bù
79.5.22	責	zé
79.5.23	於	yú
79.5.24	人	rén
79.6.25	有	yŏu
79.6.26	德	dé
79.6.27	司	sī
79.6.28	契	qì
79.7.29	無	wú
79.7.30	德	dé
79.7.31	司	sī
79.7.32	徹	chè
79.8.33	天	tiān
79.8.34	道	dào
79.8.35	無	wú
79.8.36	親	qīn
79.9.37	常	cháng
79.9.38	與	yŭ
79.9.39	善	shàn
79.9.40	人	rén
80.1.1	小	xiâo
80.1.2	國	guó
80.1.3	寡	guâ
80.1.4	民	mín
80.2.5	使	shĭ

80.2.6	有	yǒu
80.2.7	什	shí
80.2.8	伯	bó
80.2.9	之	zhī
80.2.10	器	qì
80.3.11	而	ér
80.3.12	不	bù
80.3.13	用	yòng
80.4.14	使	shǐ
80.4.15	民	mín
80.4.16	重	zhòng
80.4.17	死	sǐ
80.5.18	而	ér
80.5.19	不	bù
80.5.20	遠	yuân
80.5.21	徙	xǐ
80.6.22	雖	suī
80.6.23	有	yǒu
80.6.24	舟	zhōu
80.6.25	輿	yú
80.7.26	無	wú
80.7.27	所	suǒ
80.7.28	乘	shèng
80.7.29	之	zhī
80.8.30	雖	suī
80.8.31	有	yǒu
80.8.32	甲	jiâ
80.8.33	兵	bīng
80.9.34	無	wú
80.9.35	所	suǒ
80.9.36	陳	chén
80.9.37	之	zhī
80.10.38	使	shǐ
80.10.39	民	mín
80.10.40	復	fù

80.10.41	結	jié
80.10.42	繩	shéng
80.11.43	而	ér
80.11.44	用	yòng
80.11.45	之	zhī
80.12.46	甘	gān
80.12.47	其	qí
80.12.48	食	shí
80.13.49	美	mêi
80.13.50	其	qí
80.13.51	服	fú
80.14.52	安	ān
80.14.53	其	qí
80.14.54	居	jū
80.15.55	樂	lè
80.15.56	其	qí
80.15.57	俗	sú
80.16.58	鄰	lín
80.16.59	國	guó
80.16.60	相	xiāng
80.16.61	望	wàng
80.17.62	雞	jī
80.17.63	犬	quân
80.17.64	之	zhī
80.17.65	聲	shēng
80.17.66	相	xiāng
80.17.67	聞	wén
80.18.68	民	mín
80.18.69	至	zhì
80.18.70	老	lâo
80.18.71	死	sĭ
80.19.72	不	bù
80.19.73	相	xiāng
80.19.74	往	wâng
80.19.75	來	lái

81.1.1	信	xìn
81.1.2	言	yán
81.1.3	不	bù
81.1.4	美	mêi
81.2.5	美	mêi
81.2.6	言	yán
81.2.7	不	bù
81.2.8	信	xìn
81.3.9	善	shàn
81.3.10	者	zhê
81.3.11	不	bù
81.3.12	辯	biàn
81.4.13	辯	biàn
81.4.14	者	zhê
81.4.15	不	bù
81.4.16	善	shàn
81.5.17	知	zhī
81.5.18	者	zhê
81.5.19	不	bù
81.5.20	博	bó
81.6.21	博	bó
81.6.22	者	zhê
81.6.23	不	bù
81.6.24	知	zhī
81.7.25	聖	shèng
81.7.26	人	rén
81.7.27	不	bù
81.7.28	積	jī
81.8.29	既	jì
81.8.30	以	yǐ
81.8.31	為	wéi
81.8.32	人	rén
81.8.33	己	jǐ
81.8.34	愈	yù
81.8.35	有	yǒu

81.9.36	既	jì
81.9.37	以	yǐ
81.9.38	與	yǔ
81.9.39	人	rén
81.9.40	己	jǐ
81.9.41	愈	yù
81.9.42	多	duō
81.10.43	天	tiān
81.10.44	之	zhī
81.10.45	道	dào
81.10.46	利	lì
81.10.47	而	ér
81.10.48	不	bù
81.10.49	害	hài
81.11.50	聖	shèng
81.11.51	人	rén
81.11.52	之	zhī
81.11.53	道	dào
81.11.54	為	wéi
81.11.55	而	ér
81.11.56	不	bù
81.11.57	爭	zhēng

GLOSSARY

Pinyin	Modern Chinese	Glyph	Interpretation	Spots in the text
āi	哀		lamenting from the chest, under one's roof,	31.17.107, 69.13.51
ài	愛		loving—your heart-core stuck in your throat—	10.7.26, 13.14.71, 27.16.81, 44.4.19, 72.9.37
ān	安		calm like a woman sitting on her heels at home	15.14.74, 35.2.11, 64.1.2, 79.3.8, 80.14.52
ào	奧		secret corner—a sanctuary like that backwater place on the city outskirts where grain's arriving and divided by a great giant	62.1.6
bá	拔		pulling up so expertly by hand that it's like a running dog arriving	54.1.5
bái	白		white-clear as acorn flesh	28.7.26, 41.10.53
bǎi	百		a hundred	5.4.16, 10.11.43, 17.8.38, 19.2.7, 49.2.7, 49.12.54, 66.1.7, 66.3.19
bài	敗		being defeated—its riches hit lightly by hand, failing, decaying—	29.5.25, 64.13.54, 64.15.68, 64.17.83, 64.19.91

bǎo	寶		treasure—like a house containing cowry-riches, jade, and a lidded pot	62.2.10, 67.8.29, 69.11.45
bǎo	保		safeguarding—like carrying a child on one's back—	9.4.16, 15.15.81, 62.3.16, 67.9.32
bào	抱		bundling it all up together—in one's arms—into	10.1.4, 19.9.40, 22.7.23, 42.5.19, 54.2.7, 64.7.29
bào	報		judging and making someone answer for what's happened—handcuffing and subduing with a hand to the back	63.5.14
bēi	悲'		breaking the baby wings off one's heart-core	31.17.108
bèi	被	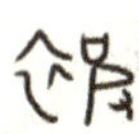	wearing like clothing—especially like a robe on the torso, like the placental afterbirth hanging from a recently pregnant woman—made of fur stripped by hand from its pelt	50.10.52, 70.11.44
bèi	倍		times—each time a person spits it out	19.2.8
běn	本		the source foundation of a rooted tree	39.15.94, 39.18.115

bǐ	鄙		a lowly rural person—kneeling, receiving from the granary, corralled on all sides	20.26.123
bǐ	彼		that—that fur stripped from its pelt on the road where you stepped slowly, only the left leg leading the way	12.10.47, 38.24.127, 72.11.43
bǐ	比		it compares, like two people right next to each other, to	55.2.5
bì	蔽		grassing over—hiding raggedy clothing that's been cut and cut into rags by lightly hitting—	15.17.94
bì	敝		raggedy as clothing that's been cut and cut into rags by lightly hitting	22.4.10
bì	臂		their arm-like the meat of a kneeling person with a chisel used to mark slaves and criminals...a ruler or dead husband	38.10.60, 69.7.27

bì	必		analytically—hands over heart-core—	30.5.29, 36.2.5, 36.4.13, 36.6.21, 36.8.29, 44.4.20, 44.5.25, 63.9.32, 63.11.40, 63.14.60, 63.15.65, 66.4.29, 66.5.37, 79.2.4
bì	弊		fraud like both hands supporting tattered cloth that's been hit lightly	45.2.8
bì	閉		blocking entry— like obstructing the double-winged gateway with the sprouting of seeds—	27.4.18, 52.6.33, 56.3.12
bì	璧		jade annulus—shaped like the backside of a kneeling slave or criminal being punished, marked with a chisel	62.10.46
biàn	辯		debating—speaking words that are emerging from a mouth like slaves or criminals branded by a chisel while surrounded by more chisels on each side	45.7.26, 81.3.12, 81.4.13
bīn	賓		receiving as a guest like a lady of the court	32.4.24

bīng	兵		carrying a short ax with two hands like a soldier or pawn	30.2.9, 31.1.3, 31.5.26, 31.6.30, 50.10.54, 50.13.67, 57.2.8, 69.1.2, 69.9.33, 69.12.48, 76.7.41, 80.8.33
bīng	冰		freezing stream water	15.9.45
bìng	病		ill as one carried on a stretcher on the third heavenly stem	44.3.15, 71.2.9, 71.3.12, 71.3.13, 71.4.17, 71.5.21, 71.6.24, 71.6.25, 71.7.29
bìng	並		side by side—like village homes on a hill or coffins in a grave—	16.3.9
bō	魄		the physical soul that stays with a body after death—that skull-white demon-faced ghost with a tail—	10.1.3
bó	薄		thinning—weak like foliage covering a great man reduced to a round-hung spindle of one inch	38.15.91, 38.21.117

bó	搏		monopolizing expertly by hand—like a big round spindle over an inch-sized spot that's as small as where you measure the radial artery pulse in your wrist—	14.5.15, 55.4.22
bó	伯		counts—people as clear as an acorn like an eldest brother or paternal uncle	80.2.8
bó	博		widely winning like ten times scattered—a courtesy name a man takes, when the moon is covered by a weapon on a pole, that's as small as that an inch-sized spot where you measure the radial artery pulse in your wrist—	81.6.21, 81.5.20
bó	泊		anchoring my vessel in simple, quiet clear, white water	20.12.49

bǔ	補		mending -- clothing such as a robe, especially that worn on the torso, like the placental afterbirth hanging from a recently pregnant woman being fixed by the courtesy name of a man after he replaces a moon with a weapon on a pole	77.6.25, 77.8.34

bù	不		the husk of the initial protective bud casing—the sepal—but not really the true inner flower of	2.2.19, 2.10.57, 2.11.66, 2.12.70, 2.13.74, 2.16.87, 3.1.1, 3.2.6, 3.3.8, 3.4.16, 3.5.19, 3.6.26, 3.13.57, 3.15.66, 4.2.7, 4.11.34, 5.1.3, 5.3.13, 5.7.32, 5.10.42, 6.1.3, 6.6.24, 7.3.16, 8.3.11, 8.13.46, 9.2.5, 9.4.13, 10.14.56, 10.15.60, 10.16.64, 12.9.42, 14.1.3, 14.3.10, 14.5.17, 14.7.25, 14.9.36, 14.10.40, 14.11.44, 14.16.68, 14.17.74, 15.3.12, 15.4.17, 16.11.40, 16.19.66, 17.5.22, 17.5.26, 18.3.15, 19.7.31, 20.7.25, 20.7.27, 21.14.55, 22.9.29, 22.11.34, 22.13.39, 22.15.45, 22.17.52, 23.3.8, 23.3.13, 23.6.25, 23.18.82, 23.18.86, 24.1.3, 24.2.7, 24.3.12, 24.4.17, 24.6.27, 24.10.46, 25.3.15, 25.4.20, 25.6.29, 26.4.16,

				27.3.13, 27.5.23, 27.7.32, 27.14.63, 27.15.68, 27.16.76, 27.16.80, 28.5.17, 28.11.40, 28.22.85, 29.2.12, 29.4.19, 30.2.7, 30.7.38, 30.11.57, 30.14.70, 30.15.72, 31.1.5, 31.3.17, 31.6.32, 31.8.41, 31.9.53, 31.11.69, 32.10.57, 33.7.27, 33.8.35, 34.3.16, 34.4.20, 34.5.28, 34.7.43, 34.9.53, 35.2.9, 35.6.31, 35.7.36, 35.8.41, 36.11.43, 37.2.7, 37.8.42, 15.17.95, 15.16.90, 15.15.85, 36.13.52, 38.1.3, 38.3.11, 38.5.24, 38.21.114, 38.23.121, 39.17.108, 39.21.125, 41.4.24, 41.4.26, 41.11.59, 42.8.33, 42.14.64, 43.5.27, 44.6.30, 44.7.34, 45.2.7, 45.4.15, 46.4.29, 47.1.1, 47.2.7, 47.5.25, 47.6.29, 47.7.33, 48.5.22,

				48.8.35, 49.4.17, 49.7.31, 50.9.45, 50.10.51, 51.6.18, 51.15.59, 51.16.63, 51.17.67, 52.4.28, 52.7.38, 52.10.48, 54.1.4, 54.2.9, 54.3.16, 55.3.13, 55.4.17, 55.4.21, 55.8.47, 55.15.76, 55.16.78, 56.1.3, 56.1.7, 56.9.32, 56.10.37, 56.11.42, 56.12.47, 56.13.52, 56.14.57, 58.14.57, 58.15.61, 58.16.65, 58.17.69, 59.4.27, 59.5.30, 60.3.15, 60.4.20, 60.5.24, 60.6.30, 60.7.36, 60.8.41, 61.12.56, 61.13.64, 62.3.11, 62.6.30, 62.12.51, 62.14.66, 63.12.49, 64.20.98, 64.20.100, 64.21.107, 64.22.123, 65.8.31, 66.6.50, 66.7.56, 66.8.65,

				66.9.69, 67.2.9, 67.4.16, 67.12.42, 67.15.56, 68.1.5, 68.2.10, 68.3.16, 68.5.27, 69.2.6, 69.4.13, 70.8.30, 71.1.2, 71.2.5, 71.2.7, 71.4.16, 71.5.20, 71.7.28, 72.1.2, 72.5.21, 72.6.25, 72.8.33, 72.10.38, 73.2.8, 73.7.37, 73.8.42, 73.9.47, 73.12.63, 74.1.2, 74.11.55, 76.7.44, 77.6.22, 77.8.35, 77.9.41, 77.10.44, 77.13.68, 77.14.73, 77.15.76, 78.7.33, 78.12.54, 79.5.21, 80.3.12, 80.5.19, 80.19.72, 81.1.3, 81.2.7, 81.3.11, 81.4.15, 81.5.19, 81.6.23, 81.7.27, 81.10.48, 81.11.56
cái	財		riches—sprouting cowry currency like seeds	53.12.41

cǎi	綵		a skein of silk dyed many colors as in with fruit hand-picked from a tree	53.9.34
cāng	倉		granaries—food stored in one's house	53.8.29
cáng	藏		hiding like storing weapons on a pole that can kill by piercing the eye under a bamboo bed below grass as is right and generous	44.5.24
cǎo	草		grass that's early, premature—like sunrise above an acorn on the jujube, that thorny plant that's used for insomnia, contraception and causes midterm miscarriages—such as herbs	76.3.14
céng	層		layers piling up—-someone bent like one who represents the dead in a rite flexing to step out of a cave has bent over the steam cooker previously many times	64.9.37

chá	察		carefully discerning—studying at home like making a meat offering by hand at an altar	20.21.97, 20.21.98, 58.3.11, 58.3.12
chài	蠆		a scorpion	55.3.10
chǎn	繟		easy-going as a solitary individual who uses a net of loose silk with weights to catch animals	73.10.52
cháng	常		the ever-present square fabric—like that which our grown men wrap around the 'little bird' top knots on their heads after receiving their public courtesy-names—or what we know as the timeless, whole head-cloth 'ji' version	1.2.5, 1.4.11, 1.7.26, 1.9.33, 3.12.46, 16.9.35, 16.10.37, 16.11.42, 16.13.47, 27.9.39, 27.11.47, 28.5.15, 28.11.38, 28.17.61, 32.1.2, 34.6.31, 37.1.2, 46.7.43, 48.6.27, 49.1.4, 51.9.35, 52.15.72, 55.10.56, 55.11.58, 61.4.15, 64.17.78, 65.12.46, 74.3.14, 74.7.29, 79.9.37
cháng	長		long as hair that has to be tied with a brooch...	2.5.31, 7.1.2, 7.2.10, 7.4.21, 9.4.15, 44.8.38, 54.6.41, 59.7.51, 59.9.59, 67.15.66

chāo	超		jumping over—transcending far like a running young man who will die young leaping off one foot, calling all together, like a blade in the mouth, like an imperious decree—	26.6.26
cháo	朝		the morning—when the sun's just rising out of the grass with a crescent moon in the sky	23.2.10, 53.6.23
chē	車		a carriage	11.2.11
chè	徹		thoroughly penetrating like a hand breaking a pot—the taxation system that was walking slowly, hitting lightly an inverted baby being birthed	79.7.32
chén	塵		leaving dusty footprints in the dirt—like a deer streaked with soil—	4.8.27, 56.7.26
chén	陳		displaying like the sun rising behind a tree in the east near a big mound of soil—ancient—like the vassal state of Chen	80.9.36

chén	臣		casting its eye down—making it surrender like a government official	18.4.26, 32.2.12
chēng	稱		being weighed, like a claw-like hand grabbing from above, holding rice or grain on a scale and called out as that	42.9.40
chéng	成		completing—that final nail in the weapon on a pole—	2.14.77, 7.10.47, 15.17.97, 17.7.35, 25.1.4, 34.4.19, 34.10.59, 2.4.30, 41.15.76, 41.19.95, 45.1.2, 47.7.36, 51.4.11, 63.13.54, 64.17.81, 67.15.64, 77.14.71
chéng	誠		speaking completely and truly—putting that final nail in a weapon on the pole—	22.21.74
chěng	騁		galloping like a horse given free rein by a chivalrous knight with frank words on a sob	12.4.20, 43.2.7
chí	馳		galloping—'oh yeah, vagina!'—	12.4.19, 43.2.6

chí	持		holding on to something—like a patron from a temple or government office that's expert at stopping and giving a hand—	9.1.1, 64.1.4, 67.9.30
chǐ	尺		one foot—measured with a bent person	69.5.19
chì	赤		bare naked and red as a great giant by a fire	55.2.7
chōng	沖		pouring water from the center, like from the hollow drum at the base of the flagpole	4.1.2, 42.6.21, 45.3.12
chǒng	寵		favoring—glorifying and pampering like a dragon or a favorite concubine gracing your home—	13.1.1, 13.3.12, 13.4.16, 13.7.29
chóu	籌		tallying—like an old man [this sub-character is the first part of Lǎo Zǐ's name] measuring the inches aloud with multiple mouths inside—	27.3.15
chū	出		stepping out of their cave	1.11.44, 5.8.37, 18.2.9, 35.4.22, 47.1.2, 47.3.14, 50.1.1

chú	除		a new posting—like moving me to a different thatched cottage on a soil mountain—	10.5.19, 53.6.25
chú	芻		wrapped straw-	5.2.9, 5.4.19
chù	處		dwelling—staying, as someone at home at the tea table, chaste and unmarried, following something slowly from behind with tiger fur—	2.9.51, 31.16.100, 31.18.116, 8.4.13, 24.10.47, 26.6.25, 30.4.20, 31.3.18, 38.20.111, 38.22.118, 66.6.46, 66.7.52, 76.9.52, 76.10.56, 77.14.74
chù	畜		rearing animals—giving them feed from a bag tied with a rope—	10.13.52, 61.12.60
chuǎi	揣		polishing a vessel by hand	9.3.9
chuān	川		Stream	15.6.30, 32.12.66
chuī	吹		blowing hard—empty boasts	29.8.40
chūn	春		springtime—vital and alive as when the grass is sprouting at camp in the sunshine—	20.11.44

chún	淳		honest—thick-tasting and flowing enjoyment like a river, like a baby with a slanting mouth at an ancestral shrine	58.2.7, 58.2.8
chuò	輟		halting like a chariot by four hands connecting repeatedly	54.3.17
cī	疵		an illness that stops a person—like on a stretcher—	10.6.24
cí	雌		femaleness—the foot stops a person here, on their footprint, at this 'short-tailed bird,'—	10.10.40, 28.2.6
cí	辭		declining into phraseology—ruling the city outskirts' hand over a hand holding a commonplace plate—like a hand from above, like that chisel used to mark slaves and criminals—	2.11.67, 34.3.17
cí	慈		benevolent as doubly-profound parental love, mysterious as two loops of string dyed black over the heart-core,	18.3.19, 19.4.16, 67.10.36, 67.13.48, 67.16.69, 67.20.83, 67.23.97

cǐ	此		this here—the foot stops a person here on their footprint:	1.11.40, 12.10.49, 14.7.22, 15.15.82, 19.7.25, 21.17.71, 23.4.18, 38.24.129, 39.18.110, 54.15.91, 57.5.23, 62.12.55, 62.13.62, 65.10.40, 72.11.45, 73.3.12
cì	次		the next one—like the second yawn, a little more deficient and lacking—	17.2.8, 17.3.14, 17.4.18
cóng	從		following in those footprints—stepping slowly with only the left leg leading the way, directly after another person, and stopping on one's footprint—	21.2.8, 23.8.34, 64.17.76
cuì	脆		fragile as crisp meat from a roof—precariously high above a kneeling person	64.3.11, 76.3.20
cún	存		surviving—on the plane of a baby with health issues, maybe a large head, but still sprouting—	4.10.32, 6.5.21, 7.8.38, 41.2.14
cùn	寸		one short inch—that spot on the forearm where the pulse beats strong	69.4.16

cuò	措		arranging—like hand-placing strips of meat to dry in the sun—	50.12.64
cuò	挫		pushing down to a sitting position on the ground	4.5.16, 29.10.46, 56.4.15
dá	達		arriving like small lambs—walking a while and stopping a while—	10.11.45

dà	大		great giant	13.2.6, 13.8.36, 13.9.44, 18.1.1, 18.2.11, 25.8.42, 25.9.43, 25.12.54, 25.12.56, 25.12.58, 25.12.61, 25.13.66, 27.17.86, 28.22.83, 30.5.25, 34.1.1, 34.8.49, 34.9.56, 34.10.61, 35.1.2, 38.19.108, 41.3.21, 41.10.52, 41.14.69, 41.15.73, 41.16.77, 41.17.81, 44.4.21, 45.1.1, 45.3.9, 45.5.17, 45.6.21, 45.7.25, 46.3.21, 46.4.27, 46.5.34, 53.2.9, 53.4.15, 60.1.2, 61.1.1, 61.6.25, 61.8.39, 61.9.43, 61.12.54, 61.15.78, 63.4.10, 63.7.24, 63.10.38, 63.12.51, 63.13.56, 65.16.68, 67.1.7, 67.3.13, 69.10.36, 72.2.6, 74.9.44, 74.10.49, 76.9.51, 79.1.2

dài	貸		lending like a retrievable arrow attached to a string with cowry riches	41.19.93
dài	殆		endangered—evil like human remains, spoken of privately, revolving around yourself—	16.19.67, 25.4.21, 32.10.58, 44.7.35, 52.4.29
dài	帶		belt, like the ever-present square fabric we know as the timeless, whole head-cloth 'ji', but around a person's waist	53.10.35
dài	代		taking the place of like a person with a retrievable arrow attached to a string or an era or a dynasty lineage	74.8.36, 74.9.43, 74.10.48
dàn	淡		bland—the flames doused by water—	31.8.48, 35.5.24
dàn	澹		calmly rippling the water—a person indifferent to fame and fortune talking, looking upward at a person on the cliff with a habitable cave—	20.23.103
dāng	當		equally—like the suburbs and field facing one another—	11.2.7, 11.4.19, 11.6.32

dào	道		The Way of the loose-haired headperson—walking a while, stopping a while, and speaking of it all	1.1.3, 1.2.6, 1.1.1, 4.1.1, 8.5.22, 9.10.39, 14.18.81, 14.21.93, 15.15.83, 16.17.60, 16.18.61, 18.1.2, 21.2.6, 21.3.9, 23.8.37, 23.9.39, 23.9.43, 23.12.56, 23.13.58, 24.7.31, 24.10.44, 25.7.36, 25.12.53, 25.16.81, 25.16.82, 30.1.2, 30.14.71, 30.15.73, 31.3.15, 32.1.1, 32.11.60, 34.1.2, 35.4.20, 37.1.1, 38.11.66, 38.17.99, 40.1.3, 40.2.8, 41.1.4, 41.2.12, 41.3.20, 41.4.30, 41.6.37, 41.7.41, 41.8.45, 41.18.85, 41.19.91, 42.1.1, 46.1.4, 46.2.13, 47.2.12, 48.2.6, 51.1.1, 51.6.20, 51.7.24, 51.10.39, 53.2.10, 53.4.16, 53.14.50, 55.15.77, 55.16.79, 59.9.64, 60.2.9, 62.1.1, 62.12.56, 62.13.63, 65.1.5, 67.1.6, 73.7.36, 77.1.3, 77.7.29,

				77.9.39, 77.12.60, 79.8.34, 81.10.45, 81.11.53
dào	盜		thievery—spitting into a bowl as an oath among thieves—	3.4.18, 19.6.21, 53.13.47, 57.9.53
dé	德		Dé—the ethical, straight way of walking awhile and stopping awhile, eye directed forward over the heart-core	10.17.69, 21.1.2, 23.10.44, 23.10.48, 23.14.65, 23.15.67, 28.5.16, 28.11.39, 28.17.62, 38.1.2, 38.1.4, 38.2.8, 38.3.10, 38.3.13, 38.4.17, 38.5.19, 38.6.27, 38.11.69, 38.12.71, 41.9.49, 41.11.57, 41.12.62, 49.5.24, 49.8.38, 51.2.4, 51.6.23, 51.8.27, 51.11.42, 51.18.72, 54.4.23, 54.5.31, 54.6.39, 54.7.47, 54.8.56, 55.1.2, 59.3.21, 59.4.24, 60.9.45, 63.5.17, 65.13.53, 65.14.55, 68.5.30, 79.6.26, 79.7.30

dé	得		hand-picking-of-cowry-shell-riches-along-the-road	3.3.11, 12.6.29, 13.5.19, 14.5.18, 22.5.15, 23.13.61, 23.15.70, 23.17.79, 29.2.13, 30.11.58, 31.8.42, 31.11.72, 39.1.3, 39.2.7, 39.3.12, 39.4.17, 39.5.22, 39.6.28, 39.7.34, 42.14.65, 44.3.11, 46.5.37, 52.3.11, 56.9.34, 56.10.39, 56.11.44, 56.12.49, 56.13.54, 56.14.59, 61.14.74, 62.15.70, 64.20.103, 74.5.22
dēng	登		is ascending—like succeeding in imperial exams while being 'of two feet, reversed' over a bean-shaped food container—	20.11.45
dī	滌		washing and arranging—like hitting lightly, stripping, and knotting twigs into slips to write on—	10.5.18

dí	敵		enemy—hostilely resisting, lightly hitting, merely speaking of 'God of Heaven,' (as we call our emperors, for they're like flower sepals connecting to above with their covering of that ever-present, timeless, whole-cloth 'ji' square fabric which our grown-men wrap around their 'little bird' top knots once they've received adult, public courtesy-names)	68.3.14, 69.8.30, 69.10.39, 69.11.41
dǐ	柢		rooted like a tree—a person standing on the ground bowing to their lineage	59.8.58
dì	地		Earth (this soil vagina)	1.5.16, 5.1.2, 5.5.22, 6.4.16, 7.2.6, 7.1.3, 8.6.25, 23.5.21, 23.6.23, 25.2.7, 25.12.57, 25.14.75, 25.15.76, 32.5.26, 39.3.11, 39.10.51, 50.4.23, 50.15.80

dì	帝		'God of Heaven'—as we call our emperors, for they're like flower sepals connecting to above with their covering of that ever-present, timeless, whole-cloth 'ji' square fabric which our grown-men wrap around their 'little bird' top knots once they've received adult, public courtesy-names—	4.12.40
dìng	定		as stable and determined as when one nails a roof over their departure—their setting out by foot on a long journey or campaign—preparing the ground for it	37.9.50
dōng	冬		the end of the year when things ice up following from behind like the knot at the end of a cord	15.6.28
dòng	動		laboring—like moving heavy bags with great strength—	5.8.34, 8.12.41, 15.14.77, 40.1.5, 50.4.20
dú	毒		poisoning—like using that toxic plant that's as virtueless as an axe-bearing soldier not-being a mother	51.13.51

dú	獨		alone as a single, old, and childless dog	20.12.48, 20.16.74, 20.20.92, 20.22.100, 20.26.120, 20.27.125, 25.3.13
dǔ	篤		honestly and sincerely as a horse under two bamboo stalks	16.2.6
duǎn	短		short as an arrow that fits in a bean-shaped food container	2.5.32
duì	兌		open mouth like that of a smiling, breathy older brother	52.5.32, 52.8.42, 56.2.11
dūn	敦		thickly earnest—hitting lightly by hand for that slanting-mouth-baby enjoyment—	15.10.49
dùn	沌		muddled and murky like water made turbid in the camp or village	20.18.84, 20.18.85
duō	多		much more—like a double serving of meat—	5.9.38, 22.6.16, 44.2.10, 44.5.23, 57.6.26, 57.7.34, 57.8.42, 57.9.55, 63.4.12, 63.15.63, 63.15.66, 65.5.22, 75.2.10, 81.9.42

duó	奪		seizing—snatching 'a spread-winged bird' with your forearm where your pulse beats strong—	36.7.27
ē	阿		'oh, familiar one,'—oh, big soil mountain around which you can purse your lips and puff 'yup, that's it, that's the big soil mound I know'—	20.2.8
è	惡		a disdained 'ugliness'—an inferior-hearted evil immediately outside, touching the house—	2.1.10, 8.4.18, 20.4.16

ér	而		and yet now, bearded,	1.12.45, 2.11.65, 2.12.69, 2.13.73, 2.14.78, 4.1.3, 5.7.31, 5.8.35, 7.6.30, 7.8.36, 8.3.10, 9.3.10, 9.7.27, 10.14.55, 10.15.59, 10.16.63, 14.8.31, 17.2.10, 20.16.72, 20.26.118, 20.28.129, 22.21.76, 23.7.28, 25.4.19, 25.13.67, 26.8.34, 27.5.22, 27.7.31, 29.2.6, 30.6.36, 30.8.44, 30.9.48, 30.10.52, 30.11.56, 30.12.61, 31.8.44, 31.9.52, 31.10.55, 32.6.37, 33.8.34, 34.3.13, 34.3.15, 34.5.27, 34.7.42, 35.2.8, 37.2.5, 37.5.21, 9.1.2, 38.5.22, 38.6.30, 38.7.38, 38.8.46, 38.9.54, 38.10.61, 38.11.67, 38.12.72, 38.13.77, 38.14.82, 38.16.92, 38.18.102, 41.1.6, 42.5.18,

				42.9.35, 42.10.46, 42.11.51, 47.5.27, 47.6.31, 47.7.35, 48.5.20, 51.6.21, 51.9.34, 51.15.58, 51.16.62, 51.17.66, 53.5.19, 55.5.27, 55.6.36, 55.8.46, 56.9.35, 56.10.40, 56.11.45, 56.12.50, 56.13.55, 56.14.60, 57.6.29, 57.11.64, 57.12.71, 57.13.78, 57.14.85, 58.14.56, 58.15.60, 58.16.64, 58.17.68, 61.11.52, 64.17.82, 64.22.122, 66.6.48, 66.7.54, 66.8.64, 67.9.31, 69.3.10, 69.5.17, 73.7.39, 73.8.44, 73.9.49, 73.10.54, 73.12.62, 74.4.17, 74.5.24, 77.8.33, 77.13.67, 77.14.72, 78.2.8, 79.5.20, 80.3.11, 80.5.18, 80.11.43,

				81.10.47, 81.11.55
ér	兒		baby son—with an imperfect fontanelle—	10.4.16, 20.13.56, 28.6.23
ěr	耳		ear [this word is the second part of Lǎo Zĭ's personal name, Lĭ Ěr]	12.2.11, 49.12.59
ěr	餌		alluring food made from rice dough—you'd love to put your mouth over that bowl [pronounced like the second part of Lǎo Zĭ's personal name, Lĭ Ěr]—	35.3.16
èr	二		two	42.2.6, 42.3.7, 67.11.37
fā	發		shot like by a bow launching 'thwang!' and levelling grass with one's feet as effectively as if by hand with a halberd	12.5.26, 39.10.57
fá	伐		bragging and criticizing—beheading another with a weapon on a pole—	22.13.41, 24.5.20, 30.9.50
fǎ	法		following standards, regulations, rules—like water coming out of a mouth between a person's legs—of	25.14.74, 25.15.77, 25.16.80, 25.17.83, 57.9.49

fǎn	反		making someone return, with one's right hand, to the cave	25.11.51, 40.1.1, 65.15.62, 78.14.64
fàn	氾		spreading out everywhere like water overflowing on a commonplace plate	34.1.3 change to node?
fāng	方		like the wide, parallel side of a tipped blade	41.14.70, 58.14.55
fāng	妨		oppositional—holding the tip of a sword over a kneeling young woman	12.7.35
fēi	非		breaking the little wings off	1.2.4, 1.4.10, 7.9.39, 31.7.36, 39.18.111, 39.19.117, 53.14.49, 60.4.17, 60.6.27, 65.2.7
fèi	廢		collapsed like a house shot by a bow, launching 'thwang!' and levelling grass with one's feet as effectively as if by hand with a halberd	18.1.3, 36.5.19
fèi	費		lavishly expending like two sticks tied together to start a fire over cowry-riches	44.4.22
fēn	紛		unravelling—separating thin silk with a blade into disorderliness—	4.6.21, 56.5.20

fèn	糞		manure—like rice kernels through a differently-masked person	46.1.9
fēng	豐		as luxuriant and lush as a pot full of flowers	54.7.49
fēng	風		as common and earthy as the wind dispersing insects altogether	23.2.7
féng	蜂		a bee -- an insect like something with two legs being followed from behind like the knot at the end of a thread through lush grown of plants	55.3.9
fèng	奉		offering a lush growth of plants with two hands	77.10.47, 77.11.55
fū	夫		that is to say, this particular grown man with a hairpin and public courtesy name	38.15.85, 38.19.110, 41.19.89, 59.2.8, 60.8.39
fú	弗		like sticks that were tied together in a bundle to start a fire—pfft!—that is, 'not'	2.14.79, 2.15.83
fú	幅		hem-width strips	11.1.3

fú	服		wearing clothes—like mourning dress as earthly and mortal as commonplace plates—subdued as a kneeling person by han—	53.9.32, 59.2.14, 59.3.16, 80.13.51
fú	福		blessings and good fortune—like a full vessel on display on an altar	58.5.19, 58.6.23, 65.9.38
fú	伏		lying in wait like a dog waiting to ambush a person	58.6.28
fǔ	腹		inside—the gut, the meat belly—	3.9.39, 12.9.41
fǔ	輔		assisting—a man's courtesy name he gets when he replaces a bucket with a weapon on a pole protecting like the wooden bars that help prevent a carriage from over-turning	64.22.116
fù	負		carrying as cowry-riches with a much smaller person or knife—that kind of load-bearing that can lead to suffering, to neglect, to betrayal, to repudiation	42.5.16

fù	父		as a beginning -- the primordial father who works by hand with a stone axe	21.15.60, 21.16.66
fù	覆		covering by walking forth and then back again, stepping slowly with only one's left leg leading the way,	51.14.55
fù	復		walking forth and then back again	14.12.47, 16.4.14, 16.6.20, 16.8.30, 16.9.32, 19.4.14, 28.6.19, 28.12.42, 28.18.65, 52.4.22, 52.13.61, 58.9.37, 58.10.41, 64.21.109, 80.10.40
fù	富		wealth—a house full of valuable vessels with lots of capacity—	9.7.25, 33.5.21, 57.13.81
gǎi	改		transforming something like a fetus or a snake—cracking lightly by hand or binding with a silk rope—	25.3.16
gài	蓋		indeed covering like grass and clay soil thatch over a chalice	50.8.37
gān	甘		sweet in the mouth	32.5.31, 80.12.46

gǎn	敢		daring—lightly hitting ears on both sides of the head—	3.13.58, 30.7.39, 64.22.124, 67.12.43, 67.15.57, 69.2.7, 69.4.14, 73.1.3, 73.2.9, 74.6.28
gāng	剛		firmly—just exactly, barely, recently cutting grass on mountains within the city outskirts with a blade—	36.10.40, 78.6.29
gāo	高		high above (a two-story building in the city outskirts)	2.6.35, 39.14.85, 39.16.95, 77.3.9
gǎo	槁		meagre and withered like a tree high above (a two-story building in the city outskirts)	76.4.25
gē	割		splitting apart a house already harmed, dense with spoken and tallied lies	28.22.86, 58.14.58
gè	各		each foot and mouth	16.6.19, 61.14.73
gēn	根		the root of the family tree—a penis—	6.4.17, 16.6.23, 16.7.25, 26.1.4, 26.9.43, 59.8.56
gōng	公		as publicly fair and impartial as a high ranking old big-balled man—a duke—	16.14.51, 16.15.52, 42.9.37, 62.9.42

gōng	弓		like a bow	77.2.7
gōng	功		real work—laboring with the force from a bladed tool, one's arm, or a plough—	2.14.76, 9.9.33, 17.7.34, 22.14.44, 24.5.23, 34.4.18, 77.14.70
gōng	攻		attacking—hitting lightly with a bladed tool, being on top	78.2.9
gǒng	拱		arching around and holding aloft like hands folded on the chest, sharing	62.10.45
gòng	共		share together	11.1.4
gǒu	狗		dogs—decorated, symbolic sacrificial objects—	5.2.10, 5.4.20
gòu	垢		humiliated like filth—clay soil next to a queen or king, the head speaker	78.10.46
gū	孤		orphaned like a big-headed, legs-swaddled baby left as a melon on the vine	39.17.106, 42.8.31

gǔ	谷		within that valley mouth between two mountains	6.1.1, 15.11.58, 28.15.56, 28.16.60, 32.12.67, 39.5.21, 39.12.65, 66.1.8, 66.3.20
gǔ	穀	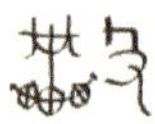	hub of a wheel on the carriage used for harvesting	11.1.6, 39.17.109, 42.8.34
gǔ	骨		that bony will that comes from a skeleton framework	3.11.45, 55.5.23
gǔ	古		ancient times—ten generations of mouths ago—	14.18.79, 14.20.89, 15.1.1, 21.13.50, 22.19.62, 62.13.57, 65.1.1, 68.8.41
gù	固		solidly, anciently—for ten generations of mouths, keeping as firm to what happened in the first place as this land surrounding and holding this nation since ancient times—	36.2.6, 36.4.14, 36.6.22, 36.8.30, 55.5.29, 58.12.49, 59.8.57, 67.21.91

gù	故		anciently, for ten generations, this lightly hits and leaves a mark of reason:	1.7.25, 2.3.22, 7.4.19, 7.10.45, 8.5.19, 8.14.48, 11.7.38, 12.10.45, 14.8.29, 15.5.20, 15.17.92, 19.8.33, 22.10.32, 22.12.37, 22.14.42, 22.16.48, 22.18.54, 23.2.5, 23.8.33, 24.10.42, 25.12.52, 27.10.43, 27.12.51, 27.14.59, 28.22.82, 29.7.31, 31.3.13, 34.10.57, 38.11.64, 38.24.125, 39.15.89, 39.20.119, 41.5.31, 42.10.41, 44.4.17, 46.6.38, 50.6.30, 50.14.75, 51.10.38, 54.9.59, 56.9.31, 56.15.62, 57.10.57, 60.9.44, 61.6.24, 61.10.45, 62.8.36, 62.17.76, 63.13.52, 63.17.75, 64.15.66, 64.16.71, 65.6.23, 66.3.16,

				66.10.71, 67.4.14, 67.13.49, 67.14.53, 67.15.62, 69.12.46, 72.11.41, 73.5.26, 76.5.26
guǎ	寡		scant as one widowed, alone —separating them from the kneeling head of the household with a blade—	19.10.44, 39.17.107, 42.8.32, 63.14.61, 80.1.3
guān	觀		keeping watch from the temple tower for	1.8.30, 1.10.37, 16.4.13, 26.5.23, 54.9.62, 54.10.66, 54.11.70, 54.12.74, 54.13.79
guān	官		official—working in a government building with many rooms under one roof—	28.21.80
guān	關		locking—like weaving a pair of the tiniest silk thread youngsters, hair still in two tufts, through the double-winged gateway—	27.4.20
guāng	光		brilliant—that shining fire over the head of a kneeling person—	4.7.24, 52.13.60, 56.6.23, 58.17.67

guǎng	廣		wide like a person with a large belly in a habitable cave in a cliff	41.11.56, 67.14.55, 67.17.75
guī	歸		returning after sweeping troops out of the hills to this	14.12.48, 16.6.21, 16.7.24, 20.14.66, 22.21.77, 28.6.21, 28.12.43, 28.18.66, 34.7.40, 52.13.62, 60.9.47
guǐ	鬼		a ghost	60.3.14, 60.4.19
guì	貴		treasuring—as if as valuable as cowry-shell-riches—	3.3.9, 9.7.26, 13.2.5, 13.8.35, 13.12.60, 17.6.32, 20.28.130, 27.16.77, 31.4.23, 31.5.28, 39.14.84, 39.15.90, 51.6.22, 51.8.29, 56.13.56, 56.15.66, 62.13.61, 62.17.80, 64.20.101, 70.10.39, 72.10.40, 75.11.52
guì	劌		stabbing with a knife like pacing off distance, one foot in front of the other, marking the passage of time like a year on a calendar	58.15.62

guǒ	果		ripened like fruit on the tree by the sun	30.6.35, 30.8.43, 30.9.47, 30.10.51, 30.11.55, 30.12.60
guó	國		this nation—this particular territory, this enclave defended by a weapon on a pole plus its surroundings—	18.4.20, 10.7.29, 36.12.48, 54.7.45, 54.12.73, 54.12.75, 57.1.4, 57.7.37, 59.6.44, 59.7.46, 60.1.3, 61.1.2, 61.6.26, 61.6.30, 61.7.34, 61.8.36, 61.8.40, 61.9.44, 61.12.55, 61.13.63, 65.6.27, 65.7.28, 65.8.35, 65.9.36, 78.10.44, 78.12.53, 80.1.2, 80.16.59
guò	過		this way of walking a while and stopping a while that's past and surpassing—like a skull mouth speaking—	35.3.17, 61.12.57, 61.13.65, 64.21.114
hái	孩		baby animal, giggling	20.13.59, 49.13.64
hǎi	海		the ocean—water lush with new life sprouting from a nursing mother—	20.23.107, 32.12.71, 66.1.2

hài	害		being harmed, like speaking and tallying many lies within the house	35.2.10, 56.12.51, 66.7.57, 73.3.18, 81.10.49
hán	寒		cold as a humble person sleeping under a desolate roof in the grass to protect themselves from winter chill	45.8.31
hán	含		to keep what's being said, in the mouth now, in modern times, in the mouth—staying stuffed in like jade, pearls, and gems in a corpse's mouth—	55.1.1
háo	號		roaring like a puffing tiger head	55.8.45
háo	毫		as tiny as the fine hair covering below the mouth	64.8.34
hǎo	好		as good as—like a woman with a child—	30.3.15, 53.5.21, 57.12.69
hé	和		harmonizing as a mouth organ	2.7.42, 4.7.22, 18.3.16, 42.6.25, 55.9.49, 55.10.54, 56.6.21, 79.1.1

hé	何		that very one about whom you can purse your lips around a cane and puff, 'yup, that's the person'—	13.3.10, 13.8.33, 13.11.57, 20.3.12, 20.5.20, 21.16.62, 26.7.29, 50.6.29, 50.14.74, 54.14.83, 57.4.16, 62.7.32, 62.13.65, 74.2.6
hé	闔		shutting it—a person with a mouth or cave between their legs withdrawing and covering an empty chalice from within the double-winged gateway—	10.9.37
hé	合		joining together from three sides over a mouth—having sex—	32.5.28, 55.6.35, 64.7.28
hè	褐		dull brown like coarse clothing—especially like that robe on the torso, or the placental afterbirth hanging from a recently pregnant woman -- we're speaking of that used to bundle up and hide	70.11.45
hèi	黑		darkness and shadiness—the illegality of someone with a criminal or penal face tattoo—	28.8.29

hēng	享		enjoying—thanks to the ancestral shrine—	20.10.40
hóu	侯		A marquis—'arrow in the cave, '	32.3.14, 37.3.9, 39.7.32, 39.14.80, 39.17.102
hòu	後		afterwards—what remains when stepping slowly with only one's left leg leading the way, leaving the tiniest of silk thread footprints, that is, one's descendants...	2.8.44, 7.5.27, 14.17.77, 30.5.28, 38.11.68, 38.12.73, 38.13.78, 38.14.83, 65.16.65, 66.5.40, 67.18.77
hòu	厚		thick like a generous cliff with a habitable cave that opposes the flow of the river, housing a baby with a large head, spread arms and swaddled legs under the sun	38.20.113, 44.5.26, 50.7.36, 55.1.4, 75.8.37
hū	乎		—pah, can you?!—	5.6.29, 10.2.9, 10.4.17, 10.6.25, 10.8.33, 10.10.41, 10.12.49, 23.7.32, 35.5.25, 39.19.118
hū	惚		can only be called 'a heart-cutting heart' because it's so elusive and difficult to describe	14.15.64, 21.4.16, 21.5.17, 21.7.27
hǔ	虎		fierce tiger	50.9.48, 50.12.61

hù	戶		the single-gate-doorway to a household	11.5.27, 47.1.3
hù	混		turbulent—waters as numerous as all of the descendants that the sun looks down, all mixing together—	15.12.59
huá	華		decorative brilliant magnificence of a flower blooming	38.17.101, 38.23.124
huà	化		transforming—a right-side-up person into an upside down person—	37.4.19, 37.5.20, 57.11.67
huái	懷		carrying in one's bosom—affectionately concealed in one's heart by clothing that's like a net over water—	70.12.46
huán	還		returning—walking a while and stopping a while in a long robe, giving something the eye, and then going back—	30.3.16
huàn	患		piercing of the heart-core with worry, with affliction	13.2.7, 13.8.37, 13.9.45, 13.11.58

huàn	渙		dissolving—dispersing like water in the city outskirts when there are so many people—	15.9.42
huāng	荒		a wasteland—desolate under the grass atop the watery uncultivated land of the lost dead...	20.8.29
huǎng	恍	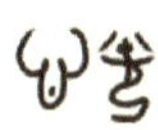	can only be called 'the heart-core of a kneeling person with shining fire over their head' because it's so brilliant yet incomprehensible	14.15.65, 21.4.14, 21.5.19, 21.7.25
huī	恢		vast—like an expanded heart restored from fire that can be toughed by hand, that is disheartened gray ashes	73.11.59, 73.11.60
huī	隳		getting destroyed—around the soil mountain, a left hand by moonlight over one's heart—	29.10.48
huǐ	虺		a venomous snake that will cut off one's foot	55.3.11

huì	諱		taboo words—words like slaves or criminals branded by a chisel emerging from a mouth to be avoided like footsteps around an enclosure as with the name of a deceased emperor or elder	57.6.28
huì	慧		wisdom—having hand-swept your heart-core with a bamboo broom—	18.2.7
hūn	昏		darkening—getting dusky as the sun bows like a person with back-swept hands—	18.4.22, 20.20.93, 20.20.94, 57.7.40
hún	渾		muddied like a river spouting from an army of surrounding carts	49.11.51
hùn	混		turbulent—like waters as numerous as all of the descendants that the sun looks down upon, all mixing together—	14.8.30, 25.1.3
huó	活		really living, like a tongue or 'clapper of a bell' licking the river water	73.2.11

huò	或		this particular territory—this enclave, defended by a weapon on a pole, plus its surroundings—	4.2.6, 4.10.31, 24.9.39, 29.7.33, 29.7.35, 29.8.37, 29.8.39, 29.9.41, 29.9.43, 29.10.45, 29.10.47, 31.2.10, 42.10.43, 42.11.48, 61.10.46, 61.11.50, 73.3.15, 73.3.17
huò	貨		transformation of cowry-shell-riches—like from a right-side-up person to an upside-down person—	3.3.13, 12.6.31, 44.2.8, 53.12.42, 64.20.105
huò	惑		confusing, deluding or hiding—like a heart-core under this particular territory, this enclave defended by a weapon on a pole plus its surroundings—	22.6.18
huò	禍		disaster—slanting mouth of a skull on a sacrifice altar—	46.4.25, 58.5.17, 58.6.25, 69.10.34
jī	積		storing and accumulating—amassing grain plants like cowry-riches under a thorn tree	59.3.20, 59.4.23, 81.7.28

jī	稽		examining—like looking at a grain plant to check its deliciousness	65.11.44, 65.12.48
jī	饑		starving—having a meal with one's mouth over a bowl of rice on a stand is carefully watched over like the smallest things, tiny silk threads, under guard by a man with a spear, by a garrison	75.1.3, 75.3.13
jī	雞		a rooster—a 'short-tailed bird' a great giant whose tiniest silk thread child is grabbed by a hand from above like a female prostitute	80.17.62
jī	基		the foundation of native earth or clay under what it holds a basket of	39.16.99
jí	及		are reaching—like grabbing a person—	13.11.51, 21.13.51, 43.7.38, 48.7.31
jí	極		in the utmost—to the highest position of a double-beamed wooden ridgepole—	16.1.3, 28.12.46, 58.7.32, 59.5.36, 59.6.40, 68.8.43
jí	吉		lucky—empty and quiet as a mouth with a soldier's axe above it—	31.12.78

jí	棘		the thorny jujube—the red date, whose fruit can be used as contraception and causes midterm miscarriages—	30.4.22
jǐ	己		binding oneself with a silk rope	81.8.33, 81.9.40
jǐ	幾		being as near as a border of fine, fine silk you'd guard with a blade to	20.3.11, 8.5.20, 64.17.80, 69.11.42
jì	既		'done'—as de facto as a kneeling person turning away after eating a bowl of rice, done	32.8.46, 35.8.43, 52.3.10, 52.4.18, 81.8.29, 81.9.36
jì	濟		helping like ferrying across that river Qi that's as even as a field of grain	52.9.43
jì	祭		a ceremony making a meat offering by hand at an altar	54.3.14
jì	忌		abstaining from—binding one's heart like with a silk rope	57.6.27
jì	伎		underhanded tricky like that person with their right hand supporting ten	57.8.43

jì	稷		the god of plants -- a plant stalk in a farmland field divided from something coming up behind as with the knot at the end of a cord	78.11.50
jì	跡		leaving tracks—speaking of this footprint, both armpits sweat this too!—	27.1.5
jì	寂		quiet as hand-husking peas at home	25.3.9
jì	寄		entrusted as one exiled east to a house of strange, great men as a punishment—but still counted on to translate there—with	13.13.68
jì	紀		binding itself with fine silk thread—a golden guide	14.21.94
jiā	佳		excellent—addressing the emperor using a stack of pointed jade tablets—	31.1.2
jiā	家		home—a pig under your roof—	18.4.21, 54.5.29, 54.10.65, 54.10.67, 57.7.38

jiā	加		putting on top of another like a mouth ordering a cow over a plough	62.5.26, 69.12.50
jiǎ	甲		shield—a turtle shell	50.10.53, 80.8.32
jiān	堅		hard and solid as a right hand through an eye cast down in surrender over solid clay soil	43.2.12, 76.2.10, 76.5.27, 78.2.10
jiān	兼		that hand holding two stalks of grain—doing two things at once	61.12.59
jiān	間		interstice—space where moonlight's peeking leisurely through the double-winged gateway—	5.5.24, 43.3.17
jiǎn	儉		frugal -- like one modest person next to people all together speaking, gathering from three sides	67.11.39, 67.14.52, 67.17.73
jiàn	賤		appearing to accumulate cheap inferior "riches"—like several tiny weapons on a pole next to a cowry	39.15.92, 39.18.113
jiàn	建		expertly hand-built by a striding person with a bamboo brush	41.5.32, 41.12.61, 54.1.2

jiàn	楗		bar—a door bolt, hand-built from a tree by a striding person skillful with a bamboo brush—	27.4.21
jiàn	見		seeing—one big eye for a head—	3.5.20, 14.1.4, 14.16.69, 14.17.75, 19.9.38, 22.9.31, 24.3.10, 29.2.10, 35.6.33, 47.2.10, 47.6.30, 52.11.50, 72.8.35, 77.15.78
jiàn	劍		a sword all together unanimous like two mouthy people walking together, gathering themselves from three sides	53.10.37
jiāng	將		soon will be—as if offering a meat tribute by hand on a table—	15.9.47, 29.1.1, 32.4.22, 32.9.50, 36.1.1, 36.3.9, 36.5.17, 36.7.25, 37.4.17, 37.6.25, 37.7.39, 37.9.48, 31.14.87, 31.15.92, 39.9.48, 39.10.55, 39.11.62, 39.12.69, 39.13.77, 39.14.86, 42.15.69, 65.3.11, 67.22.93
jiāng	江		the Yangtze River—the river that 'works like someone with a stone axe'—flows into	32.12.70, 66.1.1

jiàng	匠		master craftsmen who builds a box with axe	74.9.45, 74.10.50
jiàng	降		bestowing below—falling down a soil mountain—	32.5.30
jiāo	郊		outside of town where someone sits with crossed legs at a big soil mound	46.2.18
jiāo	交		intersecting—making friends like someone with crossed legs	60.9.46, 61.2.9
jiǎo	驕		as arrogant as a young person dangerously raving through the city outskirts on a tall horse with its mane flying	9.7.28, 30.10.54
jiǎo	角		an angled horn	50.11.60
jiǎo	皦		bright white—as if lightly hit by the tip of a blade	14.9.37
jiào	徼		delineated surface—a patrolled frontier border lightly hit with a sword tip from left to right—	1.10.39

jiào	教		This teaching—instructing a child in counting or divination, lightly hitting with a teaching cane—	2.10.60, 42.12.56, 42.13.59, 42.15.72, 43.5.30
jiē	皆		common public opinion—that clear, plain back and forth between people—	2.1.3, 2.2.12, 17.8.40, 20.15.69, 20.25.115, 49.12.56, 49.13.63, 67.1.3
jiē	竭		drained, exhausted—a person standing on solid ground making a yawning sound	39.12.71
jié	結		tying up with a knot of a skein of silk, auspiciously unused,	27.6.27, 80.10.41
jié	詰		being clearly spoken about—fathomed with words like slaves or criminals, branded by a chisel, emerging from a mouth of good luck that's as empty and quiet as a mouth with a soldier's axe above it, speaking of grass—	14.7.28
jiě	解		removing—like a blade cutting the horn from an ox—	4.6.19, 27.7.34, 56.5.18
jiè	介		a person lying in between	53.1.3

jīn	矜		commanding—gathering together from three sides over a kneeling person with a spear—	22.15.47, 24.6.25, 30.8.46
jīn	筋		sinew -- tendons, muscles, or even veins that stand out like two bamboo stalk on the meat of one's arm that sticks out from the body like a plough	55.5.25
jīn	今		what's being said—in the mouth now, in modern times—	14.19.84, 21.13.52, 67.16.67
jīn	金		gold—joined together from three sides by grinding like an axe between two blocks of metal—	9.5.17
jìn	進		walking forward awhile and stopping awhile like a 'short-tailed bird'	41.7.40, 62.12.54, 69.4.15
jīng	精		essence or spirit—like polished rice or semen or like spring's blue-green lush, ripening of that sedative cinnabar plant—	21.10.40, 21.11.42, 55.7.39

jīng	驚		startling—like how lightly hitting by hand a mouth as beautiful, honored, and circumspect as a ram's head makes a horse shy away—	13.1.4, 13.3.15, 13.5.22, 13.6.26, 13.7.32
jīng	荊		the thorny 'chaste tree'—whose fruit makes you not want sex, whose canes are used to flog wives [this character is the same as that for the state of Chǔ where legend has it that Laozi was born]	30.4.21
jìng	靜		calm peace—when the clear blue-green growth of that sedative cinnabar plant quiets a dispute between two hands on a ploughshare—	15.13.68, 16.2.5, 16.7.27, 26.2.5, 37.8.45, 45.9.32, 45.10.36, 57.12.70, 61.4.17, 61.5.21
jìng	徑		a shortcut pathway straight across—stepping slowly with only the left leg across an underground stream	53.5.22
jiǔ	九		nine (the elbow in that old way of counting)	64.9.36

jiǔ	久		enduring through time—like someone receiving moxibustion treatments with mugwort used for cramps, turning a breech baby, or other health issues—	7.1.4, 7.2.12, 15.14.76, 16.18.63, 23.6.27, 33.7.32, 44.8.39, 58.12.50, 59.7.52, 59.9.61, 67.6.20
jiù	咎		calamity—a person, something with two legs being followed from behind	9.8.32, 46.5.32
jiù	救		rescuing—lightly hitting upon request someone in a fur coat—	27.9.41, 27.11.49, 52.10.49, 67.22.94
jū	居		abiding—dwelling where birthed, sitting over ten mouths	2.14.80, 2.15.84, 8.6.23, 25.13.69, 31.4.21, 31.14.89, 31.15.94, 38.21.115, 38.23.122, 72.3.13, 80.14.54
jǔ	舉		lifting up—supporting, offering to hand-carry on one's shoulders above a fang —	77.4.15
jù	據		taking possession of like an expert hand with tigers or boars fighting one another	55.4.18

jù	懼		frightening—two eyes over 'a short-tailed bird' scaring one's heart	74.2.9
juē	攫		grabbing like an expert hand with a nervously-looking-around-with-two-eyes bird in hand	55.4.19
jué	蹶		toppling or overthrown—like stumbling or fainting as a disobedient, upside-down person yawning in a habitable cave on a cliff	39.14.88
jué	絕		severed—like a blade cutting through the silk thread of 'clinging desire,' that mythological snake who could swallow an elephant—is	19.1.1, 19.3.9, 19.5.17, 19.11.46, 20.1.1
jūn	軍		army of surrounding carts	30.5.26, 31.14.88, 31.15.93, 50.10.50
jūn	君		a lord prince administering—his hand holding a rod over a mouth—	26.2.8, 26.10.47, 31.4.19, 31.7.37, 70.6.22
jūn	均		evened out—like soil that's been wrapped up in two parallel lines	32.6.39

kāi	開		unlatching the double-winged gateway with a pair of hands	10.9.36, 27.5.25, 52.8.40
kàng	抗		opposing—expertly by hand lifting a high, arrogant, extreme like the ridge of a roof	69.12.47
kě	可		about which one can purse one's lips like a piece of cane and puff: 'Yup, that's it, definitely'	1.1.2, 1.3.8, 3.5.21, 9.4.14, 13.13.67, 13.15.78, 14.7.26, 14.11.45, 15.3.13, 15.4.18, 20.7.26, 25.5.22, 27.5.24, 27.7.33, 29.4.20, 31.11.70, 32.10.55, 34.2.6, 34.6.34, 34.8.46, 36.11.44, 36.13.53, 44.8.36, 46.3.23, 56.9.33, 56.10.38, 56.11.43, 56.12.48, 56.13.53, 56.14.58, 59.6.41, 59.7.49, 62.4.19, 62.5.24, 79.3.9
kè	克		prevailing like fire above the mouth of a kneeling person	59.4.28, 59.5.31

kè	客		a guest entering the mouth of your house under your roof on foot	15.8.41, 35.3.18, 69.3.12
kǒng	恐		afraid—your heart like commonplace dishes being scraped with a blade—	39.9.49, 39.10.56, 39.11.63, 39.12.70, 39.13.78, 39.14.87
kǒng	孔		very fine 'fontanelle' opening	21.1.1
kǒu	口		words from the mouth that are	12.3.17, 35.4.23
kū	枯		dried and withered like an ancient tree of ten generations	76.4.24
kuā	夸		as extravagant as a great giant blowing air	53.13.48
kuà	跨		stepping across—exhaling like a big man, extravagantly handsome—	24.2.5
kuáng	狂		a mad dog roaring as insanely, unrestrainedly as a king	12.5.27
kuàng	況		this river you find yourself in, brother,	23.7.29

kuàng	曠		vast as a sun -- yellow -- shining on a habitable cave in a cliff holding a person with a large belly	15.11.54
kuī	闚		flashing a look—that is to say, this particular grown man with a hairpin and public courtesy name seeing with one big eye for a head—through the double-winged gateway	47.2.8
lái	來		coming next like a stalk of wheat under foot	73.9.51, 80.19.75
lǎn	覽		reflecting like a vessel looking down, all eyes, overseeing	10.5.21
láo	牢		sacrificial animal in a pen	20.10.42
lǎo	老		an old man with long hair and a cane [this word is the first part of Lǎo Zǐ's name]	30.13.67, 55.14.73, 80.18.70
lè	樂		enjoying—like glad music played upon a wooden instrument's silk strings—	23.13.60, 23.15.69, 23.17.78, 31.10.60, 31.11.64, 35.3.14, 66.8.62, 80.15.55

lèi	羸		fleeing by moonlight with one's cowry-shell-riches and dishes	29.9.44
lěi	累		piling up—like fatigue after work in the field, with a skein of silk	64.10.42
lèi	纇		blemished as an ill head that's as bright white as husked raw rice kernels, knotted like a skein of silk	41.8.47
lèi	儽		a tired person—bound, perhaps despite being innocent like a soil margin between croplands—	20.14.60, 20.14.61
lí	離		separated—like as divided as 'a short-tailed bird' is from a failed mountain demon with 'a very prominent tail'—from	10.2.8, 26.4.17, 28.5.18
lǐ	禮		making ritual offerings at the altar with strings of jade and a drum with feathers on top	31.16.99, 31.18.115, 38.9.51, 38.14.84, 38.15.86
lǐ	里		traditional miles—that village measurement of fields on the clay soil	64.11.45

lì	利		benefiting, like by reaping grain with a sharp-edged blade	8.2.7, 19.2.6, 19.5.20, 36.12.50, 11.7.43, 53.10.36, 56.11.46, 57.7.35, 73.3.16, 81.10.46
lì	涖		arriving at an official ceremony, managing—like a person, a person standing on ground, drying up water in the grass	60.2.10
lì	立		a person standing straight up on the ground	24.1.4, 25.3.14, 62.8.37
lì	力		forceful—strong like an arm, a bladed tool, or a plough	33.3.13, 68.6.36
lián	廉		clean and incorruptible as that hand holding two stalks of grain—doing two things at once—in a habitable cliff cave	58.15.59
liǎng	兩		a matched pair, like a harness of ox yokes	1.11.41, 60.8.40, 61.14.71, 65.10.41, 73.3.13
liáng	梁		wood bridging water—with a brutal double-edged sword injury in there too—like the state of Liáng	42.14.62

liáo	飂		wafting with a high wind—dispersing insects, drifting, soaring like a thick-haired man with feathers—	20.24.108
liáo	寥		lonely as the sound of wind through a man's thick hair	25.3.11
liè	裂		rending like using a blade to tear clothing—like a robe, especially on the torso, or the placental afterbirth hanging from a recently pregnant woman—from human remains	39.9.50
liè	獵		a bristly dog beating the game toward you for the hunt, a witch hunt	12.4.22
lín	鄰		the neighboring countries that are attracting like will o' wisp light emanating from a corpse attracting a kneeling person to a grave	15.7.36, 80.16.58
líng	靈		nimbly effective as a rain shaman	39.4.20, 39.11.61

lìng	令		controlling—joining together from three sides over a kneeling person and ordering them to do something, perhaps sending them somewhere—	12.1.3, 12.2.9, 12.3.15, 12.5.23, 12.5.32, 12.7.32, 19.8.34, 32.6.36, 57.9.50
liú	流		flowing like a baby coming out head first in a river of watery waste	61.1.5
liù	六		six	18.3.13
lóng	聾		deaf—a dragon with an ice-cold bow ear—	12.2.12
lù	琭	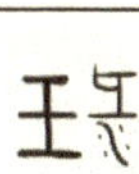	a string of carved jade-like stone totems	39.21.127, 39.21.127
lù	陸		on the land—many divided pieces of soil and big soil mound	50.9.43
lù	露		dew—rain underfoot—	32.5.32
luàn	亂		confused anxiety—one's tongue is like twisted threads with one remnant string hanging out—	3.6.27, 18.4.23, 38.16.93, 64.6.27
luò	珞		each and every pedestrian jade	39.22.131, 39.22.132

mǎ	馬		a horse	46.1.7, 46.2.15, 62.11.50
mǎn	滿		packed full—like arrowheads tightly covered with that traditional 'ji' square piece of fabric men wrap around the 'little bird' top knots on their heads once they've received their adult, public courtesy-names so no water can infiltrate—in	9.5.19
máng	盲		blind—what the eye sees is lost—	12.1.6
mèi	昧		dark— as if the sun's behind a tree with two layers of branches, tree tops not yet fully grown,	14.10.41, 41.6.39
měi	美		admired beauty—picture someone wearing a ram's horn headdress—	2.1.5, 2.1.8, 31.9.54, 31.10.56, 62.4.17, 80.13.49, 81.1.4, 81.2.5
mén	門		double-winged gateway	1.15.59, 6.3.12, 10.9.35, 52.6.35, 56.3.14
mèn	悶		gloomy—bored as a heart-core within the double-winged gateway—	20.22.101, 20.22.102, 58.1.3, 58.1.4

měng	猛		vigorous and ferocious as a dog of an eldest brother—that baby son in the chalice	55.4.15
mí	彌		far—a bow relaxing like cloth on a loom	47.3.15, 47.4.19, 57.6.31
mí	迷		getting lost—like raw rice scattered on the way of walking a while, stopping a while... bewitched, infatuated—	27.17.87, 58.11.46
miǎn	免		exempting—like a man taking off a hat	62.16.74
mián	綿		barely perceptible—like the fine, white silk threads making up that ever-present, timeless, whole-cloth 'ji' our grown-men wrap around 'the little bird' top knots on their heads once they've received their adult, public courtesy-names—	6.5.18, 6.5.19
miào	妙	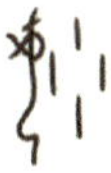	mysterious feminine essence—a few drops of that womanly mist—	1.8.32, 1.15.57, 15.2.8, 27.18.91

miè	滅		obliterating like water extinguishing a fire sheltered by a cliff with a habitable cave as surely as any weapon on a pole	39.13.79
mín	民		civilians—like the Mín people enslaved by blinding with a dagger—	3.2.5, 3.4.15, 3.6.24, 3.12.48, 10.7.27, 19.2.5, 19.4.13, 32.6.33, 53.5.20, 57.6.30, 57.7.33, 57.11.65, 57.12.72, 57.13.79, 57.14.86, 58.2.6, 58.4.14, 64.17.74, 65.2.10, 65.4.15, 66.4.28, 66.5.36, 66.6.49, 66.7.55, 72.1.1, 74.1.1, 74.3.13, 75.1.1, 75.4.14, 75.7.28, 80.1.4, 80.4.15, 80.10.39, 80.18.68,
míng	冥		as darkly profound as if there were a cover over the sun and your two hands,	21.9.35
míng	明		as bright as dawn rising on a crescent moon—enlightened—	10.11.42, 16.10.39, 22.10.33, 24.3.13, 27.13.58, 33.2.8, 36.9.36, 41.6.36, 52.11.53, 52.13.64, 55.11.60, 65.2.9

míng	名		personal, childhood naming—what it whispers to identify itself by moonlight—	1.3.7, 1.3.9, 1.4.12, 1.5.14, 1.6.20, 1.12.47, 14.2.5, 14.4.12, 14.6.19, 14.11.46, 21.14.54, 25.6.32, 25.8.40, 32.1.4, 32.7.43, 32.8.44, 34.4.21, 34.6.35, 34.8.47, 37.6.30, 37.7.34, 41.18.88, 44.1.1, 47.6.32
mìng	命		what has to be—like a command from a magistrate speaking, joining from three sides over a kneeling person—	16.8.31, 16.9.33, 51.9.33
mò	莫		nothing—eh, like the lost-in-the-bushes sinking sun—	9.6.21, 22.18.57, 32.2.10, 32.6.34, 38.9.55, 46.3.20, 46.4.26, 46.5.33, 51.5.17, 51.9.31, 59.1.5, 59.5.33, 59.6.37, 66.10.74, 69.10.35, 70.3.11, 70.4.14, 78.1.3, 78.3.13, 78.7.32, 78.8.35
mò	沒		without—because one would have to dive into the water, wrap one's hands around it to get it	16.19.64, 52.4.26
mò	末		tip-top, tree-top	64.8.35

móu	謀		consulting on strategy—speaking with a tree, words like slaves or criminals, branded by a chisel, emerging from a mouth	64.2.9, 73.10.56
mǔ	母		suckling—like being nursed by a woman—	1.6.24, 20.28.132, 25.5.27, 52.2.9, 52.3.13, 52.4.25, 59.7.48
mǔ	牡		a bull soil... male genitals	55.6.33, 61.4.19
mù	目		what the eye sees	12.1.5, 12.9.44, 49.12.60
mù	木		tree with roots	64.7.31, 76.3.15, 76.8.46
nǎi	乃		you, then,	16.14.50, 16.15.53, 16.16.56, 16.17.59, 16.18.62, 28.17.63, 54.4.24, 54.5.32, 54.6.40, 54.7.48, 54.8.57, 65.16.66
nài	奈		how, how, indeed—like a big man at an altar—	26.7.28, 74.2.5

nán	難		the solidly hard—as difficult as the dried yellow earth of Han where short-tailed birds can't find food—	2.4.27, 3.3.10, 12.6.28, 63.6.19, 63.8.30, 63.15.67, 63.16.73, 63.17.78, 64.20.102, 65.4.17, 73.6.32, 75.4.16, 75.6.26
nè	訥		mumbling or stammering—words that are emerging from a mouth like slaves or criminals branded by a chisel entering a city through its outskirts	45.7.28
néng	能		using a legendary capability—the hybrid power of that mythical bear with deer legs—for	7.2.9, 7.4.20, 7.10.46, 8.11.40, 9.6.23, 10.2.6, 10.4.14, 10.6.22, 10.8.30, 10.10.38, 10.12.46, 14.20.87, 15.13.65, 15.14.73, 15.17.93, 22.18.58, 23.6.26, 32.2.11, 32.3.17, 34.10.58, 37.3.12, 63.13.53, 66.1.5, 66.3.17, 66.10.75, 67.13.50, 67.14.54, 67.15.63, 70.3.12, 70.4.15, 77.11.51, 78.3.15, 78.8.36

nián	年		years of carrying wheat upon your back	30.5.32
niǎo	鳥		a bird with a dangling tail, paying attention already	55.4.20
níng	寧		settled as when a married woman visits her parents' home—her heart under their roof with food and wine—and she exhales	39.3.15, 39.10.55
nù	怒		angry like the heart beneath a hand capturing a woman to be a slave	68.2.11
nuò	諾		promising like someone compliantly combing their loose hair who seems to be speaking up and saying: 'this is as if... yeah, definitely'	63.14.59
pàn	泮		dissolving as half a beef in the river—like the Zhou dynasty school of that name!	64.3.13
pèi	配		matching—like an alcohol vat with a silk rope for binding oneself—	68.7.39
pēng	烹		boiling alive—a baby crying over the fire	60.1.5

pì	譬		metaphorically—ruling over the words coming out of your mouth like a ruler with that chisel used to mark slaves and criminals, making them do what you want—	32.11.59
piān	偏		assistant—just inscribed on the door, flat like bamboo tablets—	31.14.86
piāo	飄		whirling—wind roaring or flame from the west—	23.2.6
pín	貧		poor—separated by a knife from cowry-riches	57.6.32
pìn	牝		of a mother's lap—a cow with an arrow... a vagina	6.2.8, 6.3.10, 55.6.32, 61.3.13, 61.4.14
píng	平		pacified—divided and leveled as with a pestle until made even—	35.2.12
pǔ	普		universally widespread—side by side over the sun, rendering it lusterless	54.8.58

qí	其		what it holds a basket of...	1.8.31, 1.10.39, 3.8.35, 3.9.38, 3.10.41, 3.11.44, 4.5.17, 4.6.20, 4.7.23, 4.8.26, 5.6.25, 7.3.15, 7.5.28, 7.7.34, 7.9.41, 7.10.48, 9.2.7, 9.8.31, 11.2.8, 11.4.20, 11.6.33, 14.9.34, 14.10.38, 14.16.70, 14.17.76, 15.8.39, 15.10.51, 15.11.56, 15.12.61, 16.6.22, 17.2.7, 17.3.13, 17.4.17, 17.6.31, 20.8.31, 20.12.51, 20.23.105, 21.6.21, 21.8.29, 21.10.37, 21.11.41, 21.12.45, 21.14.53, 24.7.29, 25.6.31, 25.13.70, 27.16.78, 27.16.82, 28.1.2, 28.2.5, 28.7.25, 28.8.28, 28.13.48, 28.14.51, 29.2.11, 30.3.13, 33.7.29, 34.2.5, 34.9.51, 34.10.60, 35.5.26, 38.20.112, 38.21.116, 38.22.119, 38.23.123,

				39.8.41, 42.14.66, 45.2.5, 45.4.13, 47.3.13, 47.4.17, 48.7.32, 49.11.52, 49.12.58, 50.7.32, 50.11.59, 50.12.65, 50.13.71, 50.15.77, 52.3.12, 52.3.16, 52.4.20, 52.4.24, 52.5.31, 52.6.34, 52.8.41, 52.9.44, 52.13.59, 52.13.63, 54.4.22, 54.5.30, 54.6.38, 54.7.46, 54.8.55, 56.2.10, 56.3.13, 56.4.16, 56.5.19, 56.6.22, 56.7.25, 57.4.19, 58.1.1, 58.2.5, 58.3.9, 58.4.13, 58.7.31, 58.8.33, 58.12.47, 59.5.35, 59.6.39, 60.3.13, 60.4.18, 60.5.22, 60.6.28, 61.14.75, 63.6.21, 63.7.26, 63.13.55, 64.1.1, 64.2.5, 64.3.10, 64.4.14, 65.5.20, 66.2.12, 66.9.68, 67.7.22, 71.6.23, 72.3.11, 72.4.16, 73.5.25, 74.11.57, 75.2.5, 75.5.19, 75.8.33, 76.2.7,

				76.4.21, 77.2.4, 77.15.75, 78.4.17, 80.12.47, 80.13.50, 80.14.53, 80.15.56
qí	奇		remarkably cunning like the great giant about which one can purse one's lips like a piece of cane and puff: 'Yup, that's it, definitely'	57.2.6, 57.8.45, 58.9.39, 74.4.19
qí	豈		what... how? Is this 'mountains from beans?!'	22.20.70
qǐ	起		coming up like a young man who will die young running from a snake or fetus	57.8.48, 64.10.40
qǐ	企		a person on tiptoes	24.1.1
qì	器		set of valuable vessels with lots of capacity—worthy of a guard dog—	11.3.18, 11.4.23, 28.19.73, 29.3.18, 31.1.8, 31.6.35, 31.7.40, 36.12.51, 41.15.74, 57.7.36, 67.15.65, 80.2.10
qì	氣	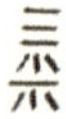	the breath of life—that vital energy, that air flow that's like rice given as a gift—	10.3.11, 42.6.22, 55.13.67

qì	棄		abandoned—like hanging a baby upside down in three leaves on a branch or generation of a tree—is	19.1.3, 19.3.11, 19.5.19, 27.10.45, 27.12.53, 62.7.33
qì	泣		sobbing a river	31.17.109
qì	契		written contract—a great giant engraving like a blade in weeds dense as three strands of hair through, up and down,	79.4.19, 79.6.28
qiān	千		one thousand—where a person reaches when extending their counting	64.11.44
qián	前		forward—the front place in battle where a step could mean one's feet get cut off as punishment—	2.8.43, 38.17.96, 66.7.53
qiáng	強		strengthening like an insect—revolving oneself as a venomous snake-like bow—	3.11.43, 29.9.42, 30.2.10, 33.4.17, 33.6.22, 36.4.15, 36.10.41, 15.5.21, 25.8.37, 30.7.42, 30.12.63, 42.14.61, 52.12.57, 55.13.69, 76.2.11, 76.5.28, 76.7.42, 76.8.47, 76.9.50, 78.2.11, 78.5.25

qiǎo	巧		craftiness—using a bladed tool on exhaled air—	19.5.18, 45.6.22, 57.8.44
qiě	且		abiding for a long time—the erect penis of a male ancestor—	7.2.11, 41.19.94, 67.16.70, 67.17.74, 67.18.78
qīn	親		intimates—like a beloved that one sees closely even in suffering like from that chisel used to mark slaves and criminals	17.2.9, 18.3.14, 44.1.5, 56.9.36, 79.8.36
qín	勤		exerting with force—working hard with the strength of an arm, a bladed tool, or a plough on the soil—	6.6.25, 41.1.5, 52.7.39
qīng	清		clear like still blue-green water—the color resembling the growth of that sedative cinnabar plant	15.13.71, 39.2.10, 39.9.47, 45.10.35
qīng	輕		as if lightweight—as lightweight as using a bladed tool in a light carriage on an underground stream—	26.1.3, 26.8.37, 26.9.40, 63.14.58, 69.10.38, 69.11.40, 75.7.30, 75.9.40
qīng	傾		leaning toward one another, head askew, as if an arrow or a fork is between them	2.6.38

qióng	窮		being used up and destitute—your pregnant self, buried with a bow—	5.9.41, 45.4.16
qiú	求		seeking and requesting—like a coveted fur coat	62.15.68, 75.8.34
qū	屈		bending—like one who represents the dead in a rite flexing to step out of a cave—	5.7.33, 45.5.20
qū	曲		bent and segmented	22.1.1, 22.19.66
qǔ	取		fetching -- carrying in your hand the ear of an enemy	38.24.128, 48.6.24, 48.8.38
qù	去		withdrawing—like a person with a mouth or cave between their legs leaving	2.16.88, 12.10.46, 20.3.10, 20.5.18, 21.14.56, 29.11.53, 29.12.55, 29.13.57, 38.24.126, 72.11.42
qù	取		grabbing the ear of—like marrying—	12.10.48, 29.1.3, 30.7.41, 57.3.12, 61.7.32, 61.9.42, 61.10.49, 61.11.53, 72.11.44
quán	全		whole like a piece of pure jade, entire as it arrived,	22.1.3, 22.19.68, 22.21.75, 55.6.37

quǎn	犬		a dog	80.17.63
quē	缺		lacking like a lidded earthen pot with a gap broken by a resolute hand with a fork	45.1.4, 58.4.15, 58.4.16
què	卻		withdrawing like a kneeling person from within that valley mouth between two mountains	46.1.5
rán	然		accomplished thus, in this manner: as naturally as dog meat over a fire	17.8.44, 23.1.4, 25.17.85, 26.6.27, 51.9.37, 53.1.4, 54.14.88, 57.4.20, 64.22.121, 65.16.64, 73.10.53, 77.9.42
rǎng	攘		their hand helping to undress, rolling up the sleeves, disturbs—throws into disorder—	38.10.59, 69.7.25
rè	熱		hot like a fire under a tree tipped and planted by a person in the clay soil	45.9.34

rén	人		that person	2.9.50, 3.7.31, 5.3.12, 7.5.26, 8.4.15, 12.1.4, 12.2.10, 12.3.16, 12.5.24, 12.7.33, 12.8.39, 20.6.21, 20.9.36, 20.15.68, 20.17.79, 20.19.88, 20.21.96, 20.25.114, 20.27.128, 22.7.22, 23.7.31, 25.14.73, 26.3.12, 27.8.28, 27.9.42, 27.11.46, 27.14.61, 27.14.65, 27.15.70, 27.15.73, 28.20.75, 29.11.52, 30.1.4, 31.10.62, 31.11.66, 31.17.103, 33.1.2, 33.3.10, 36.13.56, 42.7.26, 42.12.53, 47.5.24, 49.1.2, 49.9.41, 49.13.62, 50.4.17, 57.8.41, 57.10.59, 58.11.44, 58.13.54, 59.1.2, 60.5.26, 60.6.32, 60.7.34, 60.7.38, 61.12.61,

				61.13.69, 62.2.8, 62.3.13, 62.5.27, 62.6.28, 63.12.47, 63.16.71, 64.15.63, 64.20.96, 64.21.111, 66.4.25, 66.6.45, 68.4.20, 68.6.34, 70.11.43, 71.5.19, 72.7.30, 73.6.30, 76.1.1, 77.9.37, 77.13.65, 78.9.41, 79.4.16, 79.5.24, 79.9.40, 81.7.26, 81.8.32, 81.9.39, 81.11.51
rén	仁		being a personable person relating to others	5.1.4, 5.3.14, 8.8.31, 18.1.5, 19.3.10, 38.7.35, 38.12.74, 38.13.76
rèn	刃		a blade	50.13.72
réng	扔		your hand unexpectedly throwing away what it has	38.10.62, 69.8.28
rì	日		the sun—the day,	23.3.15, 26.3.14, 48.1.3, 48.2.7, 55.8.44, 58.12.48
róng	戎		armed like with a shield and a weapon on a pole	46.2.14

róng	榮		brilliantly flourishing—like two torches atop a tree—	26.5.22
róng	容		outward public container of private parts—like a building housing an important, older, man with big testicles, a duke—	15.5.24, 16.13.48, 16.14.49, 21.1.4, 28.13.49, 50.13.70
róu	柔		softening—to be like a tree that can be cut with a spear	10.3.13, 36.10.37, 43.1.5, 52.12.55, 55.5.26, 76.1.5, 76.3.19, 76.6.33, 76.10.54, 78.1.4, 78.6.26
rú	如		'as if—like a woman just doing as told—	5.10.43, 9.2.6, 20.10.39, 20.11.43, 20.13.54, 39.21.129, 39.22.133, 62.12.52, 64.18.87
rǔ	辱		disgracing—like vibrating oneself to life in one tiny inch as when life begins to stir—	13.1.2, 13.3.13, 13.7.30, 28.14.52, 41.10.55, 44.6.31
rù	入		entering like an arrow	43.3.15, 50.1.3, 50.10.49, 61.13.67
ruì	銳		a person speaking like an axe on metal—sharpening—	4.5.18, 56.4.17

ruò	弱		as fragile as a matching pair of decorative bows or little wings	3.10.40, 36.3.11, 36.10.38, 40.2.6, 55.5.24, 76.1.6, 76.6.34, 76.10.55, 78.1.5, 78.5.22
ruò	若		A Certain Someone compliantly combing their loose hair seems to be saying: 'this is as if...'	6.5.20, 8.1.3, 13.1.3, 13.2.8, 13.3.14, 13.5.21, 13.6.25, 13.7.31, 13.8.38, 13.13.66, 13.15.77, 15.6.27, 15.7.33, 15.8.40, 15.9.44, 15.10.52, 15.11.57, 15.12.62, 20.5.19, 20.14.63, 20.16.75, 20.23.106, 20.24.110, 32.3.16, 37.3.11, 41.2.13, 41.2.15, 41.6.38, 41.7.42, 41.8.46, 41.9.50, 41.10.54, 41.11.58, 41.12.63, 41.13.67, 45.1.3, 45.3.11, 45.5.19, 45.6.23, 45.7.27, 59.1.6, 60.1.4, 67.5.18, 74.3.11, 78.14.63
sāi	塞		cramming—both hands stuffing items into the house	52.5.30

sān	三		three [times]	11.1.1, 19.7.26, 42.3.9, 42.4.10, 50.2.10, 50.3.16, 50.5.27, 62.9.41, 67.8.28, 67.12.40
sàn	散		becoming free and loose—like bamboos lightly hit by the crescent moon, breaking apart—	28.19.70, 64.4.17
sāng	喪		circumstances associated with a disappearance, with death,	31.16.98, 31.18.114, 69.11.43
sè	色		color—like from hand-clawing a kneeling person, tinting their complexion to a feminine charm albeit sometimes lewdly or even to a perverted countenance—	12.1.2
sè	嗇		thrifty as conserving wheat in a granary	59.1.7, 59.2.10
shā	殺		killing a man by impaling a spear into the hair on his head	31.10.61, 31.11.65, 31.17.102, 73.1.5, 74.5.25, 74.7.32, 74.7.34, 74.8.38, 74.8.40
shà	嗄		hoarse—mouth like a man under a scorching sun	55.8.48

shàn	善		virtue—such as offering up a ram's head while back and forth speaking words that are emerging from a mouth like slaves or criminals branded by a chisel—	2.2.14, 2.2.17, 2.2.20, 8.1.2, 8.2.6, 8.6.24, 8.7.27, 8.8.30, 8.9.33, 8.10.36, 8.11.39, 8.12.42, 15.1.3, 20.4.13, 27.1.1, 27.2.6, 27.3.11, 27.4.17, 27.6.26, 27.9.40, 27.11.48, 27.14.60, 27.14.64, 27.15.69, 27.15.72, 30.6.33, 41.19.92, 49.3.12, 49.3.15, 49.4.18, 49.4.22, 49.5.25, 50.8.39, 54.1.1, 54.2.6, 58.10.40, 62.2.7, 62.3.12, 62.6.31, 65.1.3, 66.2.13, 68.1.1, 68.2.7, 68.3.12, 68.4.18, 73.7.40, 73.8.45, 73.10.55, 79.3.12, 79.9.39, 81.3.9, 81.4.16
shāng	傷		wounded -- a bent person with that male principle of sun shining on an altar like strands of hair	60.5.25, 60.6.31, 60.7.37, 60.8.43, 74.11.56

shàng	上		higher, ruling level	8.1.1, 17.1.2, 31.8.50, 31.15.91, 14.9.35, 38.1.1, 38.5.18, 38.7.34, 38.8.42, 38.9.50, 41.1.1, 41.9.48, 66.4.27, 66.6.47, 71.1.4, 72.2.6, 75.2.6, 75.5.20, 76.10.57
shàng	尚		elevating—aloft in a fancy house—	3.1.2, 23.6.24, 31.12.80, 31.13.84
shǎo	少		reducing to few—four little dots—	19.10.42, 22.5.13, 47.4.20, 63.4.13
shē	奢		gluttony—a big man stewing noodles or sugar cane—	29.12.56
shě	舍		handing over, like [at] a thatched inn—abandoning	67.16.68, 67.17.72, 67.18.76
shé	蛇		a serpent, a crooked snake—including certain crooked gentlemen or emperors	55.3.12
shè	涉		wading, one foot in front of the other, through a watery	15.6.29
shè	攝		taking well in hand, hearing three times over,	50.8.40
shè	社		the god of the soil to whom we build altars	78.11.49

shēn	身		one's pregnant self	7.5.29, 7.6.31, 7.7.35, 7.8.37, 9.9.35, 13.2.9, 13.8.39, 13.10.50, 13.11.54, 13.12.62, 13.14.73, 16.19.65, 26.8.36, 44.1.3, 44.2.6, 52.4.27, 52.7.37, 52.10.47, 52.14.67, 54.4.21, 54.9.61, 54.9.63, 66.5.39
shēn	深		deep as far water	15.3.11, 59.8.55, 65.14.56
shén	神	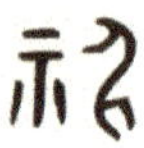	a lightning god	6.1.2, 29.3.17, 39.4.16, 39.11.58, 60.4.21, 60.5.23, 60.6.29
shèn	甚		the extreme—something pleasing in the mouth, matched so it's doubly pleasing	21.11.43, 29.11.54, 44.4.18, 53.4.17, 53.6.24, 53.7.27, 53.8.30, 70.1.3, 70.2.6
shèn	慎		prudent—your heart genuinely acting sincerely with care as with using your fork to get food right from the cauldron	64.18.85

shēng	生		birthing—a bud sprouting from the ground—	2.3.26, 2.12.68, 7.3.18, 7.4.22, 10.13.50, 10.14.54, 15.14.80, 25.2.8, 30.4.23, 34.3.14, 39.6.31, 39.13.76, 40.3.15, 40.4.19, 42.1.2, 42.2.5, 42.3.8, 42.4.11, 46.2.16, 50.1.2, 50.2.5, 50.4.19, 50.7.33, 50.7.34, 50.8.41, 51.1.2, 51.10.40, 51.15.57, 55.12.62, 59.9.60, 64.8.32, 72.4.18, 75.8.35, 75.10.46, 75.11.53, 76.1.3, 76.3.17, 76.6.36
shēng	聲		many sounds—hitting chimes with one's right hand and hearing them—	2.7.40, 41.16.80, 80.17.65
shéng	繩		a skein of silk around a striving toad	14.11.42, 14.11.43, 27.6.29, 80.10.42

shèng	聖		a grounded sage—listening and speaking, standing connected to earth as well as the heavens	2.9.49, 3.7.30, 5.3.11, 7.5.25, 12.8.38, 19.1.2, 22.7.21, 26.3.11, 27.8.37, 28.20.75, 29.11.51, 47.5.23, 49.1.1, 49.9.40, 49.13.61, 57.10.58, 58.13.53, 60.7.33, 63.12.46, 63.16.70, 64.15.62, 64.20.95, 66.4.24, 66.6.44, 70.11.42, 71.5.18, 72.7.29, 73.6.29, 77.13.64, 78.9.40, 79.4.15, 81.7.25, 81.11.50
shèng	勝		forcing a victory over—using a blade to mend a boat or roll rice into a ball under moonlight—	31.9.51, 31.18.112, 36.10.39, 33.3.9, 33.4.15, 45.8.30, 45.9.33, 61.4.18, 67.20.87, 68.3.13, 69.13.53, 73.7.41, 76.7.45, 78.3.16, 78.5.24, 78.6.28
shèng	乘		four-horse military carriage	26.7.31, 80.7.28

shī	失		dropping something—losing it	13.6.23, 23.11.49, 23.11.53, 23.16.74, 23.17.76, 26.9.42, 26.10.46, 29.6.29, 33.7.28, 38.3.12, 38.11.65, 38.12.70, 38.13.75, 38.14.80, 64.14.58, 64.16.73, 73.12.64
shī	施		putting it into place like flags flying over a corpse—yes, that too, vagina.	53.3.12
shī	師		army of 2500 soldiers stationed on a hill	27.14.67, 27.16.79, 30.4.17
shí	識		intimately knowing with the mind—recognizing those words on that weapon on a pole and saying what it carries like a plough, what it carries the meaning of	15.3.14, 15.4.19, 38.17.97
shí	實		really full like a building with strings of solid cowry-like riches as valuable as jade	3.9.37, 38.22.120
shí	石		a hard stone beneath a cliff with a habitable cave	39.22.134

shí	十		ten	11.1.2, 50.2.8, 50.3.14, 50.5.25
shí	食		having a meal—mouth over a bowl of rice on a stand—	20.28.131, 24.8.35, 53.11.40, 75.2.7, 80.12.48
shí	什		ten people	80.2.7
shí	時		seasonally timely—like when the sun is between your footprint and the position on your arm where you measure your pulse—	8.12.43
shǐ	始		beginning—like conception in and by a woman—	1.5.18, 14.20.90, 32.7.40, 38.18.105, 52.1.4, 64.12.48, 64.18.88
shǐ	使		breeding—like a gentleman holding a fountain pen making something happen—	3.2.4, 3.4.14, 3.6.23, 3.12.47, 3.13.53, 53.1.1, 55.13.66, 74.3.12, 80.2.5, 80.4.14, 80.10.38
shǐ	室		such a living space—where a wife comes to live—	11.6.36
shì	室		living space – where a wife comes to live—	11.5.31

shì	是		the sun—walking across the sundial a while, stopping a while—sees indeed	2.9.47, 2.16.85, 3.7.28, 6.2.5, 6.4.13, 7.5.23, 10.17.66, 12.8.36, 13.7.27, 14.13.52, 14.15.62, 14.21.91, 16.8.28, 21.2.7, 22.7.19, 22.11.36, 24.4.15, 26.3.9, 27.8.35, 27.13.55, 27.18.88, 29.11.49, 30.14.68, 31.10.59, 36.9.33, 38.2.5, 38.4.14, 38.19.106, 39.17.100, 43.4.18, 44.4.16, 47.5.21, 51.5.13, 51.18.69, 52.15.69, 53.3.13, 53.13.45, 56.8.27, 58.13.51, 59.2.11, 59.8.53, 63.12.44, 63.16.68, 64.15.60, 64.20.93, 65.13.50, 66.4.22, 66.6.42, 66.8.58, 68.5.25, 68.6.31, 68.7.37, 69.6.20, 70.8.27, 70.11.40, 71.4.14, 71.7.26, 72.6.23, 72.7.27, 73.6.27, 74.9.41,

				75.3.11, 75.6.24, 75.9.38, 75.11.49, 76.7.39, 77.13.62, 78.9.38, 78.11.47, 78.13.56, 79.4.13
shì	士		bachelor soldier-scholar-official appointed by the emperor—a yeoman—	15.1.5, 41.1.2, 41.2.10, 41.3.18, 68.1.3
shì	事		one's personal, manual role—what one does with a weapon, a flag, or a pen—	2.9.55, 8.11.38, 17.7.36, 23.8.35, 30.3.14, 31.12.79, 31.13.83, 48.6.30, 48.7.34, 52.9.45, 57.3.11, 57.13.77, 59.1.3, 61.13.68, 63.2.4, 63.2.6, 63.8.31, 63.10.39, 64.17.77, 64.19.92, 70.6.20
shì	勢		planting power—like holding a forceful arm, a bladed tool, or a plough on the soil to seed like testicles	51.4.10
shì	螫		stinging— both armpits sweat this too!— when hit lightly by a snake	55.3.14

shì	視		regarding like one big eye for a head seeing at an altar	14.1.1, 35.6.29, 59.9.62
shì	市		market—a bustling city at the fork in a tree	62.4.21
shì	式		a model example—like a bladed tool is for work or a retrievable arrow attached to a string is for shooting and catching—	22.8.28, 28.9.33, 28.10.37, 65.11.45, 65.12.49
shì	逝		passing—walking a while, stopping a while when a hand and axe sever life early—	25.9.45, 25.10.46
shì	恃		expecting that will be holding one's heart-core like a mother	2.13.75, 10.15.61, 34.3.11, 51.16.64, 77.13.69
shì	示		they're on display—like on an altar	36.13.55
shì	釋		releasing—distinguishing the sight of the opposite or upside-down-person-version of a running young man who will die young, that is spying on good luck or an emperor's personal favor—	15.9.48

shǒu	守		hand-defending this—one's building—	5.10.44, 9.6.24, 16.2.4, 28.2.4, 28.8.27, 28.14.50, 32.3.18, 37.3.13, 52.4.23, 52.12.54, 67.21.89
shǒu	手		their expert, convenient hand	74.11.58
shǒu	首		the head—the loose-haired headperson—	14.16.71, 38.16.95
shòu	獸		animal—as a dog on a beast—	55.4.16
shòu	受		receiving and bearing—a hand over a commonplace plate with a hand below, on bottom	78.10.43, 78.12.52
shū	疏		distant and sparse—picture a foot with a thigh above it and an upside-down baby with amniotic fluid streaming down below its head	56.10.41, 73.12.61
shú	孰		whoever—which person, like a baby with a slanting mouth of enjoyment is this	15.13.64, 15.14.72, 23.4.16, 44.1.4, 44.2.9, 44.3.14, 58.7.29, 73.5.23, 74.6.27, 77.11.50
shǔ	數		counting up—like a mother, lightly hitting, scolding her daughter—	27.3.12, 39.20.121

shǔ	屬		born to—that is the living person, a head man, who represents their dead kin or the tail-end, the most recent piece of that category—	19.8.37
shuǎng	爽		broken—a person holding nothing more than two pairs of cut-marks	12.3.18
shuí	誰		of whom 'the short-tailed bird' speaks, the one that	4.11.36
shuǐ	水		water, flowing right in the center of the Han River and spraying up on both sides—	8.1.4, 8.2.5, 78.1.7
shuì	稅		grain tax—a rice plant to an open mouth like that of a smiling, breathy older brother	75.2.8
shùn	順		smoothly going along with—like the loose-haired headperson kneeling at a river	65.16.69
sī	司		taking charge -- like a reversed queen or king, that is, head speaker	74.7.31, 74.8.37, 79.6.27, 79.7.31
sī	私	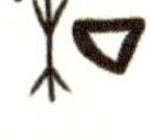	personal concerns—like about one's private grain field	7.9.43, 7.10.49, 19.10.43

sī	斯		cleverly lopping off a basket of and thereby defining	2.1.9, 2.2.18
sǐ	死		dying—going from a standing person to a pile of bones—	6.1.4, 33.8.33, 42.14.67, 50.1.4, 50.3.11, 50.4.22, 50.15.79, 67.19.80, 74.1.4, 74.2.8, 74.3.16, 75.7.31, 75.9.41, 76.2.8, 76.4.22, 76.5.30, 80.4.17, 80.18.71
sì	兕		fearsome buffalo	50.9.47, 50.11.55
sì	祀		sacrificing -- something like a fetus upon an altar	54.3.15
sì	似		it bears a side-by-side personal resemblance—like a person to a fetus—to	4.4.11, 4.10.30, 20.26.122
sì	肆		undisciplined—like the long hair that has to be tied with a brooch of one who once was skillful with a bamboo brush	58.16.66
sì	駟		driving four horses—like to pull a chariot	62.11.49
sì	四		in all four directions	10.11.44, 15.7.35, 25.13.65

sú	俗		in the common practices of the people from that difficult position in the valley between two mountains	20.19.87, 20.21.95, 41.9.51, 80.15.57
sù	素		what's plain—the elemental, like white silk being braided by hand—	19.9.39
suī	雖		although—even if 'a venomous snake' has 'a short-tailed bird' right next to it—	26.5.20, 27.17.84, 32.2.6, 62.10.43, 80.6.22, 80.8.30
suí	隨		accompanying one another—walking single file a while on a road near soil mountains, stopping a while—	2.8.46, 14.17.72, 29.7.36
suì	遂		completed—when you walk a while, stop a while after the harvest, during the time you divide up the pigs—	9.9.34, 17.7.37
sūn	孫		baby boy -- maybe a grandson like a tiny, thin silk thread	54.3.12
sǔn	損		diminishing like hands and fingers injured by the top edge of the cauldron that is the monarchy government	42.10.44, 42.11.52, 48.2.8, 48.3.9, 48.3.12, 77.5.20, 77.7.30, 77.10.43

suǒ	所		'place'— somewhere intentionally created, like a door chopped with an axe—	7.2.7, 8.4.17, 13.9.41, 19.8.36, 20.6.23, 20.14.65, 22.19.64, 30.4.19, 33.7.30, 42.7.28, 42.12.55, 50.11.57, 50.12.63, 50.13.69, 58.5.21, 58.6.27, 61.14.76, 62.3.15, 62.13.59, 64.21.113, 66.1.3, 72.3.12, 72.4.17, 73.4.21, 80.7.27, 80.9.35
tái	台		as its place name—what it says, revolving around itself	64.9.39
tái	臺		a lookout tower from which a person can shoot an arrow	20.11.46
tài	太		the utmost—the biggest, like the greatest man—	17.1.1, 20.10.41, 35.2.13
tài	忒		erring or changing—shooting a retrievable arrow attached to a string into the heart—	28.11.41
tài	泰		the excessively extravagant—a big man trying to clasp both arms around a flowing stream—	29.13.58

táng	堂		a palace courtyard	9.5.20

tiān	天		Heaven (that sky level above the human head)	1.5.15, 2.1.1, 5.1.1, 5.5.21, 6.4.15, 7.1.1, 7.2.5, 9.10.37, 10.9.34, 13.12.64, 13.13.69, 13.14.75, 13.15.80, 16.5.15, 16.16.57, 16.17.58, 22.8.26, 22.18.55, 23.5.20, 23.6.22, 25.2.6, 25.5.25, 25.12.55, 25.15.78, 25.16.79, 26.8.38, 28.3.8, 28.4.12, 28.9.31, 28.10.35, 28.15.54, 28.16.58, 29.1.4, 29.3.15, 30.2.11, 31.11.75, 32.2.8, 32.5.25, 32.11.63, 35.1.4, 37.9.46, 39.2.6, 39.7.38, 39.9.44, 40.3.11, 43.1.1, 43.2.8, 43.7.35, 45.10.38, 46.1.1, 46.2.10, 47.1.5, 47.2.11, 48.6.25, 48.8.39, 49.9.43, 49.10.49, 52.1.1, 52.2.7, 54.8.53, 54.13.77, 54.13.80, 54.14.86, 56.15.64, 57.3.13, 57.6.24, 59.1.4,

				60.2.11, 61.2.6, 61.3.10, 62.8.38, 62.17.78, 63.8.28, 63.10.36, 66.8.60, 66.10.72, 67.1.1, 67.12.45, 67.15.59, 67.22.92, 68.7.40, 70.3.9, 73.4.19, 73.7.34, 73.11.57, 77.1.1, 77.7.27, 77.11.56, 78.1.1, 78.7.30, 78.13.58, 79.8.33, 81.10.43
tián	田		a field	53.7.26
tián	畋		tilling a field, hitting it lightly, marking it up like a tattoo,	12.4.21
tián	恬		quieted—the heart-core licked by a forked tongue emerging upward from a mouth—	31.8.47
tīng	聽		hearing it, obeying like an upright person standing on earth, allowing ten nets over their heart-core	14.3.8, 35.7.34
tíng	亭		sheltering like a person in a pavilion or in a checkpoint	51.13.49

tōng	通		patiently penetrating—when the way of walking a while, stopping a while, is a path right between two walls—	15.2.10
tóng	同		when spoken of altogether in integrity—like all earthly, mortal, commonplace plates—	1.11.43, 1.13.48, 4.8.25, 23.9.41, 23.10.46, 23.11.51, 23.12.54, 23.14.63, 23.16.72, 56.7.24, 56.8.30
tōu	偷		covertly sneaking, like a man standing with his back to someone gathering themselves together from three sides after a blade cut off their foot as punishment, like from adultery	41.12.64
tóu	投		throwing expertly by hand like handling a shū weapon	50.11.58
tú	徒		follower—a foot soldier, walking awhile and stopping a while on the clay soil	50.2.7, 50.3.13, 76.5.32, 76.6.38
tú	圖		planning—plotting a chart like someone receiving by mouth from the grannies within a walled city	63.6.18

tǔ	土		clay soil	64.10.43
tuī	推		promoting along like hand-pushing that 'short-tailed bird'	66.8.63
tuì	退		withdraw—walk awhile and stop a while, retreating from the sun—	9.9.36, 41.7.43, 69.5.18
tuō	脫		they're leaving—freely stripping like a smiling breathy older brother by moonlight—	36.11.45, 54.2.10
tuō	託		trusted with—committed to caring for something like a blade of grass by speaking words like slaves or criminals, branded by a chisel, emerging from a mouth—	13.15.79
tuó	槖		a bellows-	5.6.27
wā	窪		hollow like a swampy pit as deep as the stacked jade tablets officials use when addressing the emperor in court—	22.3.7

wài	外		'outside' or foreign—the relatives of your mother, sister, and daughter who divine by the moon—	7.7.33
wán	頑		headstrong—kneeling but with a head even above one's own head as a fundamental, source, or meta-head—	20.26.121
wǎn	晚		late evening when the sun on a man in a hat is being removed	41.15.75
wàn	萬		the myriad, scorpion-medicine-dancing Ten Thousand	1.6.21, 2.11.61, 4.4.12, 5.2.6, 8.2.8, 16.3.7, 26.7.30, 32.4.20, 34.3.9, 34.5.25, 34.7.38, 37.4.15, 39.6.26, 39.13.72, 40.3.13, 42.4.12, 42.5.14, 51.5.15, 62.1.3, 64.22.117, 76.3.12
wáng	王		king—connecting heaven, man, and earth	16.15.54, 16.16.55, 25.12.59, 25.13.68, 32.3.15, 37.3.10, 39.7.33, 39.14.81, 39.17.103, 42.9.36, 66.1.9, 66.3.21, 78.13.60
wáng	亡	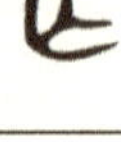	past—perished	33.8.36, 41.2.16, 44.3.13, 44.5.27

wáng	妄		improper and willful—recklessly so, like a kneeling woman fleeing—	16.12.43
wǎng	往		walking slowly toward you—like a host with a lamp, only the left leg leading the way—	35.1.6, 35.2.7, 80.19.74
wǎng	網		thin silk net	73.11.58
wǎng	枉		bent like a tree king connecting heaven, man, and earth,	22.2.4
wàng	望		gazing from a distance like a good human standing on soil below the cutting edge of a knife and the crescent moon	80.16.61
wēi	微		so triflingly small and humble as to almost not exist—as someone following something from behind, stepping slowly with only the left leg leading around the left side of three high peaks where the foot of the mountains cuts off	14.6.21, 15.1.7, 36.9.35, 64.4.15

wēi	威		pomp and power—intimidating like an axe over a woman kneeling with breasts	72.1.4, 72.2.7

wéi	為		efforting—like lifting up an elephant—	2.1.7, 2.2.16, 2.9.53, 2.13.72, 3.4.17, 3.13.59, 3.14.61, 3.14.63, 5.2.8, 5.4.18, 10.10.39, 10.15.58, 11.3.17, 11.5.30, 11.7.42, 11.8.48, 12.9.40, 12.9.43, 13.4.17, 13.10.47, 13.12.63, 13.14.74, 14.8.32, 15.1.4, 15.5.22, 19.7.29, 21.3.11, 22.8.25, 23.4.17, 25.5.24, 25.8.38, 26.1.2, 26.2.6, 28.3.7, 28.4.11, 28.9.30, 28.10.34, 28.15.53, 28.16.57, 28.19.72, 28.21.79, 29.1.7, 29.4.21, 29.5.23, 31.8.49, 34.5.29, 34.7.44, 34.8.48, 34.9.55, 37.1.4, 37.2.8, 38.5.21, 38.6.25, 38.6.28, 38.6.33, 38.7.36, 38.7.41, 38.8.44, 38.8.49, 38.9.52, 39.7.37, 39.15.93, 39.16.98, 39.18.114, 41.4.29, 42.6.24, 42.9.39, 42.15.71,

				43.4.23, 43.6.32, 45.10.37, 47.7.34, 48.1.1, 48.2.5, 48.4.17, 48.5.19, 48.5.23, 49.2.10, 49.10.48, 51.16.61, 52.2.6, 52.15.70, 56.15.63, 57.11.63, 58.9.38, 58.10.42, 61.5.22, 61.15.81, 62.17.77, 63.1.1, 63.1.3, 63.7.23, 63.12.50, 64.5.18, 64.13.52, 64.15.65, 64.22.125, 65.1.4, 66.1.6, 66.3.18, 67.12.44, 67.15.58, 68.1.2, 68.4.22, 69.2.8, 69.3.11, 74.4.18, 75.5.23, 75.10.47, 77.13.66, 79.3.11, 81.8.31, 81.11.54
wéi	唯		—oh, yes, 'short-tailed bird,' ma'am...only—	15.4.16, 15.16.89, 22.17.51

wéi	唯		essentially and only—like the mouth of 'the short-tailed bird'—	2.15.82, 8.13.45, 21.2.5, 21.4.13, 21.4.15, 41.19.90, 42.8.30, 53.3.11, 59.2.9, 67.3.12, 70.7.24, 71.3.11, 72.5.20, 75.10.43, 77.12.58
wěi	偽		'sideways' efforting—that hypocrisy where a person seems to be working hard, like they're holding up an elephant, but really they're just standing adjacent to it—	18.2.12, 20.2.5
wèi	謂		what it's called when speaking from the gut—words, like slaves or criminals branded by a chisel emerging from a mouth	1.13.49, 6.2.6, 6.4.14, 10.17.67, 13.3.11, 13.7.28, 13.8.34, 14.13.53, 14.15.63, 14.21.92, 16.8.29, 17.8.41, 22.19.65, 27.13.56, 27.18.89, 30.14.69, 36.9.34, 51.18.70, 53.13.46, 55.15.74, 56.8.28, 59.2.12, 59.3.17, 59.8.54, 65.13.51, 67.1.4, 68.5.26, 68.6.32, 68.7.38, 69.6.21, 74.9.42, 78.11.48, 78.13.57

wèi	畏		fearing—like when there's a ghost holding a stick or maybe part of a tiger with its claw—	15.7.34, 17.3.15, 20.6.24, 20.7.28, 53.3.14, 72.1.3, 74.1.3, 74.3.15
wèi	未		not yet—a tree whose top branches aren't yet fully grown—	20.8.32, 20.12.52, 20.13.58, 55.6.30, 64.2.6, 64.5.21, 64.6.26
wèi	味		tasting—reflecting on the flavor in your mouth which is still forming like a tree whose top branches aren't yet fully grown—	12.3.14, 35.5.28, 63.3.7, 63.3.9
wèi	衛		guarding—footsteps around an enclosure at an intersection	67.23.98
wén	聞		hearing at the double-winged gateway	14.3.11, 35.7.38, 41.1.3, 41.2.11, 41.3.19, 50.8.38, 80.17.67
wén	文		written description—a tattooed chest or, nowadays, literature or texts—	19.7.30, 53.9.33

wǒ	我		I/we—holding a rake-like weapon to defend ourselves and our opinion—	17.8.42, 20.12.47, 20.16.73, 20.17.77, 20.20.91, 20.22.99, 20.26.19, 20.27.124, 42.13.57, 53.1.2, 57.11.61, 57.12.68, 57.13.75, 57.14.82, 67.1.5, 67.8.26, 70.8.29, 70.9.33, 70.10.37
wò	握		gripping—holding expertly in hand like a shelter made from a cloth draped over an arrow stuck in the ground	55.5.28

wú	無		Not-Being—nobody trance-dancing with long tails flowing from her wrists—	1.5.13, 1.7.27, 2.3.24, 2.9.52, 3.12.49, 3.12.51, 3.14.62, 3.15.65, 7.9.42, 8.14.49, 10.2.7, 10.6.23, 10.8.31, 10.12.47, 11.2.9, 11.4.21, 11.6.34, 11.8.45, 13.11.53, 14.12.50, 14.13.54, 14.14.58, 19.6.23, 19.11.48, 20.1.3, 20.14.64, 20.24.111, 24.5.22, 27.1.3, 27.2.8, 27.4.19, 27.6.28, 27.10.44, 27.12.52, 28.12.45, 32.1.3, 34.6.32, 35.5.27, 37.1.3, 37.2.6, 37.6.29, 37.7.33, 37.7.40, 38.4.16, 38.5.20, 38.5.23, 38.7.39, 39.9.45, 39.10.52, 39.11.59, 39.12.66, 39.13.74, 39.14.82, 39.20.123, 40.4.21, 41.14.71, 41.17.83, 41.18.87, 43.3.13, 43.3.16, 43.4.22, 43.6.31, 46.2.12, 48.4.16, 48.5.18, 48.5.21, 48.6.29, 49.1.3, 50.11.56,

				50.12.62, 50.13.68, 50.15.78, 52.14.65, 57.3.10, 57.11.62, 57.13.76, 57.14.83, 58.8.34, 59.4.26, 59.5.29, 63.1.2, 63.2.5, 63.3.8, 63.17.77, 64.15.64, 64.15.67, 64.16.69, 64.16.72, 64.19.90, 69.6.23, 69.7.26, 69.8.29, 69.9.32, 70.7.25, 72.3.9, 72.4.14, 75.10.44, 78.4.18, 79.7.29, 79.8.35, 80.7.26, 80.9.34
wú	吾		I/we—our five mouths—	4.11.33, 13.9.40, 13.10.48, 13.11.52, 13.11.55, 16.4.11, 21.16.61, 25.6.28, 37.6.24, 29.2.9, 42.15.68, 43.4.18, 49.3.14, 49.4.20, 49.6.28, 49.7.34, 54.14.82, 57.4.15, 69.2.5, 69.11.44, 70.1.1, 74.5.21
wú	蕪		thick grass of an unused field	53.7.28

wǔ	武		military—setting out by foot with spear as one for a long journey	68.1.6
wǔ	五		five times,	12.1.1, 12.2.7, 12.3.13
wǔ	侮		ridiculing and disgracing—as a person whose lush flourishing sprouts out of suckling a kneeling woman	17.4.19
wù	物		Things cut off—all matter external to oneself like seeds, cows etc.	1.6.22, 2.11.62, 4.4.13, 5.2.7, 8.2.9, 14.12.51, 14.14.59, 16.3.8, 16.5.16, 21.3.12, 21.8.32, 24.9.38, 25.1.2, 27.11.50, 27.12.54, 29.7.32, 30.13.64, 31.2.9, 32.4.21, 34.3.10, 34.5.26, 34.7.39, 37.4.16, 39.6.27, 39.13.73, 40.3.14, 42.4.13, 42.5.15, 42.10.42, 51.3.7, 51.5.16, 55.14.70, 57.8.46, 62.1.4, 64.22.118, 65.15.61, 76.3.13
wù	惡		a house's inferior-hearted evil—seen from overhead—	24.9.40, 31.2.11, 42.7.29, 73.4.22

wù	勿		do not—seriously like blood on a blade, just don't be—	30.8.45, 30.9.49, 30.10.53, 30.12.62
xī	昔		Ancient times, when the floods covered the sun,	39.1.1
xī	希		sparse—as spare as the interconnecting threads in that square cloth men wrap around their 'little bird' top knots and heads—	14.4.14, 23.1.1, 41.16.79, 43.7.37, 70.9.35, 74.11.53
xī	兮		—Oh! A breath, like wind through tree branches! —	4.3.10, 4.9.29, 15.6.26, 15.7.32, 15.8.38, 15.9.43, 15.10.50, 15.11.55, 15.12.60, 17.5.24, 17.5.28, 17.6.30, 20.8.30, 20.12.50, 20.14.62, 20.18.86, 20.23.104, 20.24.109, 21.5.18, 21.5.20, 21.7.26, 21.7.28, 21.9.34, 21.9.36, 23.18.84, 23.18.88, 25.3.10, 25.3.12, 30.4.24, 34.1.4, 58.5.18, 58.6.24

xī	谿	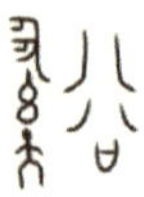	a valley—a mouth between two mountains, the tiniest little silk string of a child between a claw-like hand grabbing from above and a great giant below—	28.3.10, 28.4.14
xī	歙		sucking in—when finally a gathering of little wings isn't a sufficient target for a blade—	36.1.3, 49.10.45, 49.10.46
xí	習		practicing like flapping both wings in the sun	52.15.71
xí	襲		an inherited, raiding pattern—superposed atop like something received from the clothing or placenta of a flying dragon—	27.13.57
xí	熙		bright as a wide chin, growing with a fire below it	20.9.37, 20.9.38
xǐ	徙		moving, shifting, migrating like feces leaving a living person representing the dead in a rite	80.5.21
xì	細		small, delicate, and young -- a skein of silk fontanelle	63.7.27, 63.11.43, 67.7.23

xiá	狎		intimate with—maybe improperly familiar with—like a dog with a turtle shell	72.3.10
xiá	瑕		flawed—like what you'd see in a king who borrowed or forged a gem—	27.2.9

xià	下		down below, lower level	2.1.2, 2.6.36, 13.4.18, 13.12.65, 13.13.70, 13.14.76, 13.15.81, 14.10.39, 17.1.3, 22.8.27, 22.18.56, 25.5.26, 26.8.39, 28.3.9, 28.4.13, 28.9.32, 28.10.36, 28.15.55, 28.16.59, 29.1.5, 29.3.16, 30.2.12, 31.11.76, 32.2.9, 32.11.64, 35.1.5, 37.9.47, 38.3.9, 38.6.26, 39.7.39, 39.16.97, 40.3.12, 41.3.17, 43.1.2, 43.2.9, 43.7.36, 45.10.39, 46.1.2, 46.2.11, 47.1.6, 48.6.26, 48.8.40, 49.9.44, 49.10.50, 52.1.2, 52.2.8, 54.8.54, 54.13.78, 54.13.81, 54.14.87, 56.15.65, 57.3.14, 57.6.25, 60.2.12, 61.1.4, 61.2.7, 61.3.11, 61.5.23, 61.6.28, 61.8.38, 61.10.47, 61.11.51, 61.15.82, 62.17.79,

				63.8.29, 63.10.37, 64.12.51, 66.2.14, 66.4.32, 66.8.61, 66.10.73, 67.1.2, 67.12.46, 67.15.60, 68.4.24, 70.3.10, 76.9.53, 77.4.13, 77.11.57, 78.1.2, 78.7.31, 78.13.59
xiān	鮮		delicacies like fresh fish or ram's head	60.1.7
xiān	先		being long before—that is, an ancestor	4.12.42, 7.6.32, 25.2.5, 62.11.48, 66.5.35, 67.12.47, 67.15.61, 67.18.79
xián	賢	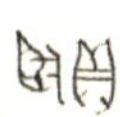	important folks—their eye looking down, surrendering, with cowry-like riches—	3.1.3, 75.11.50, 77.15.79
xiāng	鄉		a village—a rural community where people face one another over a food vessel, feasting	54.6.37, 54.11.69, 54.11.71

xiāng	相		mutually—like a seen tree and the eye seeing it—	2.3.25, 2.5.33, 2.6.37, 2.7.41, 2.8.45, 20.3.9, 20.5.17, 32.5.27, 2.4.29, 60.8.42, 69.12.49, 80.16.60, 80.17.66, 80.19.73
xiáng	祥		a good omen—a ram's head at an altar—	31.1.6, 31.6.33, 55.12.64, 78.12.55
xiàng	象		likeness—like an elephant skeleton letting us see a living elephant—of	4.12.39, 14.14.61, 21.6.24, 35.1.3, 41.17.82
xiǎo	小		very little, like three grains of sand	32.2.7, 34.6.37, 52.11.51, 60.1.6, 61.6.29, 61.7.33, 61.8.35, 61.13.62, 63.4.11, 80.1.1
xiào	笑		laughing like a dog in the grass	41.3.22, 41.4.25
xiào	肖		resembling like how a small child—a tiny three-dot-meat—looks like their parents	67.2.10, 67.4.17, 67.5.19
xiào	孝		filial piety—between, for example, a long-haired old man and a child [the old man sub-character is the first part of Lǎo Zǐ's names] —	18.3.18, 19.4.15

xié	歇		yawning—like a man deficient and lacking breath—and resting, relaxing	39.11.64
xīn	心		heart-core	3.6.25, 3.8.36, 8.7.26, 12.5.25, 20.17.81, 49.1.5, 49.2.9, 49.2.11, 49.11.53, 55.13.65
xīn	新		fresh as a newly axed tree	15.17.96, 22.4.12
xìn	信		truth-speaking—speaking words like slaves or criminals, branded by a chisel, emerging from a mouth of good luck that's as empty and quiet as a mouth with a soldier's axe above it, speaking of grass—	8.9.34, 17.5.21, 17.5.27, 21.12.48, 23.18.81, 23.18.87, 38.15.89, 49.6.26, 49.6.29, 49.7.32, 49.7.36, 49.8.39, 63.14.62, 81.1.1, 81.2.8
xíng	行		on a public road, practicing—moving with—	2.10.56, 12.7.34, 24.2.8, 25.4.18, 26.3.15, 27.1.2, 29.7.34, 33.6.23, 41.1.7, 47.5.26, 50.9.44, 53.2.7, 62.5.23, 64.11.47, 69.6.22, 69.6.24, 70.2.8, 70.4.16, 78.8.37
xíng	形		shaping with measuring lines of hair's breadth	2.5.34, 24.8.37, 41.17.84, 51.3.8

xìng	興		lifting it together—clasping hands together in front of ones' chests and all together carrying ones' shield—	36.6.23
xìng	姓		family names that women, kneeling with breasts, sprout from the ground—the common people	5.4.17, 17.8.39, 49.2.8, 49.12.55
xiōng	凶		unlucky—a hole in the ground with rock, mud, or bamboo in the bottom—	16.12.45, 30.5.31, 31.13.82
xióng	雄		maleness—left hand flipped, revolving around oneself, 'the short-tailed bird'—	28.1.3
xiū	修		studying, mastering—as when washing on a person's back and hair, hitting it lightly with water during a purification ceremony	54.4.18, 54.5.26, 54.6.34, 54.7.42, 54.8.50
xū	虛		empty—like a tiger head upon a hill—	3.8.34, 5.7.30, 16.1.2, 22.20.7153.8.31

xū	歔		snorting yawning emptiness—like a tiger head on a hill but with grass coming through the bottom—blowing through the nose of a kneeing person with their mouth open	
xú	徐		showing quiet composure—like the left side only of the 'I' pronoun used by the Shang Dynasty kings—	15.13.70, 15.14.79
xù	畜		tying animals and raising them in a pen	51.2.5, 51.11.43
xuán	玄		hard-to-see dark structure—like a figure-eight skein of string-dyed-black	1.13.51, 1.14.52, 1.14.55, 6.2.7, 6.3.9, 10.5.20, 10.17.68, 15.2.9, 51.18.71, 56.8.29, 65.13.52, 65.14.54
xué	學		learning—like hands-on teaching a child gets in school—	19.11.47, 20.1.2, 48.1.2, 64.21.106, 64.21.108
yān	焉		here—this place where that yellow bird lives around the Yangtze and Huai Rivers—	2.11.64, 25.13.72, 34.7.41, 49.10.47, 60.9.48

yán	言		speaking—words, like slaves or criminals branded by a chisel emerging from a mouth	2.10.58, 5.9.39, 8.9.32, 17.6.33, 22.20.72, 23.1.2, 27.2.7, 31.16.96, 41.5.33, 43.5.28, 56.1.4, 56.1.5, 62.4.18, 66.4.31, 69.1.4, 70.1.2, 70.5.17, 73.8.43, 78.14.62, 81.1.2, 81.2.6
yán	埏		molding clay on a potter's wheel	11.3.14
yǎn	儼		respectful—making oneself listen even when the other's excessively talkative—	15.8.37
yàn	厭		sated like by some sweet dog meat in the mouth	53.11.38, 66.8.66, 72.4.15, 72.5.22, 72.6.26
yàn	燕		calm—like the swallow for whom the kingdom Yàn is named—	26.6.24
yāng	央		ending in the center, pleading like a person with their head in the middle of a pole over their shoulders with two things on either end...	20.8.33
yáng	陽		that male principle *yáng* of sun shining on a big soil mound	42.5.20

yáng	殃		bringing harm— like bone remnants ending in the center that's pleading as a person with their head in the middle of a pole over their shoulders with two things on either end	52.14.68
yǎng	養		feeding a meal— mouth over a rice bowl, as beautiful as a ram's head—	34.5.24, 51.14.53
yāo	妖		spooky, evil like gorgeous demons—a woman with breasts, kneeling... a running young man who will die young	58.10.43
yǎo	窈		Hard to see: dim and quiet, secluded in a cave; harboring strength like of an arm, a bladed tool, or a plough caring for an infant as fragile as one fine silk thread... profoundly far-reaching	21.9.33
yào	燿		brilliant—that shining fire over the head of a kneeling person—as the plumes of a long-tailed pheasant	58.17.70

yào	要		demanding something vital—a woman with both hands pointing to her waist—	27.18.90
yé	邪	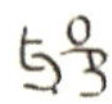	of a disastrous nature—like that disease-causing environment around Tusk Town—	7.9.44, 39.18.116, 62.16.75
yě	也		—yes, that too, vagina! —	3.13.60, 20.17.82, 24.7.32, 29.4.22, 32.2.13, 53.14.51, 55.7.42, 55.9.52, 67.7.24, 76.1.4, 76.2.9, 76.3.18, 76.4.23
yī	一		One	10.1.5, 11.1.5, 14.8.33, 22.7.24, 25.13.71, 39.1.4, 39.2.8, 39.3.13, 39.4.18, 39.5.23, 39.6.29, 39.7.35, 42.1.3, 42.2.4, 67.10.34
yī	衣		clothing like a robe—especially on the torso, like the placental afterbirth hanging from a recently pregnant woman—	34.5.23
yí	夷		as foreign as that tribe in the east—the great barbarians with bows—leveled and razed by destruction	14.2.7, 41.8.44, 53.4.18

yí	以		that carries like a plough—carries the meaning of	37.6.28
yí	遺		leaving behind cowry-like riches—like after dying— on this way of walking a while, stopping for a while	9.8.30, 20.16.76, 52.14.66
yí	宜		it's appropriate to be—like two pieces of meat in a sacrificial altar—	61.15.80
yǐ	倚		to lean—to rely on a person who's remarkable like the great giant about which one can purse one's lips like a piece of cane and puff: 'Yup, that's it, definitely'	58.5.22
yǐ	矣		—swearing on an arrow revolving around oneself, that's it!	31.11.77, 46.7.45, 63.17.79, 65.14.57, 65.14.59, 65.15.63, 67.6.21, 67.19.81, 69.13.54, 74.11.59
yǐ	已		already... finishing it in the womb	2.1.11, 2.2.21, 9.2.8, 29.2.14, 30.6.37, 30.11.59, 30.15.75, 31.8.43, 55.16.81

yǐ	故		anciently, for ten generations, this lightly hits and leaves a mark of reason—	13.12.59

yǐ	以		this carries like a plough—carries the meaning of	1.8.29, 1.10.36, 2.9.48, 2.16.86, 3.7.29, 5.2.5, 5.4.15, 7.2.8, 7.3.14, 7.5.24, 7.9.40, 11.3.16, 11.5.29, 11.7.41, 11.8.47, 12.8.37, 13.9.42, 13.12.61, 13.14.72, 14.19.82, 15.13.67, 15.14.75, 16.4.12, 19.7.28, 20.25.117, 21.15.57, 21.16.63, 21.17.70, 22.7.20, 25.5.23, 26.3.10, 26.8.35, 27.8.36, 29.11.50, 30.1.1, 30.2.8, 30.7.40, 31.11.71, 31.16.97, 31.17.106, 31.18.113, 32.5.29, 32.10.56, 34.9.50, 37.8.44, 36.13.54, 38.2.6, 38.4.15, 38.6.32, 38.7.40, 38.8.48, 38.19.107, 39.2.9, 39.3.14, 39.4.19, 39.5.24, 39.6.30, 39.7.36, 39.9.46, 39.10.53, 39.11.60, 39.12.67, 39.13.75,

				39.14.83, 39.15.91, 39.16.96, 39.17.101, 39.18.112, 41.4.28, 42.6.23, 42.9.38, 42.15.70, 43.4.20, 44.8.37, 46.1.8, 47.5.22, 48.4.13, 48.6.28, 48.8.37, 49.2.6, 50.7.31, 50.15.76, 51.5.14, 52.2.5, 52.3.14, 54.3.13, 54.9.60, 54.10.64, 54.11.68, 54.12.72, 54.13.76, 54.14.84, 54.15.90, 57.1.1, 57.2.5, 57.3.9, 57.4.17, 57.5.22, 58.13.52, 59.6.42, 59.7.50, 60.2.8, 61.4.16, 61.5.20, 61.6.27, 61.8.37, 61.10.48, 62.4.20, 62.5.25, 62.11.47, 62.13.60, 62.15.69, 62.16.73, 63.5.16, 63.12.45, 63.16.69, 64.15.61, 64.20.94, 64.22.115,

				65.2.8, 65.3.12, 65.5.19, 65.6.24, 65.8.32, 66.1.4, 66.2.11, 66.4.23, 66.4.30, 66.5.38, 66.6.43, 66.8.59, 66.9.67, 67.20.84, 67.21.88, 67.23.96, 70.8.28, 70.11.41, 71.4.15, 71.6.22, 71.7.27, 72.6.24, 72.7.28, 73.6.28, 74.2.7, 75.2.4, 75.3.12, 75.5.18, 75.6.25, 75.8.32, 75.9.39, 75.10.45, 76.7.40, 77.10.46, 77.11.54, 77.13.63, 78.4.19, 78.9.39, 79.3.10, 79.4.14, 81.8.30, 81.9.37
yì	義		righteous generosity—sacrificing a ram to the poor each year with that rake-like weapon we use to defend ourselves and our opinions—	18.1.6, 19.3.12, 38.8.43, 38.13.79 38.14.81
yì	益		overflowing like water from a vessel	42.10.47, 42.11.49, 43.4.26, 43.6.34, 48.1.4, 55.12.61

yì	亦		—both armpits sweat this too! —	23.13.59, 23.15.68, 23.17.77, 25.12.60, 32.8.45, 32.9.49, 37.7.38, 42.13.58, 49.4.21, 49.7.35, 50.5.24, 60.7.35, 65.11.43
yì	易		easily changeable to something else—going from saying 'don't' as seriously as blood on a blade to shining as sunny as the sun above—	2.4.28, 63.6.22, 63.9.35, 63.15.64, 64.1.3, 64.2.8, 64.3.12, 64.4.16, 70.1.4, 70.2.7, 78.4.20
yì	抑		suppressing like a hand pushing down on a kneeling person	77.3.11
yì	異		differently-masked person	1.12.46, 20.27.126
yīn	音		one tone—one note from a mouth—	2.7.39, 12.2.8, 41.16.78
yīn	陰		that feminine yīn principle of what's hidden and overcast as when what's being said—in the mouth now, in modern times—is said when it's dusky, like clouds covering a big soil mound	42.5.17

yǐn	隱		hidden—a soil mound as careful and compassionate as a claw-like hand grabbing from above the real work from the force of a bladed tool over a pig-head heart	41.18.86
yǐn	飲		drinking a beverage—leaning over a vase for making alcohol with one's mouth	53.11.39
yīng	應		is as it ought to be—like the heart of a person as ugly as a short-tailed bird in a habitable cave in a cliff	38.9.57, 73.8.46
yīng	嬰		an infant—a kneeling woman's, a mother's wealth as surely as a string of cowry-like riches—	10.4.15, 20.13.55, 28.6.22
yíng	盈		full to overflowing its vessel	4.2.8, 9.1.3, 15.15.87, 15.16.91, 22.3.9, 39.5.25, 39.12.68, 45.3.10
yíng	迎		welcoming—throwing a hero's parade on the way of walking a while and stopping a while with one whom you admire—	14.16.66

yǐng	營		the spiritual soul—that light of a palatial womb's crossed torches—	10.1.2
yǒng	勇		courageous and sturdy like a soldier, strong as an arm, bladed tool, or a plough—the handle of a bell	67.13.51, 67.16.71, 73.1.1, 73.2.6
yòng	用		doing truly useful work like a water bucket—by means of carrying-capacity	4.1.4, 6.6.22, 11.2.13, 11.4.25, 11.6.38, 11.8.49, 27.3.14, 28.20.76, 31.5.25, 31.8.45, 35.8.39, 40.2.10, 45.2.6, 45.4.14, 52.13.58, 57.2.7, 68.4.19, 68.6.33, 69.1.1, 80.3.13, 80.11.44
yōu	憂		grieving—the one mooning heart-core following something—	19.11.49, 20.1.4
yōu	悠		remoteness—like a person separated vertically from their own heart-core by lightly hitting—	17.6.29
yóu	猶		indeed, like a dog that rises to the top of the alcohol vat	5.6.26, 15.7.31, 32.12.65, 63.16.72, 73.6.31, 77.2.5

yóu	尤		in particular "at fault"—blamed and lamed	8.14.50

yǒu	有		Flesh-and-blood, meat-handling Being	1.6.19, 1.9.34, 2.3.23, 2.12.71, 10.14.57, 11.2.10, 11.4.22, 11.6.35, 11.7.39, 13.9.43, 13.10.49, 13.11.56, 14.19.86, 17.1.5, 17.5.25, 18.1.4, 18.2.10, 18.3.17, 18.4.24, 19.6.24, 19.8.35, 20.15.70, 20.25.116, 21.6.23, 21.8.31, 21.10.39, 21.12.47, 22.14.43, 23.18.85, 24.10.43, 25.1.1, 25.13.64, 26.5.21, 30.5.30, 30.6.34, 31.3.14, 32.7.42, 32.8.47, 33.3.12, 33.6.25, 34.4.22, 38.2.7, 38.6.31, 38.8.47, 40.3.17, 40.4.18, 41.5.34, 43.3.14, 43.4.25, 46.1.3, 48.7.33, 50.2.9, 50.3.15, 50.5.26, 51.15.60, 52.1.3, 53.1.5, 53.12.43, 57.9.56, 59.6.43, 59.7.45, 62.7.35, 62.10.44, 62.16.71, 64.5.22, 67.8.27, 69.1.3, 70.5.18, 70.6.21, 74.7.30, 74.11.54, 75.5.22,

				77.5.17, 77.7.31, 77.10.48, 77.11.52, 77.12.59, 79.2.5, 79.6.25, 80.2.6, 80.6.23, 80.8.31, 81.8.35
yǒu	牖		a window—like a boudoir window's sliver of wood that's half of a double-winged gateway and lets the moon shine in on the family's primordial father... ten hung, round spindles—	11.5.28, 47.2.9
yòu	又		again—on the right hand—	1.14.54, 48.3.11
yòu	右		priority position—right hand above mouth—	31.5.29, 31.13.85, 31.15.95, 34.2.8
yū	渝		as changeable as a river flowing against someone gathering themselves together from three sides after a blade cut off their foot as punishment, like from adultery	41.13.68
yú	愚		having a heart-core as foolish as that trampling monkey with the head of a ghost	20.17.78, 38.18.103, 65.3.13

yú	於		here—oh, black, icy raven...	8.5.21, 14.12.49, 20.27.127, 23.7.30, 23.8.36, 23.9.42, 23.10.47, 23.11.52, 23.12.55, 23.14.64, 23.16.73, 28.6.21, 28.12.44, 28.18.67, 31.11.74, 32.12.69, 36.11.46, 40.3.16, 40.4.20, 46.2.17, 46.3.22, 46.4.28, 46.5.35, 48.4.15, 53.2.8, 54.4.20, 54.5.28, 54.6.36, 54.7.44, 54.8.52, 55.2.6, 63.6.20, 63.7.25, 63.9.34, 63.11.42, 64.5.20, 64.6.25, 64.8.33, 64.10.41, 64.12.49, 64.17.79, 69.10.37, 73.1.2, 73.2.7, 75.11.51, 78.1.6, 79.5.23
yú	隅		a corner like that remote place by the big soil mound with that trampling monkey with the head of a ghost	41.14.72

yú	餘		having leftovers—excess food remains in one's house—	20.15.71, 24.8.34, 53.12.44, 54.5.33, 77.5.18, 77.7.32, 77.10.49, 77.11.53, 79.2.6
yú	輿		a carriage's sedan chair surrounded by a mortar, upheld by two hands—the masses	80.6.25
yú	魚		fish	36.11.42
yǔ	與		supporting—offering to carry on one's shoulders—	8.8.29, 20.2.7, 20.4.15, 22.18.59, 35.3.15, 36.8.31, 44.1.2, 44.2.7, 44.3.12, 65.15.60, 66.10.76, 68.3.17, 77.2.8, 79.9.38, 81.9.38
yǔ	雨		cloudburst of rain	23.3.12

yù	譽		such a good public reputation—that is, what's being spoken in words like by a slave or criminal branded by a chisel about one's support, about one's offers to carry things on one's shoulders like a broker whose fame is everything—	17.2.11, 39.20.122, 39.20.124
yù	欲		wanting—what's been eroded from this ravine—	1.9.35, 1.7.28, 3.5.22, 3.12.52, 15.15.86, 19.10.45, 29.1.2, 34.6.33, 34.6.36, 36.1.2, 36.3.10, 36.5.18, 36.7.26, 37.5.22, 37.7.41, 37.8.43, 39.21.126, 46.3.24, 46.5.36, 57.14.84, 61.12.58, 61.13.66, 61.14.77, 64.20.97, 64.20.99, 66.4.26, 66.5.34, 77.15.77
yù	遇		encountering—like walking a while, stopping a while around that trampling monkey with the head of a ghost—	50.9.46
yù	玉		jade totems	9.5.18, 39.21.130, 70.12.47

yù	育		birthing like an upside down baby below the moon	51.12.47
yù	愈	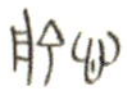	more and even more—like someone gathering themselves together from three sides by moonlight over their heart-core after a blade cut off their foot as punishment and now they've recovered from that illness—	5.8.36, 81.8.34, 81.9.41
yù	御		mastering—like a pestle halting someone who kneels to you—	14.19.83
yù	豫		a relaxed countenance—like an elephant or like two hands handing an object to one another—	15.6.25
yù	域		the soil of this particular territory—this enclave defended by a weapon on a pole, plus its surroundings—	25.13.62
yuān	淵		the deep water	4.3.9, 8.7.28, 36.11.47

yuǎn	遠		remote—not intimately close but a profound way in which you walk a while, stop a while, shaped like a big round spindle with a long robe, like the afterbirth hanging from a recently pregnant woman—	25.10.48, 25.11.49, 47.3.16, 65.14.58, 80.5.20
yuàn	怨		resenting—the heart sleeping like someone kneeling to lie down below the moon	63.5.15, 79.1.3, 79.2.7
yuē	曰		what it's called when issued on a breath from the mouth	14.2.6, 14.4.13, 14.6.20, 16.7.26, 16.9.34, 16.10.38, 24.7.33, 25.7.35, 25.8.41, 25.9.44, 25.10.47, 25.11.50, 52.11.52, 52.12.56, 55.10.55, 55.11.59, 55.12.63, 55.13.68, 62.14.67, 67.10.35, 67.11.38, 67.12.41
yuē	約		binding it—like a cord of silk keeping something in the ladle—	27.6.30

yuè	閱		inspecting a person going through the double-winged gateway—exchanging breath—	21.15.58
yuè	籥		flute—bamboo with three frets, played with the mouth—	5.6.28
yún	云		saying like a cloud	57.10.60, 78.9.42
yún	芸		as quick-growing, voluminous and numerous as the rapeseed plant—'cloud-grass,' that source of the personal lubricant canola oil—	16.5.17, 16.5.18
zāi	哉		I say, 'Oh, indeed! That hurts like a weapon on a pole wounding sprouting seeds, talents.'	20.8.34, 20.17.83, 21.16.69, 22.20.73, 53.14.52, 54.14.89, 57.4.21
zāi	載		Carrying—protecting this chariot load of sprouting seeds and talents with a weapon on a pole—	10.1.1
zǎi	宰		dominating—like the house of that chisel used to mark slaves and criminals—	10.16.65, 51.17.68

zài	在		existing sprouting—of seedlings, talents, here on earth—	24.7.30, 32.11.62, 49.9.42
zǎo	早		early, premature—like sunrise above an acorn on the jujube, that thorny plant that's used for insomnia, contraception and causes midterm miscarriages—	30.15.74, 55.16.80, 59.2.13, 59.3.15
zào	躁		impetuous, the irritable—three birds chirping in a tree along the way of walking a while and stopping a while—	26.2.7, 26.10.44, 45.8.29
zào	鑿		chiseling—with that tool used to mark slaves and criminals—	11.5.26

zé	則		after following this sacrificial blade-and-cauldron-like ritual example or regulation	3.15.64, 22.1.2, 22.2.5, 22.3.8, 22.4.11, 22.5.14, 22.6.17, 22.19.67, 26.9.41, 26.10.45, 28.19.71, 28.21.78, 30.13.66, 31.4.22, 31.5.27, 31.11.68, 38.10.58, 55.14.72, 59.4.25, 59.5.32, 61.7.31, 61.9.41, 64.19.89, 67.20.86, 67.21.90, 70.10.36, 72.2.5, 73.1.4, 73.2.10, 76.7.43, 76.8.48, 77.9.40
zé	責		blaming—a tree with thorns over cowry-riches	79.5.22
zéi	賊		using a weapon on a pole in a blade-and-cauldron ritual standard to damage or rob	19.6.22, 57.9.54, 65.7.30
zhàn	戰		battling—using a net for catching animals against a weapon on a pole—	31.18.111, 67.20.85, 68.2.8

zhàn	湛		concealed like sugar cane sweetness tucked in the ends of folded cloth and frozen like ice	4.9.28
zhāng	彰		shining forth—as obviously clear and 'enlightened' as the hair on a person standing on the ground in the early morning sun over the jujube, that thorny plant that's used for insomnia and contraception and causes midterm miscarriages—	22.12.38, 24.4.18, 57.9.52
zhāng	張		stretching—lengthening a bow string—	36.2.7, 77.2.6
zháng	長		long-haired elder	
zhǎng	長		lengthening like long hair	10.16.62, 22.16.49, 24.6.28
zhàng	丈		respected man or husband—as in, you stay ten feet from them—	38.19.109
zhāo	召		imperial summons calling everyone together like a blade out of a mouth	73.9.48

zhāo	昭		bright, bright as a blade-like imperial summons,	20.19.89, 20.19.90
zhào	兆		an omen like the cracks in a shell during divination	20.12.53, 64.2.7
zhǎo	爪		a claw like a hand grabbing from above	50.12.66
zhé	謫		banishing—the stem of speaking words like slaves or criminals, branded by a chisel, emerging from a mouth,	27.2.10
zhé	折		breaking off—cutting a tree in half with an axe	76.8.49

zhě	者		—now this is cooking with fire!—	1.11.42, 3.13.56, 7.2.13, 13.9.46, 14.7.24, 15.1.6, 15.15.84, 19.7.27, 22.19.69, 23.4.19, 23.8.38, 23.9.40, 23.10.45, 23.11.50, 23.12.57, 23.14.66, 23.16.75, 24.1.2, 24.2.6, 24.3.11, 24.4.16, 24.5.21, 24.6.26, 24.10.45, 27.1.4, 27.14.62, 27.15.71, 29.5.24, 29.6.28, 30.1.6, 31.1.4, 31.3.16, 31.6.31, 31.10.58, 31.11.67, 33.1.3, 33.2.7, 33.3.11, 33.4.16, 33.5.20, 33.6.24, 33.7.31, 33.8.37, 38.15.87, 38.17.98, 39.1.5, 40.1.2, 40.2.7, 42.14.63, 49.3.13, 49.4.19, 49.6.27, 49.7.33, 50.8.42, 54.1.3, 54.2.8, 56.1.2, 56.1.6, 61.1.3, 61.14.72, 61.15.79, 62.1.2, 62.13.64, 64.13.53, 64.14.57, 65.1.6, 65.10.42, 66.1.10, 68.1.4,

				68.2.9, 68.3.15, 68.4.21, 69.13.52, 70.9.34, 70.10.38, 73.3.14, 74.4.20, 74.7.33, 74.8.39, 74.10.52, 75.10.48, 76.5.29, 76.6.35, 77.3.10, 77.4.14, 77.5.19, 77.6.24, 77.12.61, 78.2.12, 81.3.10, 81.4.14, 81.5.18, 81.6.22
zhēn	貞		pure, chaste, and virtuous as an ancient divination cauldron	39.7.40
zhēn	真		genuine—using your fork to get food right from the cauldron—	21.11.44, 41.13.66, 54.4.25
zhèn	鎮	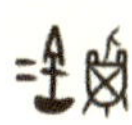	restraining—cooling with genuine virtue's ancient axed-alloy divination spoon and cauldron —	37.6.26
zhēng	爭		contending—two hands clawing over a ploughshare—	3.2.7, 8.3.12, 8.13.47, 22.17.53, 22.18.61, 66.9.70, 66.10.78, 68.5.28, 73.7.38, 81.11.57
zhèng	正		straight—upright as a nail in a footprint—	8.10.35, 45.10.40, 57.1.2, 57.12.74, 58.8.35, 58.9.36, 78.14.61

zhèng	政		politics and regulations of governing—lightly hitting to straight as if nailing setting out by foot on a long journey or campaign—	58.1.2, 58.3.10

zhī	之		what it has	1.5.17, 1.6.23, 1.13.50, 1.14.53, 1.15.58, 2.1.6, 2.2.15, 2.9.54, 2.10.59, 3.3.12, 3.7.32, 4.1.5, 4.4.14, 4.11.37, 4.12.41, 5.5.23, 6.3.11, 6.6.23, 8.4.16, 9.1.4, 9.3.12, 9.6.22, 9.10.38, 10.13.51, 10.13.53, 11.2.12, 11.7.40, 11.6.37, 11.8.46, 11.4.24, 12.6.30, 13.5.20, 13.6.24, 14.1.2, 14.3.9, 14.5.16, 14.13.56, 14.14.60, 14.16.67, 14.17.73, 14.18.80, 14.19.85, 15.1.2, 15.5.23, 15.9.46, 15.13.69, 15.14.78, 17.1.6, 17.2.12, 17.3.16, 17.4.20, 20.2.6, 20.4.14, 20.6.22, 20.13.57, 20.17.80, 21.1.3, 21.3.10., 21.16.67, 22.18.60, 22.19.63, 22.21.78, 23.13.62, 23.15.71, 23.17.80, 24.9.41, 25.7.34, 25.8.39,

				26.8.39, 26.7.32, 27.14.66, 27.15.74, 28.20.77, 29.1.8, 29.5.26, 29.6.30, 30.4.18, 30.5.27, 31.1.7, 31.2.12, 31.6.34, 31.7.39, 31.8.46, 31.10.57, 31.16.101, 31.17.104, 31.17.110, 31.18.117, 32.3.19, 32.6.35, 32.11.61, 32.12.68, 34.3.12, 35.4.21, 35.6.30, 35.7.35, 35.8.40, 36.1.4, 36.2.8, 36.3.12, 36.4.16, 36.5.20, 36.6.24, 36.7.28, 36.8.32, 36.12.49, 37.3.14, 37.6.27, 37.6.31, 37.7.35, 38.6.29, 38.7.37, 38.8.45, 38.9.53, 38.9.56, 38.10.63, 38.15.90, 38.16.94, 38.17.100, 38.18.104, 39.1.2, 39.8.43, 40.1.4, 40.2.9, 41.1.8, 41.3.23, 41.5.35, 42.7.27, 42.10.45, 42.11.50, 42.12.54, 42.13.60, 43.1.3,

				43.2.10, 43.4.24, 43.5.29, 43.6.33, 43.7.39, 46.6.41, 48.3.10, 49.3.16, 49.4.23, 49.6.30, 49.7.37, 49.13.65, 50.2.6, 50.3.12, 50.4.18, 50.4.21, 50.7.35, 51.1.3, 51.2.6, 51.3.9, 51.4.12, 51.7.25, 51.8.28, 51.9.32, 51.10.41, 51.11.44, 51.12.46, 51.12.48, 51.13.50, 51.13.52, 51.14.54, 51.14.56, 54.4.19, 54.5.27, 54.6.35, 54.7.43, 54.8.51, 55.1.3, 55.6.34, 55.7.40, 55.9.50, 55.15.75, 58.5.20, 58.6.26, 58.11.45, 59.3.18, 59.7.47, 59.9.63, 61.2.8, 61.3.12, 62.1.5, 62.2.9, 62.3.14, 62.6.29, 62.7.34, 62.13.58, 63.16.74, 64.5.19, 64.6.24, 64.7.30, 64.9.38, 64.11.46, 64.13.55, 64.14.59, 64.17.75,

				64.17.84, 64.20.104, 64.21.112, 64.22.119, 65.1.2, 65.3.14, 65.4.16, 65.7.29, 65.9.37, 66.2.15, 66.4.33, 66.5.41, 66.10.77, 67.9.33, 67.22.95, 67.23.99, 68.4.23, 68.5.29, 68.6.35, 68.8.42, 73.4.20, 73.6.33, 73.7.35, 74.2.10, 74.5.26, 75.1.2, 75.2.9, 75.4.15, 75.5.21, 75.7.29, 75.8.36, 76.1.2, 76.3.16, 76.5.31, 76.6.37, 77.1.2, 77.3.12, 77.4.16, 77.5.21, 77.6.26, 77.7.28, 77.9.38, 78.3.14, 78.4.21, 78.5.23, 78.6.27, 78.10.45, 80.2.9, 80.7.29, 80.9.37, 80.11.45, 80.17.64, 81.10.44, 81.11.52

zhī	知		firing arrows from the mouth, sure	2.1.4, 2.2.13, 3.12.50, 4.11.35, 10.8.32, 10.12.48, 14.20.88, 16.10.36, 16.11.41, 16.13.46, 17.1.4, 21.16.64, 25.6.30, 28.1.1, 28.7.24, 28.13.47, 32.9.51, 32.10.53, 33.1.1, 33.2.6, 33.5.18, 43.4.21, 44.6.28, 44.7.32, 46.4.30, 46.6.39, 47.1.4, 47.4.18, 47.5.28, 52.3.15, 52.4.19, 53.1.6, 54.14.85, 55.6.31, 55.10.53, 55.11.57, 56.1.1., 56.1.8, 57.4.18, 58.7.30, 59.5.34, 59.6.38, 65.10.39, 65.12.47, 70.1.5, 70.3.13, 70.7.26, 70.8.31, 70.9.32, 71.1.1, 71.1.3, 71.2.6, 71.2.8, 72.7.32, 73.5.24, 78.7.34, 81.5.17, 81.6.24
zhí	直		looking straight on, straight ahead	22.2.6, 45.5.18, 58.16.63

zhí	埴		clay that looks straight on—up and down—	11.3.15
zhí	執		holding tight in the hand—not letting go of, not dying young—	14.18.78, 29.6.27, 35.1.1, 64.14.56, 64.16.70, 69.9.31, 74.5.23, 79.4.17
zhǐ	止		stopping on their footprint	20.24.112, 32.9.52, 32.10.54, 35.3.19, 44.7.33
zhì	質		matter mattering with the keen and weighty quality of two axes over a cowry	41.13.65
zhì	至		reaching the extreme—like an arrow straight into the clay soil—	43.1.4, 43.2.11, 48.4.14, 55.7.41, 55.9.51, 65.16.67, 72.2.8, 80.18.69
zhì	置		installing—like a net looking straight on, straight ahead	62.9.40
zhì	智		firing arrows from the mouth—sure as the sun, on the daily—	3.13.55, 18.2.8, 19.1.4, 27.17.85, 33.1.4, 65.5.21, 65.6.25, 65.8.33
zhì	致		causing—lightly hitting and leaving a mark of	10.3.12, 14.7.27, 16.1.1, 39.8.42, 39.20.120
zhì	志		determined aspiration—stopping on their footprint over their heart-core	3.10.42, 31.11.73, 33.6.26

zhì	治		governing—regulating by harnessing the river named Happy or speaking of turning oneself—	3.7.33, 3.15.67, 8.10.37, 10.7.28, 57.1.3, 59.1.1, 60.1.1, 64.6.23, 65.4.18, 65.6.26, 65.8.34, 75.4.17, 75.6.27
zhì	制		rulers' edicts—like "blade the ox in the city outskirts!"—	28.22.84, 32.7.41
zhōng	忠		faithful as a centered heart-core like the drum with a flagpole placed in the middle of a field to gather the people—	18.4.25, 38.15.88
zhōng	中		in the center—like that drum with a flagpole placed in the middle of a field to gather the people, detect the wind—	5.10.45, 21.6.22, 21.8.30, 21.10.38, 21.12.46, 25.13.63, 41.2.9
zhōng	終		ending—the knot at the end of a thick silk skein in winter—	23.2.9, 23.3.14, 26.3.13, 34.9.52, 52.7.36, 52.10.46, 55.8.43, 63.12.48, 63.17.76, 64.18.86
zhòng	重		a heavy load—a bag carried by a man—	26.1.1, 26.4.19, 59.3.19, 59.4.22, 66.6.51, 80.4.16

zhòng	眾		the sun shining down like an eye on the people sees all this, sees	1.15.56, 8.4.14, 20.9.35, 20.15.67, 20.25.113, 21.15.59, 21.16.65, 31.17.105, 64.21.110
zhōu	舟		a boat—a dugout canoe	80.6.24
zhōu	周		meticulously organizing something into compartments—like space into circuits, time into weekly structure, money into allotments that can be distributed to help people [this word is the name of the dynasty of Lǎo Zǐ's time]—)	25.4.17
zhòu	驟		sudden—like when your horse moves quickly, say, when you're gathering and carrying in your hand the ear of an enemy in a crowd of people—	23.3.11
zhǔ	主		master—the owner and host of the lamp's flame—	26.7.33, 30.1.5, 34.5.30, 34.7.45, 69.2.9, 78.11.51

zhù	注		pouring, filling with attention like a river master—the owner and host of the lamp's flame—	49.12.57
zhuān	專		monopolizing—like a big round spindle over an inch-sized spot that's as small as where you measure the radial artery pulse in your wrist—	10.3.10
zhuàng	壯		just passing their prime -- a robust bachelor soldier-scholar-official appointed by the emperor in his bamboo bed	55.14.71
zhuàng	狀		form—like a slice of bamboo shaped to a bed or a dog—	14.13.55, 14.13.57, 21.16.68, 30.13.65
zhuì	贅		superfluous cowry-like riches—as would be the teasing uproarious action or light hitting of a person with feathers in their headdress, someone who died before taking the throne and therefore had no posthumous name—	24.8.36

zhuō	拙		clumsy—stepping out of their cave all hands and fingers	45.6.24
zhuō	斲		chopping like a keen axe cutting a stone flagon	74.9.46, 74.10.51
zhuō	銳		filed to a sharp point like an axe ground between two blocks of metal—like a keen exchange of speech with a person—	9.3.11
zhuó	濁		turbid, filthy waters like those of Shū Han—that state whose name means a seeing-person encompassing a kneeling-person,	15.12.63, 15.13.66
zī	滋		increasing as a river of double hard-to-see dark structured—like figure-eight skeins of string-dyed-black	57.7.39, 57.9.51
zī	輜		carriage carrying over field and stream—often for military supply, with a curtain—	26.4.18
zī	子		baby—arms wide open and legs swaddled [this word is the second part of Lǎo Zī's honorific name]—	4.11.38, 31.4.20, 31.7.38, 52.3.17, 52.4.21, 54.3.11, 55.2.8, 62.8.39

zī	資		supporting material—second-tier cowry-like riches—	27.15.75, 27.16.83
zí	滋		flowing like a river of hard-to-see dark structure—a figure-eight skein of string-dyed-black	57.8.47
zì	自		of course—one's self personally, right on one's nose—	7.3.17, 9.8.29, 17.8.43, 21.13.49, 22.9.30, 22.11.35, 22.13.40, 22.15.46, 23.1.3, 24.3.9, 24.4.14, 24.5.19, 24.6.24, 25.17.84, 32.4.23, 32.6.38, 33.2.5, 33.4.14, 34.9.54, 37.3.18, 37.9.49, 39.17.104, 51.9.36, 57.11.66, 57.12.73, 57.13.80, 57.14.87, 64.22.120, 72.7.31, 72.8.34, 72.9.36, 72.10.39, 73.9.50

zì	字		its public courtesy name—like that given when you're still a baby under the family roof by your parents or first personal teacher in the home-based family school but not used until a man reaches age 20 or a woman is married—	25.7.33
zōng	宗		ancestral shrine	4.4.15, 70.5.19
zǒu	走		going like a running young man who will die young on foot	46.1.6
zú	足		enough—the full leg-cut of the animal—	17.5.23, 19.7.32, 23.18.83, 28.17.64, 33.5.19, 35.6.32, 35.7.37, 35.8.42, 41.4.27, 41.11.60, 44.6.29, 46.4.31, 46.6.40, 46.6.42, 46.7.44, 48.8.36, 64.12.50, 77.6.23, 77.8.36, 77.10.45
zuì	罪		a sin or crime like a net breaking the little wings off something	46.3.19, 62.16.72

zūn	尊		honoring—like offering by hand the yi ritual alcohol vessel with the chief charged with its preparation	51.6.19, 51.7.26, 62.5.22
zuǒ	左		inferior position—left-handed work	31.4.24, 31.12.81, 31.14.90, 34.2.7, 79.4.18
zuǒ	佐		inferior position—left-handed, assisting-type work—	30.1.3
zuò	作		getting up and going to work	2.11.63, 16.3.10, 16.12.44, 37.5.23, 55.6.38, 63.9.33, 63.11.41
zuò	坐		sitting—two people staying there, on the ground of	62.12.53

CPSIA information can be obtained
at www.ICGtesting.com
Printed in the USA
LVHW030042270122
709360LV00002B/64

9 781735 793139